ALASKA
The Sophisticated Wilderness

Jon Gardey

Photography by the author

WILTON HOUSE GENTRY · LONDON

Published by Wilton House Gentry Limited,
Wilton House, Hobart Place, London SW1.
Picture design by Jon Gardey
Filmset by Computer Photoset Ltd., Birmingham
Printed and bound in Great Britain
by Redwood Burn Limited, Trowbridge & Esher

ALASKA

To Takla
in memory of an Alaskan childhood

Contents

Illustrations

All photography by Jon Gardey
The map reproduced on the endpapers was drawn by Bill Berry (© Griffin's-Alaska 1967)
The maps on pages 220 and 221 were drawn by Hilary Evans

Color Plates

following page 32
A winter swamp near Anchorage
Mount Blackburn from a lake near Chitina

following page 48
Mount McKinley from the McKinley Park road
Deneki Lakes in mid summer
Camp Denali and Mount McKinley
Harper Glacier, descent from the high camp

following page 64
The Brooks Range from the north
The Ruth Glacier. Two light planes fly through the Gorge

following page 80
A forest fire burns across the Interior
Tundra near Nabesna
Caribou on the ice of the Ivishak River
Murres on a rock in Kachemak Bay

following page 96
Halibut Cove and the Kenai Mountains
An Eskimo umiak sails into Gambell Village, St Lawrence Island

following page 112
Anchorage buildings across Knik Arm
Anchorage high school footballers' practice

Monochrome Illustrations

Acknowledgements

I would like to express my thanks to the many Alaskans and others without whose help this book would never have happened. Special thanks are due to Bill and Liz Berry, Amy Bollenbach, Chuck Champion, Alex Combs, Jack Dilley, Celia Hunter, Brooke and Wilda Marston, Bill and Ree Nancarrow, Ruth Schmidt, Gene Wescott, Bucky and Judy Wilson, Rod and Gwynneth Wilson, Ginny Wood and Teri Viereck.

I would also like to thank the following people and organizations for the help they gave me during the preparation of the book: Helen Nienhueser, Margaret McKaig, Alaska Center for the Environment; Alaska Department of Fish and Game; Karl Francis, Alaskan Arctic Gas Pipeline Company; Alyeska Pipeline Service Company; Peter Tappenden, Bryan Sage, British Petroleum London; Charles Towill, BP Alaska; Jim Kowalsky, Fairbanks Environmental Center.

My thanks to Reuel Griffin and Bill Berry for permission to reproduce Bill's pictorial map of Alaska; to Ernest Benn Ltd., London, and Dodd, Mead & Co., New York, for permission to reproduce a verse from 'The Spell of the Yukon' by Robert Service *(Collected Poems of Robert Service)*; and to Jasper Heath and Stewart N. Rothman for permission to reproduce three verses from 'God's Lonesome Trapper' by Jasper Heath (published in *This Month in Fairbanks*, Vol. 1, No. 3).

My thanks to Burt Bollenbach for help in the final editing of the manuscript.

My appreciation in anticipation for the tolerance of those who thought the climb was over: Woodrow Wilson Sayre, Norm Hansen, Norm Sanders and Jac Lasner.

Finally, my sincere gratitude to Takla for her encouragement, to Kari for her patience when her father didn't have time to play cards, and to Helen for her help and support when I needed her.

J. G.
Cookham Dean, England
May, 1976

Chapter 1

A Wild Love

Alaska is a place of love for me. It was in Alaska that I fell in love with a girl, and with the spirit of a landscape. But now the girl is dead. The spirit of the land is being diffused and robbed of its mystery. I believe it, too, is dying.

For me, Alaska was like a woman in that summer twenty years ago. A woman with moods terrifying or tranquil, but always unexpected. She would entice me into her intimate wilderness with blue skies and gentle winds, then, when I was in her embrace, she would rent the sky apart with black clouds and throw stinging snow in my face. She would color her forests in red and gold, and then in a fit of pique tear the leaves from the branches and throw them to the ground.

Alaska that first summer produced in me an almost physical longing for her mountains, her skies and her distances that has never left. Only after I had been in her wilderness and had experienced her wild moods did I realize that she was not the sort of woman I could love and forget. I didn't know it then, but my involvement with her had only begun. Like any beautiful woman, her mere presence draws men to her. Alaska has drawn me back to her beauty again and again.

But today Alaska has been split. One part is the land itself, the tundra, the mountains, and the forests that I learned to love a long time ago. The other is that part of Alaska changed by man for his own use, a process of sophistication of the Alaskan wilderness that has been carried on with ever increasing effectiveness. A process in which the intrinsic values of the wilderness are negated or destroyed by man and his technology. To build a road where there was only empty tundra before. To fill valleys with noise where once there was silence. To build a pipeline. To spread a web of hard technology over the fragile and yielding land.

Man's influence on the Alaskan wilderness is affecting not only the physical land; it is destroying Alaska's space. Man's spirit needs the mystery that the empty places of the earth can provide, and each act of his to fill these vacuums of land-space reduces the room in which his spirit can fly. The Trans Sahara Highway is being paved and filled with tourists, the Amazon basin has been severed by a road, even Siberia is becoming laced with roads; the empty places of the earth are disappearing and now Alaska's too are going.

Alaska's space is not really empty. It is a distant wind blowing across miles of wet tundra, filled with the smells of birch and spruce. It is the sweet purity of a cold cascade of air from a high mountain, or a sweep of salt air from a fresh sea. It is winter skies of purple and cobalt, infinite skies that merge with the colors of the snow so that sky and land are one. Skies pricked with the ever circling brilliance of winter stars. Skies splashed with green and white aurora. Splashed again and again until the eyes burn with the intensity and power of the magical light.

In the past few years man's destruction of the Alaskan wilderness has increased exponentially. The few early white men who came to Alaska in the late 1800's brought with them shovels and axes and used the rivers for transportation. They had hardly any effect on the land. But successive waves of these miners, military men, and now the most sophisticated of all, oil men, have found the way to the far north. They have brought, not only shovels and axes, but bulldozers to tear at the tundra, helicopters to claw at the skies. They have brought thousands of new people and have built ugly expanding cities.

Along with the spoilers others came north. They came not to exploit but merely to live. They were and are men and women in flight from the plastic cities of the 'Lower 48', the rest of America. These people had experienced the commercial and technological terrors of American civilization and had fled before them. They found in Alaska a peace that could soothe their tortured souls and regenerate their spirits. But the terrors they had hoped to leave behind have followed them. A massive influx of new people is rapidly smothering the independent life styles of those who had tried to escape. The unequal battle for Alaska's space is on.

In the summer of 1974, with the completion of the pipeline road from the Yukon River to the Arctic Ocean, man finally succeeded in cutting in half an area equal to one sixth of that of the United States, an area the size of Germany, France, Spain and Italy combined. With this one road, this one new white line of gravel across the green summer wilderness north of Fairbanks, he removed much of the awe of the Arctic, exposed the timeless secrets of hundreds of streams and valleys, secrets that had been held by the land since it was formed. That road was the first to cut that wilderness and it mattered. The roads that will surely follow will mean less, but they will come, too. Alaska is a void that will be filled by man in time. Close to the bursting monolith of America, it could not forever escape the population and technological pressures that are so near and so powerful. The summer of 1974 saw these pressures break across Alaska with the start of the construction of the Trans Alaska Pipeline.

I am not an innocent bystander at this invasion, but an integral part of it. When the four of us drove our Chevy truck across the Alaska-Yukon border in the summer of 1954, we brought another vehicle and four new people to the northern wilds. With that act, and because we, too, were part of the American consuming culture, we contributed to the need for that road across the wilderness twenty years later. We brought with us our technological and cultural needs and insisted that they be satisfied there in Alaska, as they had been in the California we had left behind.

We wanted fuel for our truck, and that required the existence of a filling station. We needed food and equipment, which meant stores and people to operate them. The food, fuel and equipment were supplied by other trucks that had passed us in clouds of dust on the Alaska Highway. Around us and others like us a machine-oriented American civilization developed in the wilderness of Alaska. We insisted on a useable wilderness, one that could fill our needs. As long as our numbers were few we found that we could satisfy our machines and still retain the wilderness.

I came to Alaska and fell in love with a beautiful landscape, but with my act of love I unwittingly destroyed a part of that landscape by my very presence and my demands. I asked and the land gave, but at a cost. Those who followed asked for more and the land gave and is giving. I can't blame those who have come north to take Alaska's treasures. It is in the nature of man to take from the earth, and, unfortunately for her, Alaska has the riches America now needs.

The new invaders are the oil companies. They come, not as individuals, but as the largest business corporations on earth. They come to the north with enormous machines, thousands of workers, and vast financial resources. They come, not for themselves, but because you and I send them. I drive a car, fly thousands of miles a year, use something made of plastic every day, my electricity is generated by oil. I cannot, while using all these things tell the oil companies to stop their invasion of Alaska. They are supplying a need developed over decades, and will continue to do so until the market place tells them to stop. If we want the invasion called off, we must use less oil. But I can see no replacement for oil as a primary energy source, at least until the year 2000.

An experience of a place is personal, and I can only tell you how Alaska has affected me. The feel and look of a place is a function of many things. When I first went to Alaska my love for a girl overflowed and extended to the new land and to the people I met there.

Alaska is to me both a place and people, and in that summer twenty years ago I discovered both. The friends made then are older now. We have progressed through long separations and have moved along different paths, but when we come together again our friendships are as fresh and real as they had been at the beginning. It was as if the spirit of Alaska had fostered the friendships and had nurtured the love.

The land and those people are now in a battle for survival. The invading forces have now spread over the towns and across the wilderness, and in their coming have trampled the lives of the people who sought solace and escape. Alaska has been taken on a new course from which there will be no turning back, for the forces at work are beyond the control of anyone—the forces of men intent on gratifying their machines no matter what the cost to their spirit.

13

Chapter 2

The Two Hundred Dollar Adventure

It was spring, 1954. Three men and a girl sat around an oak table in a pseudo-gothic building on the UCLA campus in Los Angeles. Jac's coffee had just spilled on Jill's carefully typed-out report. The total at the bottom of the paper, which appeared to read $180, was fast disappearing under a brown flood. Jill shook the coffee off on to the floor. 'It's $180 each, that is the total cost from here to the top of McKinley and back. I don't see how you guys can get it any lower unless you start walking from here.'

Norm opined that since he was furnishing his 1946 Chevy truck surely he could pay less. Jac, who was not one to give money away easily, no doubt partly, if not wholly because of his orthodox Brooklyn upbringing, vetoed that idea by pointing out that then *he* would have to pay more. 'Besides,' he looked Norm in the eye, 'you were going to drive to Alaska anyway just to see the place. Now you will not only get our charming company on the drive up, but the opportunity of carrying some of our equipment up McKinley.'

'So it's settled then.' Jill forced her way into the opening breach between Jac and Norm. '$180 each will cover food, fuel for the car and equipment and food for the McKinley climb. This is going to be the scroungiest climb of that mountain yet. The surplus stores of Los Angeles are going to see a lot of us this spring.'

Our incomes as students at UCLA were almost non-existent, and it was just as well it was a state-supported University. While not lucrative, the jobs we got while at school did enable us to spend our vacations away from the rapidly spreading suburbia of Los Angeles. During this period there were of the order of one thousand new immigrants to California *every day*. Already the air over us was taking on that brown tinge characteristic of later smogs.

Our parents and friends thought us slightly odd for wanting to spend our weekends in freezing little tents on the sides of mountains. But we felt, our 50's-style haircuts notwithstanding, that we had found something undiscovered by our fellows back in the valleys. A knowledge that couldn't be learned in the classrooms. Knowledge of our earth and its sky and something about our place in it. But comments such as these made our missions into the hills seem even more strange and questions were soon asked as to what we actually did in those funny little tents out there in the desert. We weren't saying. We told everybody that we had joined the fraternity of mountaineers as if that made us purer than the fraternity brothers of Westwood.

Many of us belonged to the Sierra Club, a California-based conservation group that at that time was fighting a losing battle to save California from itself. And in those days they had to soldier on without the popularity of words such as environment and ecology. (The Sierra Club is now trying to save Alaska, with the same marginal results.)

But we climbed and walked. We developed friendships that became somehow more real. Friendships built up in the special atmosphere of the hills, between people who tried to shake off the plastic life of Los Angeles and escape together to places where they could see the stars.

Jac Lasner is a Jew from Brooklyn who went to great lengths to preserve the stereotyped image of his brothers. His efforts at conserving money were legendary, and as such he was an invaluable addition to the group. He once took a girl to a movie and during the feature supplied her with leaves from a large head of lettuce he had acquired at a nearby grocery sale. It turned out to be the meal for the evening. On our trip to Alaska, he once mixed canned peas and baked beans together in the same pot to save fuel. It was awful. But these are not faults, merely idiosyncrasies and Jac's way of beating the system. His frugality didn't extend to personal relationships, for there he was generous with his mind and his warmth and understanding. Today he is beating the heads of the San Francisco school kids together and sending me free post cards from Harold's Club in Reno.

To Norm Sanders a mountain was another of life's problems to be solved in the most efficient manner possible. His approach, in contrast to Jac's, was methodical and organized. He liked equipment and wanted it to work. He was probably the one who kept the expedition on an even course and it was largely through his efforts that the equipment we did manage to scrape together was made workable. His early enthusiasm for the hills developed into his vocation and he is now Professor of Ecology (that word caught up with him) at the University of California at Santa Barbara. His determination and sense of what was right were put to the test a few years ago in the Santa Barbara channel off the California coast. The area is one of extensive offshore oil drilling and a large blowout had spread disgusting crude oil goo along the California beaches. When the furor died down and the oil companies wanted to site another drilling rig, Norm rowed a small boat out to the new site in the channel and paddled around in circles while the giant rig hovered nearby. Eventually the rig won, but Norm had at least satisfied his own conscience and those of many other people.

Jill Murray had had a hard break from life so far, and she went into the mountains to escape from her past and to find new friends, to find people with whom she could communicate. Jill gravitated into this group for security from her disintegrating family and to find a touchstone for a new life. Among these warm people she was happier than she had been in a long time. To come to Alaska with us meant for her a complete break from all the unpleasant associations in the Los Angeles where she had grown up. She needed us and the trip to Alaska almost for her life. McKinley itself wasn't important to her except for what it meant to us. She would climb the mountain through us, and especially me, and so share our great adventure, and our dreams.

But what gave us the right even to consider climbing such a big mountain? McKinley at 20,320 feet was in a different league from the other peaks we had climbed, and it was 4000 miles away, much of it over a gravel road, in a place called Alaska that we had only known from books and maps. McKinley had by that spring been climbed only ten times since the first ascent in 1913. Clearly it would be a big jump for us, but we wrote Grant Pearson, Superintendent of McKinley Park, optimistically asking permission to climb his mountain and enclosing a list of our hoped-for equipment and food. We also asked him for the name of at least one other climber fool enough to want to climb the mountain, for park regulations required a minimum of four people. (McKinley is U.S. Government property, in spite of its wild nature, and around its base is a sea of red tape and paperwork that must be waded through to reach the lower slopes.)

Superintendent Pearson wrote back with the information that two people in Boston were 'interested in climbing and photographing on the lower slopes of McKinley'.

We wrote to Woodrow Wilson Sayre and Norman Hansen who turned out to be planning a full-scale climb of McKinley as well. We decided to join forces. They were in their early thirties; Sayre was a philosophy professor at Harvard, a grandson of Woodrow Wilson and confessed to being 'a little bit crazy' as a result of his attempt to run for Congress from the 25th Congressional District in California. Hansen had first passed his bar exam in Alaska, of all places, so he had at least been there. Neither of our prospective colleagues had had much climbing experience, though Sayre did point out that they had read a lot of books on the subject. They had done some climbing in the Alps during the Second World War and had since learned to tie knots with the Appalachian Mountain Club. No wonder they told Superintendent Grant that they only wanted to investigate the 'lower slopes' of McKinley. Their initial letter to us spoke of the wonders of the new equipment and down clothing they would be bringing. We mulled over the thought of some real equipment for ourselves, felt in our pockets and continued our rounds of Los Angeles Army surplus stores.

We arranged to meet at McKinley Park on July 15 and wrote to Superintendent Pearson with our plans. His answer would be waiting for us at the Park.

We had done some climbing. We had begun in the Boy Scout, broken Thermos

The Two Hundred Dollar Adventure

bottle days a few years earlier in the local California hills. Then as we acquired cars and the money to buy gas for them, we drove out to the California deserts, to the Sierras, the Cascades and the Canadian Rockies. There, the summer before, we managed to clamber up Mount Robson with the help of an expert from Seattle, Don Claunch.

It was about this time that Hillary and Tensing spoiled our program of climbing increasingly difficult mountains, by taking away the ultimate goal, Everest, without asking us. But, nevertheless, our own series of mountains seemed to be getting steeper, snowier, farther away and farther north, and it was becoming harder and harder to fend off questions as to why we went to all this effort to stand for a few minutes in a freezing wind on the top of a distant peak. Since the real reasons were only just condensing in our own minds we tried the usual ploy of saying, 'because it's there'. 'So is Niagara Falls, but that doesn't mean I have to go over it in a barrel', would be the reply. We eventually said it was safer than driving on Los Angeles freeways, and the air was fresher. People still shook their heads but we didn't care and went on planning for McKinley.

We knew it would be now or never for the big mountain. Graduation would be that June, our years of close association were ending and we would soon be separating to follow different paths. It had to be this summer and for us it had to be McKinley.

Jill was still trying to assert her position as secretary and chief co-ordinator of the expedition. Smoothing the coffee-stained paper, she said, 'Honestly, I don't think you can do it on $180 after all. I think we had better allow for higher gas prices on the Alaska Highway. I hear that in some places it's up to 45c a gallon'. Jac's face had a distinctly hurt look; we nodded grudgingly. $200 it was to be.

It also meant much more baby sitting for Jill. She had put herself through University by taking care of other people's children and $200 would be an enormous strain on her finances. But she wanted to come. She wanted to keep her eye on me.

So there were to be three men and a girl. To Alaska. To McKinley. Our friends laughed. 'Good luck, but we don't think you'll make it. It's too far and too high'.

I had heard stories about a lone woman and bad luck on ships at sea. There was no precedent for a woman causing bad luck in a '46 Chevy truck on the Alaska Highway. I couldn't blame Jill for what happened; it must have been something else.

Jill in her sleeping bag was in the middle; I was pushed against one side of the tent, Jac against the other. Cavalier that we were, we let the lady sleep in the dry center of the tent. Norm was warm and dry in his Chevy as usual. Over our heads the unusually wet British Colombia rain tried to penetrate the aged fabric of the Army surplus tent and was entirely successful.

Outside in the twilight the rain refilled the potholes emptied by the day's traffic on the Vancouver to Dawson Creek road. Those potholes had already caused the demise of one of our tires and no doubt contributed to the imminent death of our brakes. But they couldn't have been blamed for the clutch bearing that disintegrated back in Washington State.

The next morning, after a breakfast of the sadistically named breakfast cereal, 'Zoom!' we arranged ourselves in the Chevy for the last few miles into Prince George, B.C. As we bounced on to the Fraser River Bridge, Jac pointed out as he followed the map that it was now only 264 miles to Dawson Creek which was the *beginning* of the Alaska Highway. From there it was another 1520 miles to the end of the road in Fairbanks, Alaska. We sighed as Norm pulled into a garage and brought the truck to a stop with the hand brake. The master brake cylinder had gone.

We piled out and made our way through the perpetual rain to a supermarket, where more food was bought for the McKinley climb. We discovered that prices tended to increase with latitude and, although we were only about 54°N, we found that the food costs were stretching our $200 budget to the limit. The parting of $25 for the brake repairs made us wonder if we would even be able to make Alaska, much less McKinley.

The Hart Highway to Dawson City had only been opened two years, although in view of its surface we thought the opening had been at least two years premature. As we twisted and bumped along, our hard-bought equipment and food gradually destroyed itself in the truck behind us as it rose and fell. Over the clatter and din, the squeaks and thuds, we could dimly hear 'Three Coins in a Fountain' on Norm's radio. Our own coins seemed to be disappearing down the potholes of the John Hart Highway.

Next morning I shook the hundreds of bloodthirsty mosquitoes off the net over the entrance to the tent and looked out. Norm was crouched over the stove like an alchemist at his pestle and mortar. He was *frying* 'Zoom!'. He was convinced there must be a better way to cook the stuff, than the usual pot of gruel we were used to. Frying, it turned out, wasn't it.

In spite of the rain and the clutching mosquitoes, we decided that to prevent further destruction of our precious food we would package it for the climb here and now, in this beautiful B.C. Road Commission gravel pit. At the first slackening of the rain we spread the eye-catching boxes and packets out over the gravel. It looked like the beginnings of a food packaging convention. When seven hours and numerous bouts with the rain later we had all the climbing food into plastic bags, we had a graphic demonstration of the wastage in commercial packaging. The pile of brightly colored boxes, envelopes and foil bags rose like a McKinley of its own over the much reduced pile of their former contents.

July 4, American Independence Day. Jac shot off a rocket into the leaden sky; its sound reverberated around the valley. 'Damn it Jac, did you have to do that?' I said, annoyed. We drive miles to escape into the wilds and he brings rockets. Jill muttered something about little boys and their toys. Only slightly chastised, Jac put the rest of his arsenal in his pack. 'It's only sound,' he said.

The next day we reached Dawson Creek and as we turned around the white phallic column marking the beginning of the Alaska Highway we felt we were really on our way to Alaska at last. We had come 2348 miles in the 11 days since leaving Los Angeles on June 24, the day after graduation. Fairbanks was 1520 miles of unknown road ahead of us. As long as more bits didn't fall off Norm's truck, and we kept it

18

on 40 mph maximum, we might just make it.

As Jill, Norm and I clustered around the ringing gas pump, amazed at the rate at which the dollars accumulated at 55c a gallon, Jac disappeared into the station office. When he returned he had four free tumblers, four pieces of hard candy and last year's copy of the *Milepost*, all of which he had acquired free. He was useful, there was no denying that. Jill added the $6.60 for the gas to her tally of our expenses and we pulled out on the road to Alaska.

We left the grain elevators and low flat-topped plains buildings of Dawson Creek behind as Jac began to read from his free *Milepost*. The book turned out to be a mile by mile guide to the Alaska Highway, heavy on advertising such as 'The Yukon Ivory Shop' in Whitehorse 'specializing in prehistoric mastodon carved ivory, genuine Yukon ivory, gold nugget souvenirs, and a variety of jade, gold dust, and gold nugget jewelry, soapstone, nugget souvenir spoons, ivory curios, and a fine selection of English Bone China' or 'SQUANGA LAKE LODGE   MILE 849.5. GULF GAS.   MINOR REPAIRS.   LIGHT MEALS.   HOMEMADE PIES.'

Jac read the first page. 'It's paved all the way past Fort St John', he announced. Our tired tires sung on the macadam as we passed the first of the 1520 white mile posts we would see on the right side of the road all the way to Fairbanks. Each 4 × 4 white-painted post was topped by a board, angled in both directions, and displaying in black numerals the mileage from Dawson Creek. They seemed to be placed further and further apart as we went north.

Jac, who was determined to educate us, continued to read from the book. He was perched on the pile of climbing equipment in the back of the truck and he had decided to make the most of the relative quiet of the paved road to tell us about the highway. Whether Norm, Jill and I, crowded in the front seat, were receptive to the idea didn't matter and he proceeded.

'It was called the "Alcan" once,' he continued, 'Built by the Army during the war— typical stupid Army lingo—so the Japs wouldn't take Alaska. Built the whole damn thing in eight months. Opened November 1942.'

'Built by the Americans and then given to the Canadians,' muttered Norm, who didn't like to give things away either. 'That was twelve years ago and they still haven't paved it,' he added, and just then the Chevvy lurched on to the gravel that was to be our running companion (with the exception of the bliss of paved bridges), all the way to the Alaska border.

The country through which we were passing was boring. On either side hills of low pine, spruce and birch rolled on in endless green waves to the gray, cloudy horizon. Occasional areas of burnt timber grew fireweed and grass that breached the monotony of the straggling forest. Infrequently, an intrepid homesteader would demonstrate his defiance by clearing away the trees and planting oats or barley. The windows of his log house reflected the same gray skies and the green hills.

Maybe it was the weather (the rain and overcast skies showed no sign of breaking), maybe it was the country, but the morale of the party was sinking fast. We had been on the way almost two weeks, confined in the tin box of the Chevy, and were getting on each other's nerves. An explosion came when Jac mixed the peas and beans in

19

the same pot to 'save fuel'. Norm blew up. 'Who do you think is going to eat that crap!' he yelled at Jac. He threw down his plate and stormed off down the road to a cafe visible in the valley below.

Jill and I couldn't eat it either, but managed to fish out the wieners he had also put in the pot and make a meal of sorts. Jill tried to point out to Jac that next time, with the cohesion of the party at stake, he should ask first before mixing weird ingredients. It is because of small things that big mountains are climbed or not.

The next day, the storms of the night temporarily abated, we found ourselves driving along the shore of a beautiful jade green lake with the ridiculous name of Muncho. The distant peaks of the Rockies across the lake, their peaks red with the evening light of a sun we thought had gone out, were the first hills of any size we had seen since Dawson Creek. We slept that night on the shore of the lake in an Army pavilion that apparently had been built for officers of the road crew in which to have their 'happy hours'. It was now propped up on oil barrels and threatened to deposit us in the lake whenever we moved.

The bright sun the next day had an amazing effect on the road surface. Within hours it was turned from a gravel-mud mixture into a dry surface of waiting dust. As soon as a tire hit it the dust was released by the action of the tumbling gravel, caught in the treads and flung into the air. The front wheels forced dust into every crack in the old Chevy and up through the holes in the floorboards into the interior. The rear tires threw the dust out from the rear of the truck, but air blowing over the body created a vacuum over the back and the flexing joints of the doors admitted clouds of the dust to join that coming from the front. The result was that we were all soon coated with a film of light yellow powder, our hair, our eyes and between our teeth. The light winds of the day failed to disperse the cloud along the road and we drove on through steadily thickening fog.

The same trucks that passed us as terrifying rock-throwing monsters during the rainy days now loomed as dim dusty demons in the murk. Their headlights bouncing as they hit the potholes, they passed us with a roar and forced us to stop in the gloom. We began to long for clouds and rain again.

We could barely make out the rough sign at mile 496 that read 'Laird Hot Springs' and turned out of the tunnel of dust into the forest. We walked a half a mile from where we parked through an obstacle course of brush, over falling-down bridges that crossed small streams and finally came to a steaming pool surrounded by hanging threads of violets and a green and gold necklace of lush leaves and flowers. Jac was the first to strip and jump into the pool followed by Norm and me and reluctantly by an embarrassed Jill. The hot spring water dissolved our coating of dust and we became close again in the womb-like warmth of the pool. The possible success of the climb to come seemed more likely as our own sense of well-being improved. We put our feet together under the water. Our situation was absurd. Three men and a girl on their way to Alaska in a tropical oasis in the northern wood, immersed in hot water. We felt close at this moment, especially Jill and I, as we locked toes under the water. I wondered about our futures beyond the mountain and Alaska.

'Let's get this show on the road' said Norm, and climbed out of the pool.

The Two Hundred Dollar Adventure

By evening the rains had returned, gas was up to 68c, and we had entered the Yukon. We were 60°N.

The road snaked over the country in an aimless fashion as though it was following the wanderings of a drunken moose. For no apparent reason it would develop an 'S' bend in the middle of an open field. Apparently back in '42 the road builders were in such a hurry that they didn't have time to push in fill, but instead merely followed gravel ridges and avoided muskeg and swamp.

Norm, his eyes red, his arms tired from turning the wheel back and forth, stared through the blurry windshield at the endless road. (He was reluctant to entrust the wheel of his Chevy to either Jac or me.) The rest of us too, bouncing and jolting against each other, looking with glazed eyes at the repetitive scenery, were lost in thought. Jill's pony tail brushed my arm. Looking back I can see now that I was too young to know what was happening. Love was something I didn't take seriously. I was wrapped up in mountains and my own life. I wasn't mature enough to include Jill in it the way she wanted to be. I hardly recognized her there, her blonde hair straight back from her forehead, the red sweater I had bought her for the trip, pale now with dust. Her blue eyes seemed to look beyond the road and the trees. She was wondering too, unsure.

I wonder what the reaction would be now if it was proposed to build a road to Alaska across such a wilderness as northern British Columbia and the Yukon. I'm sure that if the road had been built today instead of in the hysteria of wartime, the cries from the conservation groups would have been loud and clear: 'DON'T!' Today with the highway a fact, its presence as the first slash through an incredible wilderness is hardly noticed.

We crossed the beginning of the Canol Road—also built during the war by the Army to provide access to the oil fields at Norman Wells on the Mackenzie River. The road and pipeline had hardly been used, and lay abandoned.

Whitehorse! Visions of Sam McGee, gold, the Yukon, Dawson City, Bonanza, Klondike! The reality after a lurching descent from the high bluffs traversed by the Alaska Highway was of a town of log cabins, corrugated iron buildings, with a few flat-topped government buildings. The town clustered along the south bank of a surprisingly small Yukon River, but remembering that the river still had 2200 miles to go to the Bering Sea, it was off to a reasonably good start.

The streets of Whitehorse were lined by the new horses of the north—pickup trucks. Mud-encrusted, a gasoline-filled oil barrel in the back, they waited in the rain, angled in rows, their headlights staring into gem shops, hardware stores, drugstores and a dime store. At the latter we got a new bug gun (the old one had expired after its three millionth mosquito) and a pot scratcher (too many burned meals had used up its predecessor). We decided to splurge and went into a tavern. It seemed entirely populated by bearded old men who all looked as if they had been there since '98. One grizzled miner, his eyes sparkling with the anticipation of having three young cheechakos to regale with tales told a thousand times, beckoned us over. 'Buy me a beer and I'll tell you about the Gobi.' We looked at each other. 'Gobi Desert?' It

Just after breakup on the Yukon at Dawson, Yukon Territory. It was May and the trees were just beginning to bud. I walked along the muddy street of the town, past faded signs sinking to invisibility, into the gray wood of the buildings. 'Quartz', 'Gold', 'Saloon'. Perched on the edge of the river, high out of the water, was the river-boat *Keno*, dragged up and put on display for the summer tourists; in its paddles were caught the brush, blocks of dirty ice and the driftwood of the high water of the breakup. Farther on, was the old saloon, new sawdust on the floor, fresh paint on the walls, ready for the tourists taking this cutoff from the Alaska Highway on their way to Fairbanks. Towards the edge of town a couple of raggy Indian kids had put a row of empty bottles on the second floor window sill of an abandoned house and were trying to smash them with rocks. All the windows in the house, left from the turn of the century when Dawson was bursting with thousands of Klondikers, gaped empty, black and cold on this bright May day. An Indian boy and his sister wheeled a toy wagon on which was placed an empty bucket down to the single water faucet that was the supply for that part of town.

Down by the river, close to the melting ice blocks that were strewn along the river bank by the force of the breakup, and set among some willows just budding, was a house made from the collected remains of several other buildings that lay in ruins nearby. One wall consisted only of doors nailed together, the roof was of tar paper and discarded pieces of corrugated iron. It looked as though a light breeze would take the whole thing down the river. The yard was of car parts, bed springs, sheets of tin, cans, boxes. Two Indian children played among the junk, making their own houses from the pieces.

I climbed the bluff north of town to a point where I could look down on this cabin, the last in Dawson. I settled in the warm brown grass, and listened to the deep murmur of the Yukon, freed from its prison of ice. In 1898 the paddle-wheeled steamers from St Michael on the Bering Sea, almost 2000 miles away, hooted when they rounded that bend, and the people of Dawson streamed down to the river. But the river is empty now.

Sounds of laughter came from the cabin. One man came out, staggered, and fell down. His hat rolled toward the edge of the bank. He crawled after it, picked it up, and stumbled back into the cabin. A few minutes later he burst out again, but stopped at the edge and looked down onto the broad brown river. Soon the door flew open again and the other man emerged in a rush and pushed the first down the slope. They scrambled for a while in the grass, then set off for Dawson, arm in arm.

might be worth a beer, we decided. He told us a wild story of how he heard about the Klondike when a young man in Russia, and set out across the Russian steppes in the spring of '98, crossed the Gobi Desert, caught a ship at Vladivostock and eventually arrived in San Francisco. There he boarded the steamer *Excelsior* and landed at Skagway. He had made fortunes and lost them, and now would we please buy him another beer. Talking made him thirsty.

We couldn't decide whether he had been hired by the Chamber of Commerce or was telling the truth. We would never know, but we bought him another beer anyway.

By evening we had made our way to the Yukon and there high on the sands of the bank were two steamboats. They looked like misplaced Mississippi river boats. I almost expected to hear Dixieland thumping out from their saloons, but they were silent. Propped up by timbers, their funnels black and rusting, many of their paddle boards askew or missing, lay the *Casca* and the *Whitehorse*. They were used as warehouses for lumber storage, their holds full of planks and beams.

We clambered up on the deck of the *Casca* and looked in the staterooms. 'Let's sleep here tonight' suggested Jill. 'It's dry and bugless.' 'Good idea!' I said, perhaps too eagerly. So far Jill and I hadn't had any privacy on the trip and this was before the days of group sex.

Later, in our own stateroom, we nearly destroyed a new sleeping bag by trying to put two into one. As Jill fell asleep, wedged tightly against me, I looked around the room and wondered about the people who had travelled in it.

Steamboats like the *Casca* had made their maiden trips up the Yukon from St Michael on the Bering Sea, in the fall of 1898 at the height of the Klondike gold rush. Their staterooms had been filled with the hopeful on their way to Dawson City, and return journeys were equally filled with broke and despondent Klondikers as they returned to their distant homes all over the world. Steamboats like the *Casca* had also plied the Yukon from the railhead of the narrow gauge White Pass and Yukon Route at Whitehorse, downstream to Dawson City, hauling goods and people brought up from tidewater at Skagway. After a quarter of a century the boats had been hauled up on the sands at Whitehorse and there they had slowly decayed and died. (The *Casca* and the *Whitehorse* burned to the ground in the summer of 1974, in a fire probably caused by vandals. Incredibly, the event was immortalized in postcards sold all over Alaska and the Yukon.)

North of Whitehorse the rain intensified, and anticipated views of the St. Elias mountains were denied us. Rising rivers of murky, icy gray water surged down from the unseen mountains, lapped over the tops of the bridges and disappeared into the forest to the east where they would eventually join the Yukon. The pines of the northern Rockies and the Cassair Mountains, through which the Highway had passed, were now replaced by the somber black spruce of the far north. In low cold valleys these trees grow to ten feet of stunted, dusky green stalks. Their roots spread thinly over the permafrost that forms a barrier just a few inches below the mossy cover. A gentle push and the tree, really a large bush, could be toppled.

We camped near Destruction Bay on Kluane Lake in a cold fog and incessant rain. Huddled in the back of the Chevy, we cooked in a steamy environment of boiling soup and burning gasoline fumes. In an attempt to bring light to this Dantesque scene, Jac raised his voice above the noise of the primus stove and began to read from a book of Robert Service poems he had acquired in Whitehorse:

'There's a land where the mountains are nameless,
    And the rivers all run God knows where;
There are lives that are erring and aimless,
    And deaths that just hang by a hair;
There are hardships that nobody reckons;
    There are valleys unpeopled and still;
There's a land—oh, it beckons and beckons,
    And I want to go back—and I will.'

The next day the highway six miles behind us was taken out by the rushing rivers and wasn't repaired for ten days.

The black and white mileposts marched on: 1219, 1220, 1221, ALASKA!

From the road we could see the thin swath cut through the trees running north and south—the Alaska/Canada border. A battered sign read 'Welcome to Alaska', but the anticipated paved road failed to materialize. The Alaska Road Commission had decided to tear it up for repairs and the road surface deteriorated alarmingly. We crawled from rock to rock and lost one more tire before we reached the pavement 30 miles farther on.

Once on the paved road Norm was so excited that he increased our speed to a dizzy 45 mph. He didn't realize the effect the frost-heaved road was having on our overloaded Chevy. At the bottom of one particularly vicious dip the left rear wheel rim split and the tire exploded. The truck ground ingloriously to a stop and our brief moment of speed was over.

But at least the sun was coming out. Its warm rays burnt the clouds from the skies and lifted our spirits. The back of the truck remained on the ground until a kindly Alaskan came by equipped with a Handiman jack and helped us to change the bent wheel.

We were ready to go but hesitated in a field of July flowers beside the road. The sun now streamed from an almost clear sky as we took off our sweaters and parkas and stretched out on the slope of the south-facing hill. Below us the Tanana River gathered its gray water from the streams that ran down from the distant glaciers of the Wrangell Mountains out of sight to the south. But ice and glaciers were far from this warm fragrant slope. Around us fireweed, forget-me-nots, lupines, bluebells and poppies splashed their colors through the grass. Bees and butterflies flitted from flower to flower and their hum made the day seem even warmer. I lay back and looked up. The sky was so clear now that I could see a blue infinity I had never seen before. Jill looked up, too. I wanted her to find the same distances in that sky that I had found. I wanted her to respond to the country. I felt it was important for us to share this experience, to make our discovery of Alaska together. The place would have a destiny for us.

25

Joe's Bar, Stampede Bar, Gold Nugget Bar, Bonanza Bar, Girls, Beer, Girls. The lights flashed on and off in the late evening twilight. On July 10 we entered Fairbanks. The road took a bend to the right and we pulled up to a red traffic light at Cushman and Second, our first since somewhere in southern B.C. We looked around the rough town; it was 10 p.m. and its lights were just coming on in bright twilight. Second Avenue to our right seemed to consist entirely of bars with the exception of the Lacey Street Theater and the Co-op Drug. Rough looking bearded men staggered from one bar to another in the flashing light of the neon signs. Fairbanks, the end of the road. The old Chevy rattled across the Cushman Street bridge over the Chena River and Norm turned into an industrial area near the railroad yards where we found a Quonset hut. These Army surplus temporary buildings, semicircular in shape and frequently covered with canvas, seemed to clutter up many an Alaskan town. Norm disappeared and returned a while later with four cans of Rainier beer. 'To celebrate.' We crawled exhausted into our sleeping bags spread on the dusty floor of the abandoned Quonset. McKinley was now just 140 miles to the southwest.

Sunday morning. The first day since we left Los Angeles 17 days and 4000 miles back when we didn't have the prospect of a long drive ahead of us. We slept until 10 when the hot sun turned the Quonset into an oven and baked us out of our sleeping bags.

We needed more cold weather equipment, but, with the stores closed, that would have to wait until Monday. We wandered back into town. In front of the Co-op Drug were a group of natives. They seemed at a loss as to what to do with themselves and held long-distance conversations with their friends across the street. The street had the air of a prairie town that had seen better days, but then this was Sunday and perhaps the inhabitants had deserted the place for the wilds, leaving its streets to the natives for whom the concrete and frame buildings would be a novelty. It was hot. The sign on the corner bank read 88°F and we headed for the river thinking of a swim, but the murky slow moving water soon convinced us otherwise. We resigned ourselves to a rest on the grassy bank, with white drifters and native down and outs as company.

In the evening we drove out to the University of Alaska and from the elevated campus, we could see McKinley. Away to the southwest, it looked like the tip of a distant iceberg rising above the stretching forests. It was like a beacon to us, and we felt that with our goal in sight and the Alaska Highway behind us our chances were decidedly better.

A man came up behind us.

'You seem awfully interested in McKinley.'

'We want to climb it.'

'I've done a little climbing around here, why don't you come up to the house and we'll talk about it.'

His name was John McCall and his house was tucked into the birch and aspen covered hills northwest of Fairbanks. We followed his car as he turned off the University hill and headed in the direction of the low green hills we could see to the north. We turned into a narrow rutted road and pulled up to a log house deep in a forest of aspen and birch. Four kids came running out, followed by Mary Ann, John's wife. We were welcomed inside and were soon given coffee and cookies.

'You'll stay for supper won't you?' asked Mary Ann.

'Sure, thank you' we replied, almost in chorus.

I looked around the cozy, warm house. One wall was completely covered with books, many on mountains. At one end of the room was a 'Franklin' stove, a type of freestanding fireplace that could be converted into a stove by closing the doors. In one corner was an elaborate hi-fi system with a row of classical records. Along the end opposite the Franklin stove was the kitchen, with Mary Ann busy preparing moose steaks.

After the delicious meal was over (moose tastes like lean beaf), and the kids sent to bed, we settled down with the last of the wine and talked of mountains.

John was a professor of glaciology at the University of Alaska at College near Fairbanks. He spent most of his summers doing research in the mountains and had climbed McKinley in 1948. He talked about the rescue of the Thayer party in May. Elton Thayer, Les Viereck, Woody Wood and George Argus had just completed a climb of McKinley from the south. They were descending Karstens Ridge, a steep knife-edge ridge on the route we proposed to follow. On a particularly steep and exposed slope, one member of the party slipped and dragged the others off the ridge with him. Thayer was killed instantly, and the others came to rest 1000 feet below on a less steep portion of the slope. George Argus had a dislocated hip, but Wood and Viereck were relatively unharmed. They waited six days for help to come, but then when it didn't they walked out 40 miles. John McCall led the rescue teams that saved Argus. He offered to head our stand-by party, to be called by the Park Service if we ran into trouble.

In the McCalls we saw a side of Fairbanks a million miles from the sort of life we had glimpsed darting in and out of the bars on Second Avenue. Here were people who had come to Alaska for Alaska herself, for the chance to experience a new and richer life. The McCalls were open people who had rejected the artificial life in the cities of the rest of America and had come to Alaska to try to find a more valid existence. Like many others, they had built their own house out of logs, and had come to know the true meaning of living a life close to the earth and the weather. This was in 1954, long before the 'back to nature' movement grew in California and spread across America. Our stay with the McCalls was too short. We wanted to see them again but within a few months John McCall would be dead, a victim of polio.

The Chevy climbed up the ramp onto the flat car like a thankful dog onto its bed. From Fairbanks she would go by train to McKinley Park, for there was no road. We blocked her securely onto the flat car and climbed into the spartan blue and yellow Alaska Railroad coach car. The hard leatherette seats were severely functional, but the unexpected smile of the conductor more than made up for the physical surroundings. The Alaska Railroad seemed to have the friendliest conductors around. This one eyed our ropes and ice axes.

'Climbing?'

About 50 miles upstream from this point the Nenana emerges from the snout of a glacier that drains the slopes of Mt Deborah, a 12,540-foot peak in the central Alaska Range. The infant stream, nearly opaque with the rock flour ground up by the action of the ice on its bed of rock, then flows over a broad gravel bar and into a wide valley. In summer the valley is green with watery meadows and clumps of spruce. Moose wander along the edge of the widening river and beavers build dams in its tributaries. Just north of Cantwell, a railroad stop called after the former name of the river, the Nenana enters Windy Pass and begins to cross the Alaska Range. Near Deneki Lakes, the point at which this picture was taken, the blue-gray water is split by ever more frequent rocks as the stream begins to cut through the gravel beds leading to the rock walls of Nenana Canyon. Turning itself into a foaming cauldron, it races into the canyon and forces itself through the last foothills of the Alaska Range, finally losing its identity by giving up its water to the brown flood of the Tanana at the Indian village of Nenana. In another 150 miles the Tanana will become the Yukon, and a thousand miles from the stretch shown in this picture the Nenana water will flow into the Bering Sea. A strong southerly wind from Windy Pass blows along the surface of the icy water, turning the ripples produced by the rocks into small waves that will become the haystacks of the Canyon. The Nenana has become a battle ground for canoeists and the wild waters of the Canyon have taken an early toll of life.

'Yes, McKinley.'

'Be careful, had a man killed on it last spring.'

'Yes, I know.'

Jill looked at me uneasily.

'I have to do it,' I said.

I don't know why I made such a stupid remark. As a young 23 I must have thought I had some right to such arrogance. Men (and boys) think they have some unalienable right to put themselves in deliberate danger, regardless of the cost in mental anguish to those who love them. I think now that they do it because of some primal drive, perhaps derived from the dangers and risks inherent in hunting. Man no longer must hunt, but the drive remains. He must prove himself. The ego devil within him must be satisfied and climbing a mountain is one way of doing it. But for those who wait it seems, and perhaps is, pointless extravagance.

The train crossed the broad brown Tanana River at the village of Nenana. A black and white sign down among the docks read 'Nenana Ice Pool'. Every spring in late March or April a large wooden tripod is placed on the ice in the middle of the Tanana. It is connected to a clock on shore by a wire. The ice usually goes out of the Tanana in a rush and when it does it takes the tripod with it and stops the clock. The bets on the time of the break-up run to over a hundred thousand dollars, and come from all over Alaska and the Yukon.

The mountains opened again after the confinement of the Nenana Canyon and the train pulled into McKinley Park Station. There on the platform, surrounded by a wealth of brand-new climbing equipment, stood Norman Hansen and Woodrow Wilson Sayre.

Chapter 3

McKinley

Woody Sayre handed me the letter:

> Messrs Lasner, Sayre, Gardey, Hansen & Sanders.
> Dear Sirs,
>   Your expedition appears to be well organized and equipped, with the exception of food, for your attempt to climb Mount McKinley via Muldrow Glacier and Karstens Ridge. It has been recommended that at least one and one half pounds of dehydrated food per man per day be provided. Your check list of food does not meet the recommended amount. Therefore, permission is granted for your attempt to climb McKinley with the following provisions:
> 1. Maximum of 30 days departure from Wonder Lake and return.
> 2. Forward climbing must stop and the return trip be started, regardless of 30 day time limit, when your food supply reaches full rations for five men for four (4) days.
> 3. Supplies and caches of food and equipment to be found on Muldrow Glacier are the property of the National Park Service and not to be used, moved or molested in any way except in case of life and death.
> With best wishes for a successful climb and safe return.
>
> Grant H. Pearson
> Superintendent
> Mt McKinley National Park

On January 4, 1960 a sun with no warmth rose over the Chugach Mountains and spread a yellow light on these black spruce laced by an overnight hoar frost. By the summer of 1974 this snow-covered swamp, just seven miles from the center of Anchorage, was gone. The straggly spruce, heaved to and fro by frost action, struggling to grow in the watery tundra of the swamp, were wrenched out by bulldozers and the swamp filled in with gravel. Sewer and water mains were buried in the gravel, roads built on the surface, and then came the houses. Forty houses were constructed in this swamp, split levels, three-bedrooms, four bedrooms, five bedrooms, kitchens with dish washers and eye-level grills, wall to wall carpets, sliding doors for the view of the neighbour's sliding glass door. The houses were warm and the hundred or more people who came from the southwestern states to live in them found it hard to believe the thermometer outside the kitchen window. Eventually they became used to the cold and decided to enjoy the winter. So soon the driveways of the houses were filled, not only with cars, but with snowmobiles, skis, trail bikes and sleds. The new people that had come to live in the houses had become Alaskans, determined to fill their lungs with fresh cold air, to use the great outdoors to enrich their lives. So they bundled themselves up, fired up the snowmobile and set off. But where? By the time they had the snowmobile turned around, that great open swamp with its fresh snow, that was just beyond their housing development, had been filled in with houses, too, houses much like the ones they lived in. And the next, and the next, until the city climbed up the distant Chugach. So they rode along the roads, prohibited to snowmobiles, late at night when there were no cops around. That soon became boring, and anyway it didn't seem to satisfy their desire to get into the open country, so next Sunday they put the snowmobile in the new trailer behind their car and set off down the Seward Highway. They found themselves in a long line of cars headed in the same direction, but at Thompson Pass, 60 miles from Anchorage, they reached their goal, turned into a parking lot already filled with cars and unloaded their snowmobile. Following the directions on the sign beside the road restricting snowmobiling to one side of the road only (the other side was reserved for skiers), they joined a growing herd of other snowmobilers in a noisy celebration of their freedom.

Mount Blackburn, 16,523 feet, in the Wrangell Mountains. This lake without a name is about 20 miles along the road from Chitina to McCarthy. Chitina was started in 1908 as a railroad and mining center, and reached its peak in the 20s when the rich copper deposits at McCarthy, 30 miles farther on over to the right of Blackburn, were being exploited by the mining interests of J. P. Morgan and Simon Guggenheim. They established the Kennecott Mine at McCarthy, and by the time the mine was closed by a strike in 1938, it had produced over $200 million dollars worth of copper for its backers. The copper was taken to a port at Cordova by means of the Copper River and Northwestern Railroad, constructed for the purpose. It is on the roadbed of this railroad that the gravel road to McCarthy has been built. It is the desire of the state of Alaska to rebuild the railroad right of way from Chitina to Cordova as a road, but this plan has been opposed by conservation interests on the grounds that the area has potential as a park.

The lake is silent, the air calm. Even the mosquitoes have settled down in the cool of the July evening. The sun is in the northwest, lighting only the higher foothills and the snow peaks. The Alaskan summer is at its height, the slopes of the foothills are green to the rocks, the lily pads full grown, the lake grass luxuriant. The air has a nip, but then in the sub arctic it always does without the sun to banish the threat of winter cold that is never far away. I pull my parka closer and lean against the rough mossy bark of a black spruce. The small tree leans under my weight, then stops. I hear nothing louder than the beating of my heart.

'And somebody called Oscar Dick is coming around tomorrow to see if he can break our ice axes!' said Norman Hansen.

Jac and Woody were two of a kind and therefore took an initial dislike to each other. They were both demonstrably extrovert, each wanting to hold the floor. As they couldn't both do their acts at the same time, a jockeying for position ensued that wasn't pleasant to watch. In our group of three we hadn't thought of a leader, merely that we all wanted to climb McKinley, for whatever reason. With such a single-minded goal in mind, we felt we could do without the para-military cast a leader would give the party.

We would have climbed the mountain ourselves, were it not for Superintendent Pearson's regulations, and only reluctantly joined Woody and Norm. This was unfortunate, because I feel that if we had planned the climb together from the beginning it would have been a happier experience. As it was, two separately equipped parties from opposite ends of America, a generation apart, were now together and the climb had to begin.

We felt too, that we were being used (as I suspect they did too). I'm sure they looked on us as green young students with some climbing experience behind us, but little other experience of life. Hence, they treated us diffidently at first, and assumed the roles of father figures, in this way hoping to hold the party together when things got difficult.

Norm, like his namesake in our group, was a man of few words. He and Sayre had been close friends since their days together in the Army in Europe, and they obviously formed a social unit of their own.

But it was the meat bars that did it. In the camp to which we repaired after unloading the Chevy, we dumped all our food on the ground to see if we could convince Superintendent Pearson to give us more time. Foil wrappers glinting in the sun, the crowning glory of their pile was an enormous quantity of concentrated meat bars. At 75c each this costly item was way beyond our budget, but they had a hundred of them.

Jac read off our list: 51 lbs of food each, consisting of Baker Boy confection roll, instant potato, instant rice, lemon and chocolate bits, peanuts, oatmeal, Ralston, Brex, Grape Nuts, logan bread, pilot bread, Ovaltine, Nemo, tea, lemon powder, rice soup, raisins, fruit cookies, dates, fig bars, bouillion cubes, margarine, canned Uruguayan beef, salt, sugar (35 lbs), candy, cocoa, cheese. It worked out to 5500 cal. per man per day. He also brought out a map made for us by John McCall, showing the position of the caches on the mountain that were 'not to be used, moved or molested in any way except in case of life and death.'

Our equipment was meagre. Jac was to borrow Jill's sleeping bag, and I her air mattress and her ice axe, though I did have a new parka bought for $17.95 in Seattle. Most of the rest of our gear was Army surplus, olive drab and heavy. In contrast, the Sayre contingent had the latest down clothing and a mouth-watering array of food including canned butter.

Oscar Dick, Chief Ranger, rested his official foot on my ice axe as it leaned against a rock. It bent but didn't break. 'All right,' he said grudgingly.

He gazed at our motley pile of equipment that looked as though it had been left by a retreating army. 'That it?' We nodded. 'All right,' he acquiesced, 'But remember— 30 days and you should be down. We don't want to waste the taxpayer's money getting you off that thing, do we!' We nodded in deference to officialdom.

Grant Pearson, when we visited his office, turned out to be friendly and easy in contrast to his official-sounding letters. He told us a little about his 1932 climb of McKinley which had followed the same route we proposed, but he had started from where we were then, Park Headquarters, 100 miles from the mountain.

'Used dog teams' he said, in answer to our quizzical looks.

During our conversation he mentioned that he had first come to Alaska in 1925.

'But there wasn't any Alaska Highway then,' he added. 'Could only get here by ship from Seattle.'

I asked him why there wasn't any road to the Park. It seemed a lot of trouble for everybody to put their cars on the train.

'No money,' he explained. 'Anyway, I'm not sure it would be a good thing. This Park is fragile. It can't take too many people. Good luck on your climb. I hope the weather lets you have a chance.'

We piled our gear into the Chevy. All six of us climbed into the protesting machine and we set off on the last 85 miles to our starting point. According to our map, the road ended 91 miles out at an old mining town called Kantishna, after passing a place marked Camp Denali.

The Chevy, in its lowest gear, ground up Polychrome Pass. As we edged around the loose varicolored cliffs that dropped away to a glistening river far below, the temperature gauge pegged at 'H' and a cloud of steam blossomed from beneath the hood. Norm eased into the parking area at the top, the Chevy sounding like a fire-breathing dragon with indigestion.

Parked next to us was a gray jeep. Leaning against the fender and munching an apple was a red-headed fellow with a smile that was verging on a laugh.

'Looks like you guys could use some water; I've got some here.'

He helped Norm lift the hood and introduced himself as Woody Wood.

'Not *the* Woody Wood!' I exclaimed. We bombarded him with questions about the mountain on which he had so recently almost perished. It was unfair to question him so about an accident in which he lost a close friend and almost his own life, but we were hungry for information about McKinley, and he was willing to give it. In fact I took an immediate liking to his welcoming manner. His response to complete strangers was similar to that of the McCalls back in Fairbanks.

I began to see Alaskans as individuals, as people I would like to know and not as some vague group of pioneers scattered about in the north woods. And what is more, they all seemed to know each other. There was a communication between those people that easily spanned the physical distances between them. It turned out that the three people we had met so far, John McCall, Grant Pearson and Woody Wood, were all good friends. We mentioned our major lack of a pair of snowshoes to Woody who immediately suggested we ask his wife, Ginny, at Camp Denali.

We left Woody at Polychrome Pass and puffed and steamed through the foothills of the Alaska Range. McKinley itself was lost behind ridges and clouds ahead

Most of Alaska receives surprisingly little snow. In the mountains along the coast, along Prince William Sound and over those of Southeast Alaska, mountains that take the full force of Pacific storms, snowfall is high, and when melting begins in April it can be 30 feet deep. But over the vast Interior, over Cook Inlet and the Copper River Basin, only a couple of feet will accumulate on the ground in an average winter. In the arid Arctic there will be even less, while in Southwest Alaska and the Aleutians, areas that experience frequent winter thaws, snowcover will occasionally disappear completely. Here, at Deneki Lakes, it is late December and there is about two feet of cold, powdery snow on the surface of the lake. The air temperature is about 20 below F., there is no wind and it is noon. The sun has reached its highest point for the day, just the height of a tree on the south of the lake, and in a few hours the crystal skies will blaze with stars and aurora.

Alaskan winter weather usually runs in cycles of a week or more, a week of cloudy, snowy weather followed by a week of clear, cold skies. Rarely is there a day to day alternation of storm and sun as is the common pattern of weather in the temperate zone. High pressure in Arctic winters can build for weeks, allowing the snow-covered ground to radiate what little heat it has retained from the warm days of September, for there is no heat in that sun, barely able to climb above a tree. After a week of the clear skies produced by the high pressure, the temperature will be 40 below F., another week and it could be 60 below. Extremes below minus 80 have been reached, and it is on days like those that the appearance of clouds on the southern horizon, like these creeping up over the Alaska Range near Windy Pass, will lift spirits. For clouds mean warmth, a retreat from deep cold, a veil drawn across the awful void of space that is robbing the earth of its vital heat.

somewhere, but all around us were hills of unique beauty. They had a beauty not borne of classic concepts of mountains with snow on top and trees below for there was neither snow nor trees. At 3000 feet we were above the sub-arctic timber line and the 18 hour-a-day sun had melted all the snow except that lying in protected valleys, and the few patches of permanent ice visible on the mountains to the south. The hills were bare and stark. They loomed dimly under their cloud shadows like lurking giants. We could see no-one on the road ahead of us and seemed to be moving into a world of dark mystery as the afternoon clouds closed low over the peaks. Looking up toward Highway Pass I could see nothing but the grass-covered slopes turning to rock and merging into cloud. We saw no animals. The way ahead was as empty of life as though an Arctic wind had come in mid-summer and taken it all away.

Gradually the narrow dirt road wound down out of the ominous hills and the gray clouds, and what seemed to be an enormous golden cloud appeared before us, lit by the setting sun. The cloud was McKinley. We stopped, and stared. Its two lofty peaks crowned what seemed to be an entire mountain range pushed together into one mountain, so huge did it appear. The wall on the right, three vertical miles of snow, rock and ice, rose like a fountain into the slanting rays of the northern sun. The mountain was a presence. Even when I turned my back on it, I could feel it. We looked at each other, all with the same doubt and fear on our faces. The top didn't beckon to us. It was a remote, other world of ice and snow. Distant.

By the time we reached the base of the road leading up to Camp Denali, the country was in deep twilight. I cranked the old Army field phone. A confident voice came back. 'Yes, we were expecting you. Come on up!'

Ginny, Woody's wife, greeted us with a strong handshake as we met her in the cluster of tent cabins at the top of the road. Just below them on the edge of the sloping shelf on which the camp was built was a small tarn. Beyond that, like a giant ghost in the twilight, was McKinley, now 25 miles away. We were led into the largest tent cabin which served as dining room, and there met the third member of the trio that ran Camp Denali, Celia Hunter. Both Ginny and Celia had that matter-of-fact easy welcome I had now come to expect from Alaskans. They set us down and put coffee and cookies in front of us. We talked of McKinley and Alaska. Alaskans seemed eager to talk to anyone about the territory.

After supper I pored over the camp library, thumbing through the extensive collection of books on McKinley and Alaska, books I had never seen before. By the light of the hissing Coleman lantern I read the history of the big mountain.

Frank Densmore, a 200 lb miner from the Klondike was the first white man to see it at close range, and it was called Densmore's Mountain for years among the miners in Alaska and the Yukon in the late 1800's.

The Russians called it Bulshaia Gora, the Athabascan Indians, Denali, The Great One, and W. A. Dickey, a prospector, good Republican, and an American not to be taken in by these previous names, called it McKinley in honor of a man running for U.S. President, a man who had never seen it. Unfortunately, we are stuck with the name, thanks to Dickey. At least he didn't name it after himself. (A campaign is now under way in Alaska to change the name to Denali).

The first sighting of the mountain by a white man was contained in the records of George Vancouver who, in 1794, mentioned 'distant, stupendous, snow mountains' to the north. He had the grace not to name them, but then he had already scattered his name around the Pacific Northwest.

A hundred years or so later, after the U.S. had bought Alaska from the Russians, Dickey appeared on the scene, and in his footsteps followed the U.S. Geological Survey in the persons of George Eldridge and Robert Muldrow. With their plain tables and transits they fixed McKinley's height at 20,464, though it has since been lowered 144 feet. Both these men left their names on McKinley's glaciers. Eldridge's flows out of the southwest side of the massif and Muldrow's is the 40-mile-long ice river on the northeast, the upper part of which we planned to ascend.

In 1903 Judge Wickersham tore himself away from his official duties in Fairbanks and with four others packed in the 140 miles from the new boom town. They decided on a direct frontal assault and began to climb the stupendous 15,000-foot north face of the mountain. At a point 8000 feet above sea level, at the very base of the wall, they gave up an obviously futile exercise, and returned to Fairbanks. Wickersham left his name on the wall he tried to climb.

The next man to appear in the McKinley saga was a fraud, Dr Frederick Cook. He was either suffering delusions of grandeur or an inferiority complex, but he approached first McKinley and then the North Pole purely as a means to enhance his personal image. In the case of McKinley he first surprisingly spent a considerable time in genuine exploration of its southern and northern approaches. Then with a single companion he disappeared for a few weeks in the direction of the mountain. He returned with the claim that he had climbed it and produced photographs as proof. The climbers of the day were deeply suspicious but Cook, his ego bursting, wrote a book, lectured and became known as 'The Conqueror of McKinley'. His undoing wasn't to come for seven years.

Meanwhile the boys in the backroom decided to have a go. Pete Andersen, Bill Taylor and Charlie McGonagall sat around a rough table in Billy McPhee's Fairbanks saloon and decided that it was high time somebody from Alaska got up the damn thing before some outsider actually made the top. They *knew* Doc Cook was a fraud. There were a lot of quick-buck characters in Alaska then and he looked a likely candidate to them. 'By just looking at that mountain, we knew he was a liar.' Billy McPhee and two other Fairbanks saloon keepers each gave them $500. They talked three of their more daring friends into going with them and the party of six set off into a late March snowstorm in the general direction of McKinley. They had a leader by the name of Tom Lloyd and an idea that they would follow a route through a pass later named after McGonagall, which they had explored earlier while hunting for gold in the McKinley foothills.

They had no esoteric reasons for climbing McKinley. They merely wanted to show their friends in Fairbanks that they could do it. They approached the problem in the frontier spirit of the day: take what you can, while you can. It is an aggressive way to do things, a good American 'go get 'em' policy. It gets things accomplished; the oil companies tried the same thing years later. The consequences of the policy depend on what you are doing. In climbing McKinley it can be spectacularly successful. If you are invading a wilderness with men and machinery it can be a disaster.

But first the sourdough climbers ran into an internal problem. Two of the party had an argument with Lloyd in the foothills, said 'to hell with you', and trudged back to Fairbanks. The rest continued up the Muldrow, and with remarkable determination reached 12,000 feet. Here Lloyd became ill and could go no farther. That left three—Pete, Bill and Charlie. On April 10 the weather improved and Charlie poked his two companions. 'Get up you louts, it's clear!'

With primitive equipment they plodded up Karstens Ridge into the whitening heights above; taking turns carrying the 14-foot flagpole they were going to plant on top. At 16,000 feet Charlie gave up but Pete and Bill managed to drag the flagpole to 19,000 on the North Peak, then they went down to pick up Charlie and return to camp at 12,000 feet.

Two days later, with a picnic lunch, they climbed up again, finished the climb to the summit of the North Peak at 19,470 feet, and put their flagpole in some rocks near the top.

When the sourdoughs reached Denali Pass, at 18,200 feet between the higher South Peak of McKinley and the North Peak, they knew which way to turn—to the right, up the North Peak. That peak was visible to their friends (girl and otherwise) in Fairbanks. They wanted to be seen to have climbed this mountain. Why else carry that damned flagpole to the top?

A week later they were back around the table in Billy McPhee's saloon. The increased business they brought in with their stories more than repaid Billy's $500.

The sourdough climbers were a welcome change in the line of distinguished visitors to McKinley, for the next pair in 1912 were the physicist and university professor Herschel Parker and his friend, a well known painter named Belmore Browne. They planned to follow the same route as the sourdoughs, but, as befitted their position, to follow it in a sophisticated and organized manner. They pored over maps, planned camps and equipment. They started in late February from Seward on the Pacific, 300 miles from McKinley. By June they too were at the head of the Muldrow at 11,000 feet. But they didn't have that clear April day that the lucky Fairbanks prospectors had. Instead the blizzards lashed at McKinley's upper slopes with an unremitting frenzy. Parker, Browne and one of their two companions, La Voy, struggled into the darkness of the storms above. For days they waited at 16,000 feet. Finally the weather cleared and they decided to try for the top—the South Peak this time. But within hours the storms gripped the mountain again and they turned back—300 feet below the top. Another attempt a day later failed 1000 feet below the peak and they began their descent, dejected and full of 'dull despair'. This expedition was their third to McKinley and it too was to end in failure. They were unlucky, or were they?

On the evening of July 6 the party was camped in the tundra just north of the range. Browne remarked that the sky was a 'sickly green color and the air seemed heavy and lifeless'. He couldn't have known that 400 miles away on the Alaska Peninsula, Mount Katmai had been erupting since June 6 and in the first 60 hours had poured

7 cubic miles of pumice and ash into the air. No wonder the sky looked 'sickly green'. Earthquakes had been occurring along the Alaska Peninsula for almost a month.

Suddenly, a 'deep rumbling' came from the Alaska Range . . . 'a sinister suggestion of overwhelming power that was terrifying'. 'Good God! Look at Brooks!' exclaimed Aten, the fourth member of the party. The entire range, including the 12,000-foot Mount Brooks, was avalanching as the ground shook in a violent earthquake. Tons of ice and snow cascaded from all the peaks in a thunderous roar and spread out in a swirling cloud of ice particles. Soon the tiny camp of the climbers was engulfed in a stinging storm of ice and snow that almost swept them away. Had they stayed a few more days on McKinley they would certainly have been killed.

I looked at Brooks through the dining-room window. The soaring white summit ridge of the peak glowed in the moonlight, peaceful, calm and apparently solid. In ten years I, too, would learn to mistrust the earth. I pumped the flickering Coleman and read on.

It was an Archdeacon this time. Building on the experience of the previous parties, the Rev. Hudson Stuck, Episcopal Archdeacon of the Yukon climbed the south peak of McKinley with a four-man party on June 7, 1913.

Let me quote the Archdeacon's words as he stood on the top. They describe how one man came to terms with the illogicality of his position.

> Only those who have for long years cherished a great and inordinate desire, and have had that desire gratified . . . can enter into the deep thankfulness and content that filled the heart . . . There was no pride of conquest . . . no gloating over good fortune that had hoisted us a few hundred feet higher than others who had struggled and had been discomfited. Rather was the feeling that a privileged communion with the high places of the earth had been granted; that not only had we been permitted to lift up eager eyes to these summits, secret and solitary since the world began, but to enter boldly upon them, to take place, as it were, domestically in their hitherto sealed chambers, to inhabit them, and to cast our eyes down upon them seeing all things as they spread out from the windows of heaven itself.

And he saw the sourdough's flagpole still stuck in the north peak, and also disproved for all time the fraudulent claims of Doc Cook.

The second ascent wasn't made until 1932 and included our friend Grant Pearson in the party. In the same year the first two deaths occurred when Carpe and Koven, two members of a scientific expedition on the upper Muldrow, fell into a crevasse and froze to death. During the war the Army took over McKinley as a test site for equipment, and in the succeeding ten years the total number of parties to make the South Peak had come to eleven. We hoped to be the twelfth.

I went to sleep that night with the Archdeacon's words in my head: ' . . . a great and almost inordinate desire . . . ' I only hoped that our own desire would be strong enough to take us through the storms that would lie ahead.

Within the city limits of Anchorage is a park called Russian Jack Springs. In winter it is laced with ski and snowmobile tracks and those of the few moose that still wander in to the edges of the city. The relatively warm stream is giving up the last of its summer heat in vapour to the calm 10 below air that hovers over its surface.

Beyond the distant spruce lies a jumble of houses and trailer courts and beyond that is a large area set aside by the army. For years this large tract of land has been coveted by Anchorage real estate agents for development as an area for housing. Cut by the two forks of Campbell Creek, it supports a beautiful growth of spruce and birch and its rolling hills rise to join the Chugach. It must be worth millions on the real estate market. It would make a good park too, but I would say that the chances of that occurring are nil.

Jac went across first. Below the little hand car, suspended from the thin cable, the waters of Moose Creek ran fast and clear. At the lowest point Jac's feet dragged in the water, and then he pulled himself up to the far bank. I pulled the car back and put Jill in it and sent her down towards the water. After a few minutes we were all on the far side and walking towards a low log cabin. The walls of the cabin were hung with snowshoes, traps, pans and gear of all sorts. Standing in the door was a short man with a big smile on his face, Little Johnnie. He was of indeterminate age, one of those people who beyond a certain time seem to age no more, but merely look wiser and happier.

As soon as we were all inside the cabin Little Johnnie disappeared down a trap door in the floor.

'Be right back', were his parting words.

I looked around. The big logs of the cabin were dark with the smoke of a thousand fires. The one room had all Little Johnnie needed to survive. A couple of bunks, a stove, and shelves and cupboards filled with every imaginable bit and piece necessary to fix anything. Watches, snowshoes, dog harnesses, clothes.

Little Johnnie returned with some bottles.

'What is it?' asked Jill sceptically.

'My brew,' said Johnnie. 'Just molasses, hops, rice and sugar. It's good!'

Jill's face told me she was questioning the hygiene of the glasses into which he was pouring the dark liquid, but I'm sure the alcohol in that brew would have killed anything.

'Ginny up at Camp said you might have a pair of snowshoes we could borrow,' began Norm.

'Yep, I got some you can use—going up McKinley?'

'Yes, we'll need them about a month.'

'Don't matter. Time don't matter to me. No snow here until September anyway.'

Johnnie Busia was half the population of Kantishna. He had come to Alaska from Croatia in 1918 and had spent most of the time since then in the hills of the Kantishna. Eight months out of every year he spent alone. Kantishna once had a population of 2,000 during the gold stampede of 1906, but now there were only two, and the other fellow was only there in the summer. Johnnie was one of those men left behind in the north long after their reason for going there in the first place had disappeared. He had come for the gold, but now the gold had run out and in the isolation and silence of the Alaskan wilderness he had found something more valuable, an inner contentment and a harmony with the world around him. It showed on his face and in his easy smile. For his life he used what the land around him had to offer. He canned its berries and the vegetables from his garden near the cabin. He killed just enough of its caribou to provide for his needs. He trapped foxes, but only enough to bring him the money to buy the things he couldn't find around him in the Kantishna. He didn't need visitors, though he was compassionate enough to welcome us and to loan us his snowshoes. He was already drawing his world in around him as he grew older. Finally, it would consist only of him. Then he would look out on the familiar Kantishna hills and be at peace, with himself and with the wilderness world around him.

44

McKinley

Little Johnnie died in the Kantishna three years later, in August 1957.

With the borrowed snowshoes under his arm, Norm led the way back across Moose Creek and we headed for Wonder Lake. Our own attempt to find out something about ourselves was about to begin.

I couldn't get up. I used my ice axe as a prop, but I still couldn't get up. Jill pulled and pushed on my pack and I managed to get to my knees. I was only with difficulty able to stand erect. The sweat poured from my forehead and my knees quaked. Was I supposed to carry this 110 pounds up McKinley? I could barely stand, much less walk.

We set out on the trail to the mountain. Jill would come with us as far as the Bar Cabin on the banks of the McKinley River. She had found a job washing dishes at Camp Denali and would wait there for our return.

From the pool of mud on the trail, into which my boot had just sunk, to the top of McKinley was 39 miles, but I could see already that I, at least, would not be able to carry this much weight very far. If I could make the Bar Cabin two miles away I would be doing well. The walk through the spruce forest was no doubt pleasant in the soft evening light, but I didn't notice. My heart pounded in my ears as it vainly tried to force blood through the arteries in my shoulders, pinched by the pulling straps of the pack. I staggered through the forest in a daze, always in imminent danger of toppling over into the dripping muskeg. The others seemed to be doing much better, especially Norm Sanders who strode ahead of the group oblivious of the enormous weight on his back. But it was midnight when we reached the cabin; it had taken us two hours to walk two miles.

The Bar Cabin was one of several remote cabins scattered throughout McKinley Park. It served as a refuge for winter dog-sled patrols of the Park. There was no-one there when we arrived, and we collapsed in a confused array on the cabin floor, too exhausted to talk.

The sun next morning filtered weakly through broken clouds as I watched Jill enter the spruce forest again. She was going back to work at Camp Denali. We had been intensively living together, taking in new impressions and sensations, both of each other and of the vibrant country to which we had come. We both needed now to pull apart and look around us as individuals again. We were not yet ready to assume a dual outlook on the world, nor too close a look into each other. I looked after her disappearing figure with a mixture of relief and regret.

We shouldered the horrendous packs again and set out to cross our first obstacle, the McKinley River. The snout of the Muldrow Glacier about ten miles to our left disgorged a great quantity of icy gray melt water that spread into several channels over a wide gravel bar. At our crossing point this bar was two miles wide. We crossed the first seven channels without incident.

I stood on the bank of the eighth channel. Hansen, who had crossed before me, had stumbled close to the opposite bank and was just pulling himself dripping from the water.

Crossing the other channels of rushing ice water had built up in me a fear of

Alaskan glacial streams that never left during all the climbing I did there. The relentless rush of opaque water spoke of death. Once caught, the river would never release me, or so it appeared.

Halfway across and the water was up to my waist, pulling at my legs, foolishly clad in trousers. My legs and feet were numb from the cold and wouldn't function properly. My right foot stepped on a rolling rock and I was down. The climbing rope, tied around my waist and held by Woody, went taut and I was pulled under; my pack pressed my head to the bottom. I forced myself up. 'Let go!' I gasped and went down again, but with the rope released I was moving downstream in the waist-deep water and could work my head above the icy flow. At last I was washed up on a shallow bank near the far side and crawled weakly onto the gravel.

I assessed the damage. One lost ice axe meant we would have to use our spare. My left arm had lost feeling and was almost uncontrollable. Apparently the pack had pinched a nerve; it would be ten days before I could control the arm again.

We decided to divide our loads in half and relay at least to 10,500 feet at the head of the Muldrow. By that time we would have cached and eaten enough to enable us to make the final climb with one manageable load.

The way ahead to the foothills lay over tundra. Most of the lowlands of Alaska and the Arctic are covered with this demonic mixture of grass, small bushes, water and mud. With permafrost only a foot or two down, rain and melt water remain near the surface, and our stumbling, sucking progress was depressing and discouraging.

As we picked our way through the swampy grass, each step released a cloud of mosquitoes that swarmed around our eyes and ears. The mosquito dope we spread over our faces and hands was soon washed away by our sweat. Although it was raining slightly, and the mountains were obscured in cloud, the air was warm. We were at the low point of the climb—1200 feet above sea level. We had 19,000 feet to go.

In the evening of the third day we made our camp on a sandbar in the middle of the Clearwater River, in an effort to escape the mosquitoes. We were only moderately successful. The bloodthirsty bugs swarmed around the netting on our tents in clouds almost as thick as the wet fog that had now enveloped everything.

Sunday, July 18. The sun. Steam rising from sodden but drying sleeping bags. Spirits rising in depressed climbers who were beginning to wonder if this were some sort of purgatory before the white gates of McKinley would open.

Woody, wearing the black hat that made him look like a bad guy in a Western, disappeared into the brush. When he returned an hour later, his hat was inverted in his hands.

'Peace offering' he said, and handed the hat around, full of blueberries. The gesture alleviated somewhat the tension that had been building up on the walk from the McKinley bar. Small things that create friction such as how to break a candy bar into five pieces, when to stop and rest. With our loads cut in half we moved much better. But we students put on a silly display of arrogant youth in walking fast and then waiting impatiently for the 'old men' to catch up with us. It was foolish and was beginning to separate the two groups. Woody was trying to smooth over a blow-up which occurred earlier when he tried to tell us to slow down.

McKinley

'Thanks for the blueberries, Woody,' said Jac. As we dug into the fresh food, I looked around at the circle of faces, their teeth becoming blue with the berry juice. Jac with his blue and gold UCLA rooter's cap and straggly week-old black beard looked like a confused prospector, Norm's beard was more promising and he looked more like someone actually in the process of climbing a big mountain. Woody and Hansen settled back in their down parkas. Woody seemed pleased with the response his blueberries had produced, and his face broke into a blue-toothed smile when our eyes met.

By the next afternoon we were at McGonagall Pass with half our loads. Charlie, the sourdough, had been through the pass forty-four years earlier with his 14-foot flagpole. We sat on the slate-colored rocks in the warm late-afternoon sunlight. This pass marked the end of the tundra and rock and the beginning of the ice. From our right the blue-white river of the Muldrow Glacier swept down from the darkening shadows under McKinley and disappeared to our left in a haze of dirty ice and fog. Between us and the ice wall of the glacier was a stream of liquid ice and at that moment none of us could see a way across. High up beyond the head of the glacier, the North Peak soared into a deep blue sky, distant, remote, and irrelevant to our prosaic pack carrying. We turned our backs on the spectacle of this fantasy world and returned to the familiar one of mosquitoes, tundra and, by 9 p.m., more rain.

By the next evening we were back, but the North Peak, the Muldrow, everything was gone in rain and fog. The three of us crowded into the old Army tent, dripping wet and cold. Sayre and Hansen were only slightly better off in their more spacious tent.

During the night I thought the rain was stopping; its patter on the fabric had become a gentle hiss. I looked out (it was my turn to have my head at the entrance end). A dim blue white world of swirling snow presented itself to me. Snow!

I looked out again the next morning. Woody's face appeared at the entrance to his tent about five feet away. Between us a rush of snowflakes muffled our words.

'Damn weather,' I said, in place of 'Good morning'.

'Damn weather,' he agreed.

'What should we do?'

'Wait.'

'Can't wait too long or we'll run out of time. Week's gone already.'

'Can't see a thing out there on the Muldrow, can you?'

'No,' I said, craning my neck around to look, my eyelids blinking away snowflakes. 'Damn weather.'

Three hours later I had finished a Somerset Maugham story or two and looked out again. It was the same.

'Woody!'

'What,' came from the opposition.

'It's still snowing, can't see a thing,' I announced superfluously.

'So?'

'We'll have to move, or we'll never get up the damn thing.'

'All right. But let's wait till this evening. Maybe it'll stop.'

Mount McKinley from the east. The ridge in the right foreground rises to the summit of Mount Koven, 12,210 feet, then drops along a snow ridge to the base of Karstens Ridge, at the notch below the small gray cloud. Karstens Ridge then rises through the cloud to a break, and above the break is the arching crest of the Coxcomb that ends on the rocks of Browne Tower at 14,600 feet. Just to the right of Karstens Ridge the ice of the Harper Glacier falls into the broken blocks of the Harper Icefall, the lower end of which is lost behind the snow ridge of Mount Koven. The Harper Glacier itself rises in a series of small steps or icefalls to Denali Pass, 18,200 feet at the extreme upper right of the picture. On the right of the Harper Glacier the sharp dark rocks of a ridge lead to the North Peak, off the right edge of the picture. The small peak on the top skyline is called the Archdeacon's Tower, after Archdeacon Stuck, and its top is 19,650 feet. The skyline ridge climbs through a cloud to the summit of the South Peak, 20,320 feet, the highest point in the picture.

Only the top half of McKinley is visible in this picture, taken with a telephoto lens from Eielson on the McKinley Park road 30 miles away, near the place where we had our first sight of the mountain. Our camp that was almost destroyed by avalanches was in the shadow just beyond Browne Tower, and our route crossed the Harper Glacier to hug the right side below the North Peak. The wind blowing over the South Peak is from the north, probably about 40 knots, and a small lenticular cloud clings to the slope below the summit. It was probably a cloud similar to this that pinned us to the snow on our last day, though the cloud looks innocuous enough from this distance. It is July, about the time of year we were on the mountain. The sun has melted some of the snow from the south (left) slopes of Mount Koven, but otherwise the sub arctic mountain shows little change from winter to summer.

Deneki Lakes and Carlo Mountain, mid summer.

Mount McKinley from Camp Denali.

We have climbed it. Good weather continues and Woody Sayre is the last to leave our camp at 16,400 feet (beyond the seracs at upper left) for the descent across the Harper Glacier toward the upper end of Karsten's Ridge. The snow that fell during the fierce storms earlier in the climb has been packed by the wind into a reasonable firmness that allows us to move with ease. Days of sun have melted the trail we made on the climb up into the white line visible on the right, and we are using it as a guide around the crevasses that mark the beginning of the Harper Icefall, down which the glacier plunges just out of the right of the picture. It is a glorious afternoon; there is no wind now and the vast bowl (it is just over a mile to the rocks of the North Peak, whose summit is just to the right of the sun) is warm with the reflected light of the sun. Our spirits are high for at last we can descend, but deep in our bodies there is the fear of the climb down Karsten's Ridge, with its exposure and memories of tearing storms. We are walking through a beautiful blue-white trap, and the only way out is down that ridge. Another series of storms and we would perish, for our food is low, our reserves of strength even lower. We push our felt boots into the cold powder snow without sensation. There is no conversation, no real appreciation of the beauty of our surroundings, not yet, both will come later when we have survived. I took this picture while waiting for Woody, but as I wait my feet begin to feel the cold of the snow. I pound them to restore circulation, the snow I've packed squeaks and soon I have a small platform. The others are behind me, now approaching the rocks of Browne Tower. I'm getting colder. I long to descend the ridge, to finish this madness. 'Woody! Come on!' He's tired and I am too, but my mind is frazzled by the altitude, my sense of survival tells me not to wait. I hold on until he is almost to me, then I turn and without a word plod after the others.

I settled back with a soggy Maugham. Jac and Norm, their heads at the other end separated by my feet, were asleep. I squirmed down between them and tried to ignore the increasingly wet nature of my sleeping bag. Over me the sweating tent slowly dripped water on to my bag, the dark water stains spreading out to merge. I felt myself gradually lower onto the cold rocks of McGonagall Pass as the air leaked out of my air mattress.

Occasionally, as I read, I looked across at the white wall of the Muldrow, barely visible through the blur of snowflakes. The level of the stream between us and the glacier gradually dropped as its source of melting snow and ice decreased in the continuing storm. By 9 p.m., five cold, sodden climbers emerged from their dripping tents, waded across the icy stream and set foot on the living ice of the Muldrow.

Around us the blue-white world of snow, fog and cloud was illuminated by the all-night summer twilight of 63° north. Nowhere on the flat expanse of the glacier was there anything to give us a direction. We merely headed out from the stream and turned right. From there on we were blind. Every 60 feet we pushed in a 'wand', a rose bush support of bamboo, one of hundreds we had brought in a nursery in Los Angeles. We shuffled on skis and snowshoes through the deepening snow and the wands marked our path. Without them to lead us back to our camp at the Pass we would have been lost. By 2 a.m. we were back in camp; half our load was somewhere out on the Muldrow. At least we were moving.

I retrieved the last of the wands from the snow as we reached the cache for the second time 24 hours later. We still didn't know where on the three-mile-wide glacier we were, only that we must be moving up the ice since we were going slightly up hill. It was our only reassurance in the everlasting fog and snow.

A dim sun tried to penetrate the fog the next morning, but only intensified the glare from the brilliant white of the new snow into a dazzling spectacle of crystals. All around us the air was filled with ice particles that turned and floated in the light of the sun, presenting their millions of facets as tiny mirrors and prisms, crowding the air with light and color. But we still couldn't see anything. We set off again in the only reasonable direction, uphill.

Woody, leading the first rope, saw them first.

'Look! Seracs!' he exclaimed.

Ahead dark shapes loomed in the lowering twilight and fog. We had been moving forward in silence, lost in our own thoughts, trying to blot out the misery of our situation. The seracs meant we had been lucky; ahead was the lower ice fall of the Muldrow.

A glacier is like a slowly flowing river. The ice is always moving; the pressure of the weight of the 500 feet of ice beneath our feet was pressing on the rocks below, becoming plastic in its lower layers as it did so. Thus the glacier could flow over the irregularities of the rocks below. But the ice near the surface of the glacier is hard and when the mass of the glacier descends rock slopes it cracks and breaks, forming crevasses—horizontal cracks that sometimes stretch across the width of the glacier, and can be 200 feet deep, and seracs—blocks of ice pushed up out of the body of the glacier by pressure from upstream.

McKinley

We were now almost halfway to the head of the Muldrow and we thought we must be at 7,600 feet, $4\frac{1}{2}$ miles up the glacier from McGonagall Pass. The storm returned with renewed fury that night, but it was its last blast. The sun rose in a clear sky the next morning.

We found ourselves in an unbelievable world, a world of blue and white. The white of the glacier met the surging ice-hung walls bordering the ice just a mile away to the south. The walls rose screaming into the depths of the blue-black sky, piercing it. The Muldrow climbed in waves above us, crevassed and broken until it disappeared into the bowels of the mass of McKinley, a mass of white and rock that blocked our westward gaze like a hunching giant.

'God, that feels good,' said Jac, his eyes closed against the burning sun. He seemed to be making love as he stretched out on his sleeping bag and flung his arms sideways in a gesture of acceptance to the sun goddess.

The sun warmed our blood and turned our brains into positive thinking organs again. Our soaking equipment steamed and began to dry.

Woody passed around a pot of melted snow water into which had been dissolved lemon powder and sugar.

'Drink up! There's 500 calories in this stuff. A hundred apiece.' It was so sweet my teeth retreated in protest. But it was liquid and it came from Woody, who was still trying to keep us together. I think he felt that as the oldest member of the group, it was his duty to look after our moral needs. I was too immature to realize how important inter-relationships are in a climbing party, and did my bit to foster division by joking about 'the other tent' and their idiosyncrasies. Woody, with his offers of blueberries and lemonade, at least made gestures toward harmony.

By late afternoon our equipment had dried and we began moving again.

We were strung out on two ropes. Jac and I were struggling along on inadequate short skis, while the others shuffled along on a variety of snowshoes. We were negotiating a route through the seracs, over snow bridges and around crevasses. Crack! My right ski broke, my foot tipped sideways, and I was down. Our good luck with snow bridges seemed to be changing. I found myself above a blue crevasse that dropped away below me to a depth I didn't contemplate. The rope around my waist compressed my stomach as both Jac and Norm on either end forced their ice axes into the snow and held on. I edged off the snow bridge as though I was crawling across glass. The tinkling of the ice and snow particles as they fell into the depths below me reminded me of the fragility of my position. Sanders pulled me to the uphill side and I was on solid ice again.

Snow bridges form when wind blows and drifts across the crevasses. They can be 5 feet thick or delicate traceries of snow barely able to support their own weight. They attain their maximum strength when they are cold; by early afternoon on a warm day they can be unstable and unsafe, as we found. We began to climb at night.

Another Sunday, July 25, and we had all our gear, 525 lb, above the lower icefall. It was 6 a.m. and a sunrise spread magenta and gold over the snow around us as we climbed into our tents for a day of sleep.

Midnight. A shallow fog settled around the seracs. Above us the crests of Mounts

Carpe and Koven felt their way into the dark sky. We worked our way over the snow bridges and edged past the looming seracs like a party of trolls on their way back to their mountain hideout. On our second relay, made after the sun had risen, my packframe disintegrated into a random collection of aluminium tubing. I tied it together with wire and rope. First my skis, now my pack. And the inner baffles had torn in my sleeping bag, so that my nightly ordeal as I tried to squirm into it soon made Norm and Jac wish for a different sleeping partner.

All appeared to be going smoothly in the relative comfort of the Sayre/Hansen tent. The meat bar wrappers thrown out at supper time together with the surprisingly appetizing aroma of their contents being cooked told the story of a pair of climbers well equipped and comfortable, oblivious of the squalor and degradation only 5 feet away.

The old Army tent was holding up well enough though, even with three where there should have been two, but it had a characteristic habit of sweating. Moisture from our bodies and from cooking condensed on the waterproof fabric and then fell on us as a gentle drizzle. By morning, when the tent had cooled, this moisture would freeze and we would be greeted by a shower of ice particles.

The Great Icefall, our next problem, failed to live up to its advance billing of difficult climbing and we found ourselves camped at the head of the Muldrow at 11,000 feet in yet another blizzard.

A further conference took place from tent to tent through the haze of streaming snowflakes.

'Two weeks today, Daddy O,' I yelled at Woody's grizzled face peering at me from the other tent.

'Nice weather we're having, isn't it,' came back the reply.

'Let's take ten days of food up Karstens. That will leave us six days to get back to Wonder Lake before Oscar Dick gets his posse together.'

'Yeah. Damn weather.'

It seemed useless to carry on and I settled back into my sleeping bag, which was getting wet again. Climbing a big mountain requires a lot of waiting, I was discovering.

July 28, our fourteenth day. At 5 p.m. the storm was fading. Shreds of clouds were caught on rocks high above us, but the sky was clearing rapidly. I looked to the right. The etched line of Pioneer Ridge disappeared towards the North Peak. Ahead of us the stupendous icefall of the Harper Glacier hung suspended—a frozen cascade of ice poised over the Muldrow. From its lip, blocks of ice the size of railroad cars occasionally broke off and plummeted down the granite cliffs to be dashed to crystals in a roaring cacophony of sound. Our way was blocked, or would have been if it hadn't been for the existence of Karstens Ridge.

The Ridge soared in a seemingly perfect sweep almost 4000 feet to the base of Browne Tower, just above the Harper Icefall. This ridge, the scene of Thayer's recent tragedy, was our next problem.

9 p.m. We cached food and equipment for our return, put on our packs and began the climb. Foot by foot we pushed our boots into the deep, new snow. Each step made by the leader was used by all of us and leads were changed frequently. The

weather was, for once, clear, and the view improved with each step. We climbed through the night.

4 a.m. A level bench on the ridge. We set up one tent and cooked a stew. We had now been climbing seven hours. The sun rose behind us, but overhead ominous-looking clouds were spreading over the sky from the west. A light breeze began.

5 a.m. We resumed the climb. The new snow clogged our crampons and so we tied them to our packs and continued without them. Two ropes, two and three men. The ridge narrowed to a knife edge and arched steeply above us. Ahead of me, as I took a lead, I noticed the wind beginning to blow particles of snow from the crest of the ridge. I planted my feet in the top of the ridge and tried not to look down. To my right was a 2000-foot slope to the Muldrow, the same slope down which the Thayer party had fallen, to my left a dizzying cliff of ice and rock walls that ended in the West Fork of the Traleika Glacier 3,500 feet below. I put one foot in front of the other, carefully.

Even in those days, when I was doing a lot of climbing, I was never happy with 'exposure'. To some climbers, to cling insecurely to a mountain with nothing below them but air and distant rocks is exhilarating. I always found it nervewracking and, to a degree, terrifying. I enjoyed the mountains, and still do, but I enjoy them more when I am not in fear of death. In climbing that ridge it would not have been impossible for one of us to mis-step and slide down the slope. It would have been difficult for the others on the rope to stop him. Death would surely have followed, as it had Thayer.

There were risks on Karstens Ridge and we took them as though we had a right to. But did we?

I had told Jill in my arrogant way on the train that I had to climb McKinley. I thought of her now, back in the green lowlands. I tried to see her face as they told her of my death. My hands broke into sweat under my gloves, and I plunged my ice axe into the snow, forcefully, with each step. Behind me Jac was silent, staring at his feet, moving them upward into my just-emptied footsteps.

I suddenly wanted to be off the ridge, off McKinley and back with Jill in the safe valleys. To stare at death on either side of my feet was more than I could bear. I had no right to be here; this was a place for a real climber with no fear. Who was I to put myself on this big mountain and with my fear jeopardize the safety of my friends? I stopped and looked to either side, shaking. Behind me Jac continued upwards, slackening the rope, which was unsafe. 'Let's go, Jon,' he said, and I once again pushed my boots into the top of the ridge until it was time to change leads.

Noon. We had been on the ridge fifteen hours. The crest of snow fanned upward into the Coxcomb. It became steeper but now the awful abyss below us had disappeared in cloud. Above us, too, the pink granite of Browne Tower had vanished in mist and snow showers. Karstens Ridge was suspended in space, detached from the earth. A white route from cloud to cloud.

3 p.m. We were hit. Suddenly, visibility dropped to zero and a furious gale tried to wrench us from the Coxcomb. I gripped my ice axe and forced it deeper into the hard snow of the ridge. My face burned in the stinging hail of ice particles flung at me by the 75 mph gale. Ice froze to my eyelashes and around my mouth. I couldn't

see and my lips and beard were a solid mass of hard ice. We stopped. We held on to our ice axes in fear and terror. We could not descend the ridge, we could only go up. Up into the dark, screaming storm.

4 p.m. Crampons. Got to get them on. Moving again. Slowly . . . upwards. We had been climbing for 18 hours and were near exhaustion. Slowly, the slope began to relax. Rocks ahead. Dim rocks that came and went like ghosts in the tearing snow and cloud. Browne Tower.

6 p.m. Stop! We must stop! It's level here. We pulled a tent out of a pack and without putting it up just crawled into the wildly flapping bag. We huddled together for warmth and contact. We had made it.

Later we set up the tents and slept a sleep of exhaustion through a night of bucking fabric and roaring winds. We awoke at noon the next day.

Sunday. Dim sun glimpsed through racing cloud. We managed to dry some of our clothing, but by 2 p.m. the storm had returned. Once again we clung to the tents, for our lives depended on them. There was nothing between us and the storm but thin nylon. I watched the gusts ripple across the old tent. It had to hold. I thought of death again and how we would die if the tent ripped. Frozen into the snow, quiet, peaceful, painless.

We had to move. The tents couldn't stand much more of this. We struggled to pack up and staggered into the fog and snow toward Harper Glacier. The snow was deep and drifted and in five hours we had done only four hundred yards.

We set the tents up on the lower edge of a crevasse below a large pinnacle. It was the best place we could find in the dim light, but at least the wind was less.

As we groped around in the gloom to set up the tents I heard Woody remark to Norm Hansen, 'I don't like that slope above us. What if it comes down? Do you think those guys know what they are doing?'

'God knows,' said Norm. 'Hand me that ice axe, I've got to tie this tent down to something.'

We settled into the tents and slept. Late in the night I suddenly awoke choking, with the roof of the tent pressing into my face. Snow from a rip in the fabric near my head poured down my neck. From the other end I could hear Jac and Norm fighting their way through the door. I forced the heavy snow from my chest and clambered out. A bank of snow from the pinnacle above had fallen on our tent, ripping it in several places and breaking three of the four poles. The Sayre tent was torn slightly.

We looked at each other in the darkness and snow.

Woody began.

'Let's move.'

'Yes, but where?' I looked around. All I could see was ghostly gray snow and when I stepped off the small platform we had packed down, I sank to my waist.

'I think we should move,' said Jac. 'That whole slope looks to me like it could come down.' He gazed ruefully upward at the pinnacle.

'Aw, it won't avalanche again,' I suggested hopefully. The prospect of trying to find another camp in the storm was too daunting for me to contemplate.

'Let's go to bed,' said Norm Sanders and we propped up the tent, sewed up the rips and crawled in. The altitude was beginning to affect our reasoning.

An hour later it happened. For a few seconds I could feel the ground vibrate and then I heard a dull whoosh. Then silence. An avalanche. It was close.

Jac looked out. The Sayre tent was gone.

We flew out of the tent again. Norm Hansen, who had been outside sewing their tent, was already digging with his bare hands into the snow. I could dimly hear Woody's muffled voice under the snow. In a few minutes we had dug an air hole to him, but it was an hour before he was out. Their tent had been buried under five feet of snow, its poles broken, its fabric ripped. Woody had almost suffocated.

'Jesus Christ! Let's move!'

We moved.

This time we put the battered tents farther down the slope, away from the avalanching snow. The rest of the day we recouped our energy and repaired the tents as best we could.

August 2, Monday. Our nineteenth day. Sun and blue sky, but the wind continued, and blew the snow in sheets across the glacier. In the early afternoon we packed up our partially dry gear and started up across the Harper Glacier.

At almost 15,000 feet, the lonely mountain was a world of its own. To our right the black cliffs of the North Peak were crowned by the pristine white cornice of the peak itself. Ahead and to the left breaking waves of snow and ice soared upward to obscure any sight of McKinley's South Peak.

At 16,200 we were numb with cold. 'Let's stop' said Woody through swollen chapped lips, his breath coming in short gasps. The wind at that moment roared down the glacier in a gust that made us turn our backs to its icy blast, and decided the issue.

After our usual instant-potato-and-canned-meat-followed-by-sugary-tea meal, all of it luke warm at this altitude, I performed the exasperating act with my sleeping bag.

'Fucking hell, Jon, what did you buy that thing for?' shouted Norm Sanders as I shoved my knee into him for the one thousandth time.

'Guy in the store said it was good. English bags are supposed to be good.'

'They aren't,' came the reply. 'Next time get an American one.'

I put on my last available sweater and tried to sleep. (We always slept in our clothes to keep warm.) The wind tugged at the tent and tried to throw it down the glacier. My thoughts wandered aimlessly. Suppose I married Jill. Should I continue to climb? Would it be fair? The thoughts drifted in and out of my oxygen-starved brain like ghosts. I couldn't reason or carry a complete thought through to its conclusion. I reached down for a cookie, but the bag had turned to crumbs. I couldn't sleep, I merely languished, shivering occasionally in my lousy English sleeping bag.

It was clear and calm the next morning, our twentieth day.

'Let's try it,' suggested Jac.

'Okay, let's,' I said unenthusiastically. The altitude had even begun to sap my obsession.

In a demonstration of solidarity on this fateful day, Woody offered the use of his more efficient stove for our morning pot of hot chocolate. We managed to gag down a few cookie crumbs and set off.

By noon we were near Denali Pass at 18,200 feet, 2000 feet above our camp. We looked for the first time down the west side of McKinley. Mount Foraker surged out of a layer of clouds that stretched westward.

19,000 feet. Woody and Norm Hansen were dropping behind. We sat on our packs and waited. In a half hour Norm appeared, but Woody was still far down the ridge.

Norm sat down without speaking for a few minutes, his head between his legs as he gulped in what oxygen there was.

'I think Woody and I will hold you people up. Go ahead and we'll follow at our own pace. If we can't make it we'll turn around. The weather is good—it'll be okay.' His eyes were full of the tears of defeat.

It was a hard decision and our oxygen-starved minds were in no condition to make it. When we decided to go on and leave Woody and Norm trailing up the ridge, it was a gut decision. Our emotional obsessions took over from our feelings for our fellows. We rationalized that the weather was good and the way back to camp obvious and easy. They would be okay, if nothing happened. The top was 1000 feet above us. We said goodbye to Norm and set off.

Jac with his finger on our map, torn from a copy of the National Geographic Magazine, suggested a route. We were on a large open slope and ahead lay the final summit pyramid.

At 4 p.m. we began to climb a long slope hip-deep in new snow. We were near exhaustion and my breath came in choking bursts. I stopped and looked around. Far below Woody and Norm were going down, their decision made for them by their bodies. Mine was screaming its protest at the unremitting punishment I was giving it. But I forced myself forward, driven up this final climb by an obsessional desire. My body would have to obey my mind and the mind was in a world of near fantasy. I was becoming a non-human. The muscles lifting my legs pulled by sheer chemistry.

The snow, the sky, the mountain, gone! We were hit again. Once again the ice crystals tore at our faces, the wind pounded us into the snow and we stopped. We could go no farther. No farther. We would meet the same fate as the Browne party and fail a few feet from our goal. We huddled together not hoping, not praying, not thinking, just waiting.

After a half hour the storm subsided, the clouds and wind disappeared into the void from which they had come. We edged on to the summit ridge. We hardly dared look anywhere but at that small cone of snow, just ahead. We moved towards it, single-minded, step by step until we were there.

We stood and looked. There was nowhere higher to go. All the mass of McKinley was concentrated in this snow cone. Below us the giant slept and permitted us our brief walk on his back. We didn't analyze, we didn't wonder, we didn't think. That could come later. We just looked and felt relief. Relief that we no longer had to satisfy our illogical drive to climb up. The beast within us was satisfied at last and we could now descend, our minds freed from his tenacious obsession.

We hardly said a word to each other as we looked around. Our dull minds were befuddled by having their task of driving our bodies upward suddenly taken from them. I reacted only dimly to the scene before me. The sky seemed very close and much bigger, without the bulk of McKinley filling it as it had done for the past twenty days.

The feeling of finally reaching the top was for me a very gentle one. I sat in the snow, weak and tired, while a diffused euphoria spread over my mind. I was released and had been given a freedom from a beast within me. I could now look beyond McKinley; it no longer dominated my future, my mind.

Jac handed me the tiny piece of notepaper for my name to be added to theirs and we put it into a can in the snow. Why? For the damn ego-beast to eat.

Down. Down. Down. We stumbled and fell, but gravity pulled us ahead. Four hours later we were at the camp and the moment spent between earth and sky had vanished forever.

For three days we waited while Woody and Norm tried. Our obsession to climb was now transformed into one of descent. Our bodies cried to be taken from this too rare air. The good weather couldn't last. Soon the storms would return and we would be trapped. Our food was low.

Jac's diary, written while we waited at 16,200 feet:

Aug. 6. Friday. Urine can working overtime early A.M. . . . Weather is superb—how long will it last? . . . anxious to get off the mountain but have to wait for Woody and Hansen who certainly must have made their second attempt yesterday and are now coming down from their high camp at Denali Pass this morning. It is now 9:30 a.m. and I am trying to melt this cursed snow for cereal (notwithstanding Sanders' unreasonable request to go outside to urinate—not being inclined to use the can as the rest of us, thereby causing a complete disorganization of the cooking arrangement which is in the doorway.) Cooking and waiting . . . melting tons of water (our throats are constantly parched). Sanders' lips hurt so much he can hardly feed himself. Conjecture on their doom and destruction keeps me thinking as Jon and Norm doze on the sunny coated warm tent . . . on slope just below final icefall before Denali Pass. Time drags on in this timeless cold, white, silent world, high above the smelly thick oxygenated, noisy bustling underworld. Civilization can barely reach us except for the occasional jet plane casually playing above 'our' peak. Please Woody and Norm make all your enticing blasted summit and come down! Waiting for you 3 days with nothing to do—imaginations jaded as our appetites—a vain attempt at 20 questions—especially after we made the monster and are frantic to get back to liquid water, green life and new foods and people. God—this makes you appreciate life's most elementary gifts—air and water. Here they come! A jolt and a head out of our miserable igloo door shows two floundering figures . . . staggering out of the upper world we gladly left 3 days before. 1:30 p.m.—what took so long? 'We left for the summit 8 a.m. yesterday from our high camp near the Pass and made the summit at 5:30—back at 9 p.m. This morning we were slap happy and had a hard time dragging ourselves down to this camp! Well let's get down the ridge while the weather is perfect . . . '

Karsten's fearful ridge. The threat of death that the ridge had brought to us on the ascent had been in the backs of our minds all the time we had been above it, though we had not admitted the nagging fear, except to ourselves.

The day after Woody and Norm had joined us in the high camp we found ourselves on the top of the Coxcomb, peering down the twisting snow crest of the ridge. We hesitated, our minds unwilling to commit our bodies to further danger. The procrastination was helped by the arrival of a single-engine Super Cub that buzzed like a fly around and around below us, over the Upper Muldrow. Try as it could it seemed unable to reach our 14,300 foot altitude.

'I wonder if it's Woody Wood from Camp Denali,' I asked nobody in particular. 'Maybe Jill is with him.'

'Maybe,' said Jac absently. 'Let's go.' The plane gave up its struggle and spluttered off down the glacier.

Norm Hansen finally led off and immediately disappeared from sight as he dropped down the steep descent. Soon we were strung out along the knife-edged crest and I found that the angle of the ridge forced me to stare deep into the space below, down the falling slope of snow and rock that ended in the finality of a maze of crevasses that shattered the surface of the Traleika Glacier. I obtained temporary relief from this awful exposure by lifting my eyes to the sparkling circle of snow peaks that glistened in the bright morning sun.

In four hours it was over, and we walked out onto the flat snow of the Muldrow.

'I think we might say now that we have climbed it,' said Woody, soon regretting the smile that shattered his chapped lips.

'I don't know,' I replied, 'Just below here is the place where Carpe and Koven fell into a crevasse.'

With this thought in mind we shuffled carefully off down the Muldrow on our motley assortment of broken skis and patched snowshoes.

Sunday August 8, our 25th day. The party was almost at the end of its psychological tether, as a result of living too close for too long. Jac and Norm Sanders gave vent to their undying hatred for each other at every tiny squabble, even when sharing the last dregs of a pot of potato water. The continued noises of cooking from the Sayre/Hansen tent frustrated us as our food began to run out. The pile of meat bar wrappers grew outside 'their' tent, but little sharing of the supplies took place. Instead, they seemed preoccupied with their own rows and a series of ever more heated arguments rent the clear air.

By the time we reached McGonagall Pass and had left the ice world for the familiar one of dark rocks and rain, everyone was feeling better. Our cache there had been broken into by mice. The remaining mouse-tasted and declined food was made into a thin soup and I poured it into five assorted receptacles.

Down into the dark canyon below the pass. The fantasy world of ice and snow had been left behind, and around us now were life sounds and sights. Grass, moving and burbling water, scurrying animals. heavily scented air and warmth. We lived on blueberries and the remains of the mouse-tasted food.

We all now had a single thought—to stop. Twenty-six days of movement and struggle had exhausted us mentally and physically and we had to stop, but not yet.

Across the McKinley River—less trouble this time. Its channels were lower, but maybe our thinner bodies offered less resistance to the rushing water. We clambered up the bank and flopped down inside the Bar Cabin.

An hour later the door burst open and there was Jill, her arms full of food, her face exploding with life and love.

Chapter 4

A Beginning and an End

Five emaciated climbers sat around a long table in the Camp Denali kitchen/dining room. We contrasted sharply with the well-fed lowlanders who plied us with a ham dinner. It was the evening after our return and Sayre and Hansen had decided, as a parting gesture, to buy us a dinner. They would begin their trip back to Boston the next morning, unaccountably anxious to leave. Whether it was us they were leaving in such a hurry, or the recent trying memories of a bout with the Alaskan wilderness, we never learned. All was harmony on this last supper. The conversation went to mountains, McKinley and news of the distant real world outside. Irrelevant news, best forgotten, but dredged out of the others around the table in a reflex action.

Nothing that would really affect us had happened in the world, of course. Throughout our lives we had had news available every day and we now felt deprived; our month away from a diet of doom, disaster and destruction had caused a condition of news starvation. So we asked and the old news was given and our minds were refilled with information they wanted but didn't need.

With us around the table were the 'camp people', Woody Wood (it had been Woody with Jill in the Super Cub), his wife Ginny, Celia Hunter, Liz and Bill Berry, who had come to Alaska for the first time that summer from Los Angeles, so that Bill would be able to paint wildlife. They, like Jill who sat beside me, were earning their keep by chopping wood, cooking, hauling water to the scattered cabins, digging privy holes in the permafrost, and building. It seemed that the camp existed on this sort of volunteer labor. No one seemed to mind working for food. It was a direct way of bartering labor without the intervening unpleasantness of money.

A Beginning and an End

After a time I found exhaustion, both with the conversation and within myself, creeping up. Jill and I left and wandered down the slope toward the cache where she had been sleeping. Ahead of us, reflected in the tarn and framed by several spruce was McKinley, pale and blue-white in the twilight.

The cache was like a miniature log cabin built on stilts about ten feet above the ground. It is a trademark of the Alaska bush and is usually used for food storage. The legs are ringed with flattened tin cans to prevent red squirrels and other hungry denizens from climbing up. It is normally bear proof too, though a determined bruin could solve the problems of entry if the ladder is left down. All the food had been taken out of this one and our sleeping bags were put on the 7 ft by 7 ft floor. The door faced McKinley.

As we squirmed into our bags, I felt my exhaustion take second place to an emotion that had kept my mind preoccupied during much of the McKinley climb. It was an emotion that made my stomach churn in anticipation. I looked up at the small logs above me and then over at Jill. She was on her side, gazing at me.

'I thought you would just fall instantly to sleep, you were so exhausted', she said.

I couldn't even answer her then, but looked away again to the logs. The emotion welled up again and this time I couldn't keep it down.

'I think I love you,' I blurted out, ineptly.

Jill smiled, her face partially hidden by her sleeping bag. 'Yes . . . ?'

Commitments were hard for me to make then. My independence, my ego, everything in my future was at stake. But I made the commitment anyway.

'I think we should get married.' Half statement, half question but it was the best I could do.

Jill drew her arms from inside her sleeping bag and put them around my neck. We pulled each other together in a tired, warm embrace. After a while we fell asleep. We slept the sleep of decision, complete and finally made.

The next morning we talked. About Alaska, about us. We filled in all the blanks that had occurred while I was on McKinley. At least for the moment I was able to tell her my weaknesses. Later I would find it more difficult and it would separate us. But for now we were close and at the beginning. She said she hadn't missed me, really. I was just there, on the mountain she could see from the Camp when the clouds parted. She knew I was realizing a dream, satisfying an obsession and would return a more complete man. She could wait, happily.

She was right. I think I did grow a little on that mountain. For one thing the climb had crystallized my relationship with her into the commitment made the previous night. And it wasn't just absence from Jill that made me want her, rather that I had matured to the point where I was able to make the decision.

I told her that I had put her name on the tiny slip of paper we had put in the can on the top. I wrote on it that I had used her ice axe or some such silly sentimental words.

She had had a happy time at Camp Denali during the month we were on the mountain. She had come to know the people at the resort and that morning she filled me with her enthusiasm for them and for Alaska.

61

Alaska had meant a release for her. An opening out of her life and thoughts. Ginny, Woody, Celia, Liz and Bill had all fled the south, all found they needed this release and all had found it in Alaska. The place provided freedom for their minds and room for their feet.

Jill had grown too. Grown on the country, but especially on the thoughtful food given freely to her from the minds of these people. Jill's dream too had been realized— to be free forever from her beginnings, her restricted and difficult life in Los Angeles. She was very happy that morning.

Sayre and Hansen left. The trail of dust from the camp station wagon taking them back to McKinley Park Station settled again on the road far below in the valley. I watched them go, without regret. They had not really helped us to climb the mountain, nor we them. I believe each of our two parties could have climbed it separately. Our co-operation was minimal and I think each of us was equally to blame. They had climbed their mountain, and ours. Each for his own reasons and now we would all separate to reflect on what we had done, and what McKinley had given each of us.

Ginny broke up our atmosphere of thoughtful goodbyes with the remark that if we wanted to eat lunch we would have to do a little work, though supper would be courtesy Camp Denali. Norm started a new privy hole with a blow of a pick into the rock-hard ice of the permafrost. I offered to continue the construction of a trail down the hill to Moose Creek. I was still weak and the leisurely building of a trail downhill would be a good way to build up my strength again. Jill disappeared into the kitchen. Jac disappeared.

I enjoyed the trail building. It was like returning to the sand box as a child. It isn't often one has a chance to return to childhood and build things. Alaska, it turned out, was a good place for this journey back in time. I attacked the blueberry bushes with what gusto I could muster, and I planned the gradient and line of the trail with relish and care. But by lunch I was exhausted again.

The spaghetti supper that camp gave us that evening was our last together as climbers. Jac and Norm were to head back to Fairbanks the next morning. Jill and I wanted to stay. We convinced Celia, Ginny and Woody that we would work and they agreed.

The climbing partnership formed the previous spring around the table on the UCLA campus broke up the following morning, when Jac and Norm clambered into the old Chevy truck, and with a few waves and goodbyes were gone. We didn't have much to say to each other anymore. Living too close for too long had exhausted our capacity for conversation. We were saturated with each other's personalities and wanted to step back and renew our friendships again.

Jill and I turned back up the hill toward the kitchen. Liz Berry was busy over the stove. She was short, with her light brown hair brushed tightly back into a pony tail, like Jill's. Her eyes flashed. She seemed to have a vital source of energy that never ran down.

'Got ten guests for supper, Jill,' she began. 'Woody is bringing them through the Park from the station this afternoon. He saw three grizzlies last trip.'

'Who comes here anyway,' I asked, curious as to who would pay $200 a week for a rustic wilderness vacation.

'Oh, people from all over. In this trip today are a couple from Pennsylvania and one from England. We get a lot of lawyers, doctors and businessmen. People who want to get away. It's funny, but even when they pay they sometimes end up working. For most of them it's the first manual work they've done in years.'

'Speaking of work, I had better get back to my trail,' I said resignedly.

I was more tired than I thought.

I found Bill Berry near the end of my new trail with his sketch pad on his knee. His presence provided a good chance to sit down.

'Better than Los Angeles,' I said as I stretched out on the warm, sunny hillside. McKinley was in clouds, but Wonder Lake was a blue piece of the sky set among the distant hills. Bill had grown up in Los Angeles, too. We both knew what that particular bit of civilization was like.

'Yeah, that smoggy hole. How are you? You still look like a starving refugee.'

'Better, but weak.'

I looked at his sketch. It was of a branch of a blueberry bush, its leaves already turning in mid-August. He sharpened a burnt sienna pencil to shade in a portion of the tiny stem. I admired his precision and detail. He had more patience than I thought possible. I preferred photography. It was quicker. I would find it impossible to work for two hours on a sketch of a branch. But Bill probably got more out of the country than I did. He saw the small things in the land and when he did his paintings was able to use the detail as the bones of the picture and build on it. His pictures were intense and real, done by a knowledgeable and intelligent man.

About a week later on August 17 the first frost of the new winter whitened the ground, and when the clouds cleared from McKinley after a storm on the 19th the snowline was down below the foothills. Below the snow the tundra had turned a brilliant red, interspersed with pale yellow. The reds of the alpine bearberry contrasted with yellow willows and dwarf birch. The leaves of the few birch and alder trees along Moose Creek had begun their spectacular golden funerals.

On August 20 the caribou hunting season opened. Camp Denali, on its ridge, was about three miles from the National Park boundary, and in that three miles hunting was allowed. The McKinley herd that migrated each summer from the foothills of the Alaskan Range out into the endless, flat, forest-covered region toward Lake Minchumina was subject to hunters here, as the animals left the Park.

On the evening of opening day we heard a shot below along the bank of Moose Creek. Shortly thereafter the field phone in the kitchen rang. It was the hunter at the camp entrance.

'Could I borrow your small bulldozer to bring out the meat?'

'Hell no,' barked Woody. 'We're not going to chew up the tundra just for your caribou. We'll pack it out.'

In the fading light, we carried empty packs across the mushy tundra for about two miles. The bull caribou was lying on his side, looking slightly prehistoric in the hissing white light of the gas lantern. Its long antlers, just beginning to lose their velvet, had been pushed into the mud when it fell.

63

The Brooks Range in the region of the upper Ivishak River, in early September. The peaks, most of which are just below 8000 feet, have received a first dusting of winter snow. Below the high peaks the slate colored sedimentary rocks blend into the reds and browns of tundra in the last stages of its annual growth cycle. The land is essentially treeless. Scattered willow grow in the depths of the valleys, and here and there in unusually sheltered places are a few poplars, but that is all. For about a month in mid summer the mountains lose all their snow. Little snow falls in the winter in this Arctic desert where the annual precipitation is only four inches, and 24 hour sun melts the thin snowpack from the hills by mid July. A few retreating glaciers remain, mostly in north facing valleys on the highest peaks, those near 9000 feet, in the eastern part of the range. About 70 miles west of the area in this picture is Dietrich Pass, the pipeline route over the range.

It is easy to see how vulnerable this land is to human intrusion. The tracks left by a bulldozer driven over the tundra will remain for tens of years, since in this extreme climate the plants that make up the mat of tundra vegetation grow with difficulty, and very slowly. So far, the hills in the Arctic are relatively track-free, but the vast lake dotted flats that stretch a hundred miles behind me to the Arctic Ocean, have been scratched with the many lines of oil exploration crews, who in the early days of the search for oil in the Arctic were both unknowing and uncaring of the damage they were doing. Regulations have corralled the oil men to some extent, but now there are more of them, and the tearing of the tundra continues. It seems this land must be sacrificed for fuel, in the same way that the old forests of Europe were cut to the bare land for fire and ships.

The glacier beneath us was named by Dr Cook for his wife, Ruth. Flying 'Charlie' off to the left, is Lowell Thomas, Jr., now Lieutenant Governor of Alaska. With me in the silver Cessna 180, on the side of which are reflected the walls of the Great Gorge of the Ruth Glacier, is Don Sheldon.

Don had a special place in the hearts of mountain climbers from all over the world. His broad smile and welcoming hand helped many a climber into his Cessna or Super Cub to begin their own great adventures in the snow peaks that clustered around McKinley, only a few miles from his home at Talkeetna. For 27 years Don flew in his mountains with care, never needing a rescue himself. But his ultimate danger was not to come from a rock wall looming out of the swirling clouds, but from cancer. Still in his early 50s, he died in Providence Hospital in Anchorage in January, 1975.

Just ahead of us on this brilliant May morning, the Ruth will open out into a vast ampitheater of snow and ice. There, some years ago, high on a rock and accessible only by ski plane, Don built a tiny wooden cabin that he called his 'Mt McKinley House No. 1'. That beautiful snow basin, over which the empty windows of his cabin gaze, will be named in honor of him.

It was the first time I had seen an animal butchered and I was revolted by the blood and gore. I was relieved when I could pick up my portion of the 200 lb. of meat the animal produced, and leave.

Stumbling back through the irregular tufts of tundra I saw a ghost, or what I thought was a ghost. It was a white moose. Up on a ridge just above the road he stood for a second in the dim light and then turned and faded into a dark ravine.

'Yes,' said Celia when she caught up with me, 'we saw him last year too. An albino moose. Pretty rare, but they do exist.'

It was a shame it was real. I would have preferred an Arctic ghost moose, forever pounding the tundra in his lonely search for a mate.

For Jill and me the two weeks at Camp Denali were a sheer delight. We were in the first warm flush of a new relationship, a commitment had been made to each other and our course was set. Life seemed simple, straightforward and obvious. We were surrounded by new friends and a beautiful wilderness. McKinley had been climbed and we both felt ourselves being drawn into Alaska. Our love for each other was enhanced by our growing love for the country. To leave seemed a sacrilege, but we had to. The Air Force had promised to teach me to fly, in exchange for three years of my life. That commitment had been made before we discovered what Alaska could have done for us.

The drive back through the Park in late August was a wrenching and tearing-away at every turn. Woody, who was driving us in to the station, helped us by his good humor and a promise to give us a job at Camp when (he didn't say 'if') we returned to Alaska. The mountains were clear this time. New snows had covered the bare rocks of summer and the Alaska Range and McKinley seemed higher than ever with the snow line down into the valleys. A high north wind over the peaks blew snow from the ridges in long plumes. The two peaks of McKinley were almost obscured in a blizzard of snow torn from the high rocks and flung out to the south. I reluctantly turned away from the sight of the beautiful mountain and looked ahead down the winding gravel road. We turned a corner and descended into a valley. McKinley disappeared behind us.

We were early for the Fairbanks train and Woody suggested we visit his good friends the Nancarrows at their homestead on Deneki Lakes, south of the station.

As we pulled off the rough gravel road that continued to Cantwell, a railroad village twenty miles further south, we were greeted by a chorus of barks and howls from some fifteen huskies chained to their houses. They were Bill Nancarrow's dog team. Woody told us that when the road closed in late fall the dog sled was Bill's only means of transportation. His lifeline to Fairbanks and Anchorage was the Alaska Railroad which ran all winter, but he was ten miles from the station.

Bill was in the middle of the dogs, peeling the bark from a log for a new cabin. His round face broke into a grin as Woody introduced us.

'After Oscar Dick told me about your equipment, I had my doubts that you would make the top. Glad you did, though. Coffee?'

He led us down to his log house on the edge of Deneki Lake, one of two small lakes, that this calm autumn afternoon reflected the freshly snow-covered slopes of Carlo

Mark Berry and his dog on Deneki Lakes.

Mountain that rose just to the southeast.

Woody and Bill had been rangers together in McKinley Park and at about the same time in 1951, each had decided to build wilderness retreats. Woody's turned into Camp Denali, Bill's into his year-round home.

Ginny Nancarrow already had the coffee on, the barking of the dogs had announced a visitor and her hospitality was always ready. She was surrounded by bowls of blueberries just picked and ready for canning. Her easy smile crossed her face as she shook hands with us.

The log room was small but beautifully furnished. Almost everything had been made by either Bill or Ginny. From the trees he felled he had built the house, and with his small sawmill had fashioned the lumber for the furniture. Ginny Nancarrow had made all the curtains and rugs. I was surprised and pleased to see a large collection of classical records. When darkness fell, a small generator would supply electricity for the player and for lights.

I looked out of the large window at Carlo Mountain and its reflection in the lake, as I sipped the cup of hot coffee Ginny had just given me. It was idyllic. Music, a wilderness just out of the window, and good company. I resolved to come back to Alaska someday. She had caught me. A bull moose emerged from behind a group of spruce on a small island, feeding on plants on the bottom of the shallow lake. The ripples from his movement ran across the water and dissolved the reflection of Carlo Mountain. It was time to go—we had a train to catch.

The shock of returning to the Fairbanks version of civilization late that evening was severe. We found ourselves back in a world of cars, buildings and a sudden increase in the number of people around. We gratefully accepted the ride given us by an old Fairbanksan in his equally aged Ford. He told us he worked on one of the few gold dredges still operating near Fairbanks.

''Bout finished, though' he said. 'Got to raise the price of gold, or we'll quit. I guess then we'll get the tourists come to see the dredge. Can get some money out of them.'

He sounded bitter. Fairbanks was founded on gold, but now it was gone. The U.S. Army and Air Force supported the town. We had passed several huge bases southeast of town on our way up the Alaska Highway in July.

It was a relief when he dropped us at the rough dirt drive that led back into the trees toward Woody's house. He had loaned the place to us for a few days.

Aspen and birch trees closed in around us as we made our way toward a log cabin dimly visible in the dark forest. I opened the door and turned on the lights to reveal a cozy cabin similar to Bill Nancarrow's. Books and records again lined the walls. There were a few bunks against one corner, another corner was the kitchen, and the ever-present Franklin stove occupied a place of honor against one end. I had just made a fire in the grate, and Jill had poured the coffee, when there was a knock at the door.

'Oh, I thought Woody was home . . . Saw the lights . . . I'm Bucky Wilson.'

I didn't know it then, but this first meeting with Bucky was the beginning of a long friendship.

'If you need anything, my cabin is just up the lane. Come around tomorrow evening, we're having a small party. Good night.'

A Beginning and an End

And he was gone.

The next morning we had Stravinsky's *Firebird* with our breakfast. The music sounded strangely precise and civilized in this forest. I could almost imagine the firebird with her dazzling wings flying through the shafts of sun. Flitting from shadow to sun, brushing the golden leaves from the aspens with her feathers. It was a beautiful image; the place was given to them.

After breakfast Jill and I wandered through the forest until we came to a clearing. Before us a broad valley spread out to the Alaska Range far to the south. The clear autumn air revealed the big snow peaks of the range—Deborah, Hayes, Hess.

'I can read your mind, Jon. You're thinking of more climbs, aren't you?'

'Yes, I suppose so. Someday. Do you think we'll come back here?'

'I want to, very much.'

'I would have to find work here. But first the Air Force. I hope Alaska won't change too much in three years, I like it the way it is.'

Bucky's party that night became a farewell party for us. The people we met and the way we were received so easily into their circle convinced us even more to return.

With packs in hand we set out the next morning to hitchhike to Anchorage. We had decided to take the Alaska Steamship Company's SS *Aleutian* from Seward to Seattle on September 7. Anchorage was 437 miles away.

The first ride with a soldier from Fort Greeley, a large Army camp near Big Delta, took us back down the Alaska Highway again. From Big Delta a native with an old Plymouth took us down the Richardson Highway to the Glenn Highway. Most of this road was gravel and the clouds of dust brought us instantly back to the miseries of the Alaska Highway in the Yukon. The native, Harold Simpson, was from the Indian settlement at Copper Center.

'Don't usually pick up whites, but you two looked desperate for a ride. Going to Anchorage? Drop you off near Glennallen.'

Our speed was incredible. The old car protested without result at the treatment it was getting. Rocks and gravel flew in a clattering spray to each side. I didn't know it was possible to move so fast over a gravel road.

The ride from Glennallen to Anchorage was considerably more sedate. The old couple from Iowa, who had just survived the Alaska Highway, were on their way to visit their new grandchildren.

'Damned if I'm going back down that road,' said Henry Plumb.

'Going to sell this thing in Anchorage and fly home.' His wife, Martha, nodded agreement. But we had to admire them for driving to Alaska in the first place. We thought we had accomplished some heroic deed by forcing the Chevy up the Highway. We were duly chastened by the fortitude of this old couple.

The last few miles into Anchorage were by courtesy of the military. 'Keep Out' read the signs lining the road, 'Fort Richardson Military Reservation.' This part of Alaska seemed to be in the hands of the Army.

Henry Plumb dropped us in front of an old frame house near Merrill Field that had been propped up on oil barrels. It looked as if it was about to be moved, but we hoped it would be stationary for at least the two nights we wanted to spend in Alaska's

69

largest city.

Martha was dubious. 'Sure you'll be all right there?' 'Yes, thanks. Thanks for the ride'. We stood by our packs as the Plumbs disappeared into the night down the dusty, unpaved street.

When we awoke the next morning we found a drunk sleeping it off in another room of the house and decided to find another place for the next night.

Anchorage had two dominant buildings, both apartments, both fourteen stories, and identical. They must have been built by some brave developer who had saved money on his plans. The rest of downtown consisted of a motley mixture of cabins, frame houses, low concrete buildings and bars. Anchorage seemed to have Fairbanks beat in the number of bars. Both sides of East 4th Avenue were lined with signs that jumbled onto one another, each vying for supremacy: 'Scandinavian Club-Bar', 'Sam's Liquor Store', 'Pawn Shop', 'Arcade', 'Loans'. Many of the people on that end of 4th Avenue were the same mixture of drunk whites, drunk natives and down and outs we had seen on 2nd Avenue in Fairbanks.

As Jill and I walked for the first time down Anchorage streets on that cloudy Monday in early September 1954, I felt alienated. I think it was partly the fact that we now suddenly found ourselves in a big city, at least by Alaskan standards. Our experience of Alaska had, up to then, been of her wilderness, interrupted only briefly by the small-town homeliness of Fairbanks. In Anchorage the citizens had the determined look of people on the move. The smiles were fewer, the heads hung lower, the strides were quicker. In 1954 the economy of the two cities was essentially the same with military and government employers providing the payroll, so I couldn't imagine where all those people thought they were going. I think, even then, Anchorage had its manifest destiny in mind. It was, and always would be, the largest city in Alaska with half the state's population, and that responsibility weighed heavily on the shoulders of its inhabitants.

To the east, the backdrop of the Chugach Mountains were receiving their first coating of snow. 'Termination dust' the construction workers called it. In those days its arrival meant the end of seasonal outdoor construction, and the workers fled south with the birds. There was neither rain nor snow in town, though, only a cold wind off the murky tidal waters of Knik Arm that forced us into our sweaters and parkas.

We walked. To the 'good' end of 4th Avenue where the 4th Avenue Theater was showing *The Caine Mutiny*. After a couple of banks, a jewelers, a souvenir shop and a pet shop we stopped in front of a cafe called the Milke Way that advertized 'Foot Long Hot Dogs'. The coffee at the Milke Way was hot, served with the ubiquitous canned cow, congealed milk around the two openings in the top of the can. I scraped away the dried condensed milk with the end of my spoon, and offered the can to Jill.

'Well, what do you think of Anchorage?', I asked, the tone of my question implying at least some doubt on my part.

'Oh, I don't know . . .', her attention was distracted by the figure of a passing businessman, complete with overcoat and briefcase.

'It doesn't seem very, well, Alaskan to me', she went on, 'But I suppose these people have to make money somehow, don't they?'

'Yes. It seems a shame that we have to come down to earth so fast. Money. That's what Anchorage is about.' I had begun to think that McKinley, Camp Denali and the Alaskan wilderness were all a beautiful dream. The realities of Alaska were like realities anywhere.

How would I live here? I was a meteorologist, just graduated. I could probably get a job in weather forecasting, but the main office of the Weather Bureau was in Anchorage and the most interesting work would be here. But then I would be living in a city in a wilderness, visiting the wilderness, that I had come to think of as the 'real' Alaska, only at weekends and in vacations. I would be in Alaska, but not of it. At that time I could see no other solution to the economic problem of trying to live in Alaska; it would be a compromise.

We walked. Along Spenard Road to a run-down suburb of the same name. The mud-splattered cars that plunged into the water-filled potholes of the unpaved road forced us frequently into the bushes as we tried to avoid the brown spray. The buildings of Anchorage dissolved into the ramshackle hodge-podge of Spenard. Spenard seemed to be the Fairbanks of Anchorage where everyone built how and where they liked, without the annoying restrictions of planning regulations—trailers, junk cars, more bars, hardware stores and gas stations lined the winding muddy road all the way to Lake Hood, where it all stopped abruptly at the airport boundary.

The lake was lined with float planes, and ringed with trees. At the end of the road was Anchorage International Airport. But just before the airport was a rather forlorn clump of trees, bounded on one side by the airport road, on the second by a Union 76 gas station, on the third by the Lake Hood/Lake Spenard runway, and on the fourth by the airport parking lot. We camped in this glen for the night.

'Can't camp here.' The fat airport cop loomed even higher and fatter from my vantage point in my sleeping bag on the ground. His tin star caught the morning sun and flashed in my eye.

'Could we make breakfast first?' I inquired, but from his already programmed expression I knew what the answer would be.

'Naw. I go off at 8 and I want you two out of here by then.'

'All right.' Damn cops. I muttered to myself. He stood watching us until we had rolled up our sleeping bags, then followed us out of the tiny forest.

'And I don't want to catch you there again.' He finally turned and waddled off back to the airport, no doubt satisfied with a good night's work. We made sure we were out of his sight before we started hitching rides.

Stomachs growling, we stopped at a tiny cafe on the Seward Highway, just south of Anchorage. After a breakfast of coffee and soggy doughnuts, we were just walking down the creaking wooden steps when Jill spied a Chevy pick-up with the back full of crab pots, fishing gear, a couple of outboard motors and a sticker on the back window that read: 'Seward Silver Salmon Derby'.

Jill rushed over to the driver just as he was pulling out.

'Could you give us a ride to Seward? We want to catch the boat to Seattle,' she said in her most appealing manner.

'Yeah, I guess so. Hop in. Throw your gear in the back'.

The road led southwest from Anchorage toward Turnagain Arm, then east where it was squeezed between the Chugach Mountains and the Arm. Turnagain Arm appeared to consist almost entirely of mud.

'Where is the water?' I asked our driver, who turned out to be a commercial fisherman living in Seward. He was a man used to long lonely hours at sea and was given to the barest minimum of conversation.

'Low tide.' His eyes never left the road, which by now was on a ledge over the mudflats.

Several miles of silence passed, then suddenly further information came forth.

'Tides up to 33 feet. Highest in the world.'

I was under the impression that the Bay of Fundy had the highest tides, but obviously Jim the fisherman thought Alaska had the biggest and best of everything. He had lived in Seward for fifteen years and had been a fisherman for most of that time. As we drove on around the end of Turnagain Arm he relaxed and became more vocal.

'Portage. You should see the glacier up that road.' His clear blue eyes briefly left the road, the crowsfeet at their sides deepening as he squinted up at the white hanging glaciers above a valley of cottonwoods. 'Icebergs right up against the road at this end of the lake. Want me to let you out?'

Noting the sparse traffic, I declined his offer and we left the possible icy delights of Portage Glacier for our eventual return to Alaska.

For the remaining eighty miles to Seward we never left the vertical pleasures of the Kenai Mountains. Red tundra climbing up to freshly snow-covered peaks. But in the valleys was something new. The road descended toward the sea through forests of big trees. Spruce and hemlock. A sea-modified climate produced a change in our visible world that brought a new dimension to our concept of Alaska. It was not entirely the land of tundra and black spruce we had experienced in the Interior. We were entering the domain of the mild Pacific. Warm winds and a longer growing season were evident in the forests of moss-hung trees. Thick green undergrowth filled the spaces between the trees.

'Bears in there.' Jim suddenly broke my scientific musing. 'Moose too.'

We didn't see either. The fact of the hunting season had presumably been made known to the animals and they had fled. The way the road signs were shot up by frustrated hunters attested to the threat the wildlife was under at this time of year.

We were four miles from Seward when Jim suddenly turned off the road into a drive that led to a large log house. I thought we were being kidnapped, but his next ration of words reassured us.

'Alice will make us something to eat. You must be hungry after all this time.' I had to confess we were. The doughnuts had been assimilated a couple of hours back.

'Alice!' he called into the house in his best chauvinistic voice, after pushing open the door. 'Got a couple of starving people for lunch!'

A plain, and obviously overworked woman poked her head out of the kitchen.

'Hello, sourdough pancakes and eggs okay?' she asked, wiping her hands on a flowered apron and getting right to the point.

'Yes, if it's convenient,' I answered apologetically, feeling uncomfortable in the role of a forced guest. Alice soon put us at ease.

'No problem. Be ready in a minute,' and she disappeared back into the kitchen, from which the smell of cooking blueberries ensued. Everybody in Alaska seemed to be canning blueberries at this time of year.

Jim relaxed in a large chair and suddenly broke into his version of conversation.

'Getting the *Aleutian?*'

'Yes.'

'Almost her last trip. Airlines taking away the passenger service. Soon'll be only freight from here to Seattle.'

'How long has the steamship service been running?' I asked, trying to keep the conversation going.

'Don't know.'

'Oh.' Obviously the wrong question.

'You should walk up Marathon this afternoon; boat doesn't leave until late.'

'What's that?'

'Mount Marathon. 'Bout 3000 ft. Good view. Every 4th July we have a race and give $1000 to the fastest runner up and back. Record so far is 52 minutes. Probably take you two longer.' His attempt at humor coincided with Alice's 'ready!' from the kitchen.

It was late afternoon when we said goodbye to Jim at the small boat harbor. He was going out into the Gulf of Alaska near Kodiak to put out his crab pots. The king crab measured six feet across their arms, he said, but then everything in Alaska was bigger and better to Jim. He loved the place. We discovered later that he was right this time.

Seward reminded me of a frontier town transferred from Wyoming to Norway. The milky blue waters of Resurrection Bay reflected parallel rows of peaks as they marched to the Pacific. Tucked between the steep walls of the mountains and the bay, on a level area just big enough for it, was the town. Mostly wooden clapboard buildings this time, with the waterfront given over to the Alaska Railroad. Seward was founded in 1903 to provide a supply point for the building of the railroad. (Anchorage was started for the same reason in 1914.) The names of the streets read like a government memo. A, B, C, D. 1, 2, 3, 4. Washington, Adams, Jefferson and, of course, Government Road. Alaska, in the early days, was a victim of the dull bureaucracy of Washington thousands of miles away.

At the town pier was the SS *Aleutian*. Big (to us) black with white superstructure, smoke from her single funnel drifted down the bay in the light evening breeze. It was after 4.30 p.m. and we could board. Sailing would be at 2.30 a.m. for the six-day voyage to Seattle, via Juneau and Ketchikan. We joined a sparse and in general elderly group of passengers for the last leg of our $200 adventure. This particular limb would cost us $60 each, but that included food.

Mr Hickman, the Chief Purser, was uneasy about letting an unmarried man and woman share the same cabin, but we assured him we did intend to get married eventu-

73

ally and that seemed to pacify him. But every time we passed him during the voyage he tried not to notice us, as though we didn't really exist. Since it was almost the last voyage of the *Aleutian* I guess he considered a slight infraction of the rules would be all right. But it still disturbed his puritan ethics.

When we awoke in our cabin of sin the next morning we were at sea. Off to the north the snowy peaks of the Chugach north of Prince William Sound formed a ring of white on a base of dark forested islands and peninsulas. The water was almost calm in spite of the Gulf of Alaska's reputation for storms. The *Aleutian* throbbed comfortingly eastward toward Southeast Alaska and Juneau.

That evening after a dinner of Pâté de foie-gras, Baked Alaska (of course), Black Cod, Roast Beef, and Steamed Fruit Pudding, among other things, Jill and I went up on deck. To the northeast, distant and orange in the light of the setting sun, was Mount St Elias, the peak we had tried to see in the rain on the Alaska Highway back in July. I mused that it must have been from near where the *Aleutian* was then that the clouds had parted for that great Dane, Vitus Bering. It was in 1741 that Bering, on an expedition of discovery for Peter the Great of Russia, first saw St Elias and the Alaskan coast and began the 226-year history of Russian occupation of Alaska. This occupation only ended in 1867 when W. H. Seward, U.S. Secretary of State, bought the place with $7,200,000 of the taxpayers' money. 'Seward's Folly' the sceptics said.

We were up early for our arrival at Juneau. Mists were dissolving into the clear air as the *Aleutian* edged up Gastineau Channel toward the capital of Alaska. To our right was the giant abstract ruin of the Alaska-Juneau gold mine, empty and rusting. Joe Juneau's discovery of gold in 1880 led to the town of Juneau. It was designated the capital in 1890 when the only other town of any size was Fairbanks. When the big mine closed in 1944, Juneau fell back on government payrolls for its existence, like Anchorage and Fairbanks.

Jill and I pounded up and down the wooden stairways and walks of Juneau in an effort to see as much as possible before Captain Brastad whistled us back to his boat. The town was a jumbled confusion of wood houses and concrete buildings that ran steeply up into the trees of a mountain that seemed as if it could topple on the place at any minute. A cobweb of telephone and electric lines threaded up and down every street and tied the buildings to each other. I felt claustrophobic. The combination of encroaching mountains on all sides and the confining town forced us down to the open harbor well before Brastad's whistle. Juneau would have to wait for a better frame of my mind. My Alaskan experience had been nurtured on the open spaces of the Interior. Juneau was a different, closed place: vertical without relief. Tight and isolated—a place with little sky. An odd location for a capital. Only history could have put it in such a place. (History would take it away, too. In 1974, Alaskans voted to move it to the Talkeetna—Anchorage area.)

The *Aleutian* threaded a circuitous course through the fjords of Southeast Alaska. Forested, green mountains fed their trees to the sea on either side, sometimes seeming too close to be safe. Brastad brought us through.

Not every ship has been so lucky in the devious waterways of Southeast Alaska.

74

A Beginning and an End

In 1918 the Canadian ship SS *Sophia* ran aground on a reef near Juneau. The 349 people on board waited hopefully for rescue, but gales and snow prevented boats from approaching. After a day the *Sophia* slipped off the reef, and took all 349 with her.

The *Aleutian* docked at Ketchikan under rainy skies the following morning. Jill and I, poncho clad, sloshed along the slippery wooden walks of the town. Ketchikan was wood, fish and rain, 150 inches of the latter a year. The harbor was choked with fishing boats that formed a confused maze of masts, rigging and fishing gear against the leaden sky. A totem pole on a downtown street corner stared forlornly into the rain. A roaring tumbling stream, swollen by the rain, penetrated the center of the town, the sound of the water merging with the now heavy rain in a watery concerto.

'Let's go back, I'm getting soaked,' pleaded Jill, water dripping from her nose.

'Okay.' The rain had started to run down my neck by then.

By the time we had changed and had come back on deck, Ketchikan had disappeared into the fog.

The forested channel down which we were sailing gradually widened and we were left in a gray world of cloud and sea. Alaska and our summer of discovery of a love for a land vanished into the mists like a dream.

Chapter 5
Spring 1958

On July 23, 1957 Richfield Oil Company's wildcat well on the banks of the Swanson River, fifty miles southwest of Anchorage, struck oil and the first major oil field in Alaska had been found.

The well represented the first confrontation between conservationists and oil men since it had been drilled on the Kenai National Moose Range, near the nesting lakes of the almost extinct trumpeter swan.

Alaska did call us back. We followed our dreams—dreams that had been conceived in the summer of 1954 and had gestated during our forced absence in the Lower 48. (Alaskans have a difficult time deciding what to call the rest of America. Most of the terms they come up with—'Lower 48', referring to the 48 states not including the islands of Hawaii, 'South 48', or 'Lesser States'—carry an intentional connotation that Alaska is superior to those other places. A common phrase is 'Outside' which gives the impression that Alaska is one large in-group, though the word 'Inside' is never used for obvious reasons. Government agencies searched through their dictionaries and came up with 'contiguous states'. They are the only ones who use it.)

The decision to return had been made in '54, but, as with any place at a distance, the dream of a life in Alaska had become more ideal as time went on. When my Air Force tour ended, we packed up our old lives, broke connection with our families and left for Alaska. My own parents had done much the same, when towards the end of the 30's depression they took off for the golden land on the Pacific, California. But others had followed them to the cornucopia of the West and that horn of plenty was soon emptied. In our dream, Alaska had, not only space and a job, but a richness of wilds and people, and a hope for us of a more fulfilling life. We wanted to lift ourselves from the civilized ruts we saw being dug by those around us. Perhaps Alaska could change the direction of our lives.

We should have realized that our dream, born in that brilliant summer, was an idealized version of Alaska. We had been truly lucky then. Lucky to have spent our time in Alaska's wilderness and not in its cities. Lucky to have met amicable and forthcoming people who let us into their lives and hearts. People who themselves had done just what we were proposing to do, and who had succeeded. Their lives *had* been changed and made more complete by Alaska. We wanted ours to be changed too.

But, in our enthusiasm, after I received an offer of a job with the Weather Bureau in Anchorage, we had forgotten that discussion of economics and compromise in the Milke Way cafe. Those two issues were to have a profound influence on our future in Alaska.

We would be going to a place that was half a city trying to be whole, and not to the wilderness that had charged us with such a new force. Some of the super sophistication we wanted to leave behind in Los Angeles had already made its way to Anchorage. The real change wasn't to come to the town for over ten years, but the seeds had been sown.

I hadn't considered the importance of time. Alaska, I was to discover, was a place that devoured time. Its wilderness was a place of no time, where the winds and the skies were endless. To try to experience it on a weekend, as I would have to in my new job, would be like taking an inch square section out of a painting and from that experiencing the whole. By taking a secure job in Anchorage I would be forfeiting a large part of that identity the Alaskan wilderness had helped to give me.

Why not homestead? Why not build our own Deneki Lakes? No guts. Both Jill and I were city bred, we had no feeling for working the land. We were intellectual wilderness lovers. We saw the wilderness as an antidote to our inbred sophistication. We recognized our need for it, but, I think at least then, to immerse ourselves completely in its isolation would have been a shock to strain our psyches to breaking point. In the 50s, we hadn't experienced that rich liberation of mind that young people can enjoy so freely today. As a result we were caught in yes/no thinking, and a solution too far beyond our previous experience was discarded as unworkable. If I were in my twenties now, with a dream of Alaska in my head, I would at least try to come to terms with her wilderness by living in it. If I were twenty-five today I would need it more, too.

We made our compromise and settled for the secure economics of the Weather Bureau. Perhaps Anchorage would give us a new life after all. As we stepped from the Seattle plane into an Anchorage April of rain and snow with the mountains obscured and the squalor of Spenard to greet us, I began to think of retreat. But we had made a life commitment to each other and now to our Alaskan dream. The awakening would be hard.

It was breakup time in Anchorage. The solid grip of winter was relaxing into a watery mush. Patches of dirty snow fed their melt water to rapidly growing lakes on the roads.

Two-year-old Takla, who sat between us on the back seat of the Yellow Cab that lurched along Spenard Road, pointed to the soggy flakes as they splattered against the windshield. 'Sno?' 'Snow', I said. Snow for Easter.

We eventually found an apartment that fitted our budget but little else. It was in a three-story building under the final approach to Merrill Field in the eastern part of Anchorage. The house on barrels where we had spent our first night with the drunk was nearby. (It was still there and still on barrels.) Paint was peeling from the walls of our apartment and a thousand children ran up and down the central stairway, past our door on the second floor. But it was warm and cheap; our Alaskan reality.

Our world became Anchorage. We drove our VW bus, when it finally arrived by ship from Seattle, up and down the streets with names like 'Northern Lights Boulevard', and 'Arctic Boulevard', in search of a house. Our sights gradually lowered from what we wanted to what we could afford. My dreams of emulating the log houses we had seen near Fairbanks receded into the improbable. The Fairbanks and bush style of house didn't seem to fit into the emerging sophistication of Anchorage, even then. Anchorage was trying to become the metropolis of Alaska and its citizens were building their city like those they had left behind in the Lower 48. Most of the houses were frame or concrete block, the few log houses seemed to be left over from an earlier era when Anchorage was smaller and closer to Alaska.

One day in early May, as the lakes on the roads were beginning to dry up in the bright and almost warm sunshine, a note appeared on the bulletin board at the Weather Bureau. 'For Sale. Two Bedroom House. Raspberry Road. TEL: FAirfax 2-1249'.

Sand Lake Road led past the airport to Raspberry Road. We were at that desperate stage that most house hunters go through when the primitive drive for shelter begins to become irrational. As I turned the VW from the gravel of Sand Lake Road to the just passable mud of Raspberry Road, I began to decide to take the house. The Merrill Field apartment with its noise and total disassociation from anything we thought of as Alaskan was making our whole move look foolish.

Ahead the Chugach, still with snow on the north-facing slopes, rose into the clear spring sky and gave Anchorage a sorely needed background of beauty.

The 'For Sale' sign was plunked into a lawn of gray-green grass, trying to rise now that its winter weight of snow had melted. At the end of the lawn was a flat topped board and batten house of simple design: it was a box.

Inside it was empty except for a space heater that provided minimal heat and kept the plumbing from freezing; but it smelled of fuel oil. The walls were made of the characteristic 4×8 ft sheets of veneer plywood that seemed to adorn nearly every house we had seen. It was pseudo mahogany this time. The checker-board pattern of green and cream floor tiles was fixed to cold hard concrete.

Jim Watson, the previous owner, had followed his wife and family back to Oklahoma in March. She had been a victim of 'cabin fever' which frequently strikes many new Alaskans toward the end of their first winter. The long hours of darkness, coupled with cold and snow become claustrophobic. This psychological disease particularly affects wives left at home in small houses with small children. By about February they find they can no longer cope with another two months of winter and want to return home to the sunnier and warmer winter they think they remember from home. The husband is usually better off, able to lead a more interesting and varied life at his work away from the forced confinement of a stuffy, kid-filled house. Jim Watson had reluctantly given up his job as a carpenter with an Anchorage contractor and had ended his attempt at a new life. It was either Alaska or his marriage.

Along one side of the house was a small grove of old birch and black spruce and the back lawn ended in the tattered, mouldy remains of last year's vegetable garden. Our possible future neighbor on one side, visible through the birch grove, lived in a house that consisted only of a basement. It looked like a bomb shelter with a raised door at the top of a stairway that led into the depths. This was a common way of building a house in do-it-yourself Alaska. A family would save enough to hire a Cat to dig a hole in the ground and in this they would build the concrete block basement of their future house and live in it. As spare money became available they would buy a few boards and begin the house. By this method it took Bill Margolis four years to finish his house. As I peered through the birch, I could see he already had six children who were playing in two junk cars that had been set up as play houses in the front yard. By the time his house was finished he had seven kids, but the same two cars were still there. Such, we were to discover, was the character of Raspberry Road, and a good many other Anchorage roads as well.

On the other side was a trailer with a plywood lean-to attached to one side. A strip of chrome had peeled off one side of the pink trailer and was swaying back and forth in the cool afternoon breeze. The inhabitants of the trailer suddenly emerged in a rush. They were natives.

Up to then, I suppose I hadn't thought much about Alaskan natives. In '54 we had met Harold who had given us that ride down the dusty Richardson Highway, but he was the only native I had actually met. The impressions I had of them were not good. I had seen them hanging around the bars in Fairbanks and Anchorage or sitting in dejected solitude on park benches. Those city natives, displaced from the relatively simple environment of their villages, separated from their families, looked like losers. They had struggled against the sophistication of a white man's town, but were not emotionally or culturally equipped for the fight, and lost. And in those days their white neighbors didn't have much time for them and tended to treat them, especially in the towns, as a necessary nuisance. I eyed our future neighbors with misgiving. My narrow middle-class life so far had not prepared me to live next to them either, and my emotions were a jumble of doubt, guilt and fear.

I couldn't understand the relationships between the trailer occupants. There were three men, two women and three children in the group that climbed into a '51 Chevy and rattled off down Raspberry Road. I later discovered that none of the men was married to either of the women. The devious ways of welfare in Alaska made that arrangement more profitable. The lack of most of the exhaust system added to the

A forest fire burns unchecked through the spruce and tundra of the Interior. The west wind has carried the smoke high into the air and the two of us in the Super Cub almost choke when a swirl of it comes into our path. In a bad fire summer the smoke from the tens of fires can blanket most of Interior and south central Alaska, changing the clear air into a strange pall that brings an unfamiliar sensation of claustrophobia to Alaska. The rains of late August and September usually put out the last of the summer's fires, those beyond the capabilities of the fire fighting crews. Sometimes the fires will dig themselves into the vegetable mat of the tundra to smolder all winter, and flare again when summer comes. A fire like the one in this picture, far from a road, was probably caused by one of the many thunderstorms that occur in Interior summers. But it could also have been started by a fisherman or hunter who flew his float plane into one of those lakes, built a campfire on its shore, and then left the embers to smolder.

In times past most of this forest was probably consumed by lighting fires, and there was no one around even to consider how to put them out, or if it was necessary. Nowadays, with oil to pay the state's bills, the trouble and expense of fighting hundreds of fires every summers is being questioned. The timber burnt is usually small and of low commercial value, and the effectiveness of the arsenal of aircraft and other fire fighting equipment doubtful. But it was hard for me to fly over the licking flames of this fire, watch them eat into the habitat of thousands of animals, to see moose fleeing in panic, and not want it put out. With the growth rate of these sub-Arctic plants and trees so slow, it will be a lifetime before this blackened land is regrown.

Tundra and spruce near Nabesna.

Caribou on the ice of the Ivishak River on the North Slope.

Around Alaska are 35,000 miles of shoreline, 38 per cent of the total shoreline of the United States, and nesting on the rocks and along the tidal flats are millions of birds. In Kachemak Bay, about halfway between Homer and Halibut Cove, an isolated rock supports the nests of cormorants, puffins, kittiwakes, gulls and murres. In July the nesting bird population is at its peak and packed colonies here protest loudly at a gull cruising overhead. Just up Cook Inlet a Shell drilling platform waits for permission to begin drilling for oil in Kachemak Bay. So far, they have been thwarted by conservation groups, especially the Kachemak Bay Defense Fund, a group of Homer residents and fishermen who see oil development in southern Cook Inlet as harmful to shrimp, crab and other fishing, and a disaster to the beauty of the area. Oil spills could be a threat to birds such as these. Those bird populations around Prince William Sound will be the first to feel the effects of oil development as Alyeska's tankers, in October, 1977, begin their twice a day voyages from Valdez. The greatest threat to coastal wildlife, is, of course, oil development along the outer continental shelf in the Gulf of Alaska, and the Bering Sea coast, which could become larger, and even more tempting, sources of oil than the Arctic.

occasion of their departure.

We bought the house.

It wasn't much, but we now thought of ourselves as Alaskans. As I was soon to discover, Alaskans were all on an ego trip and I found I was now joining them on their journey. Jill, who had less of an ego problem anyway, found she could cope with her situation by immersion in the daily routine of life in Anchorage. I joined the large group of Alaskans, who, though they wouldn't admit it, were a bit uncomfortable up there on the edge of the Arctic. They puffed themselves up into slightly superior beings and looked down from a height on lesser mortals such as tourists and people who have the misfortune to live elsewhere in the U.S., especially those poor souls in Los Angeles. By this ruse they immediately felt better, the winters became shorter and milder, the summers warmer and sunnier and their wives more likely to stay. After several years in Alaska the need for this self-deception disappeared as those in the south, who watched you go on your (to them) foolish northern experiment, gradually lost contact and wrote you off. The Alaskan could then relax and restrict his social intercourse to his fellow Alaskans who knew the true score anyway. But he had survived the first few years. The only disadvantage to this method of coping with the realities of Alaska is that after all that puffiness it is hard to live anywhere else.

We went to Alaska in an attempt to recapture the experience of a summer, and probably made a mistake in that we didn't follow our dream far enough. I tried to justify my halfway measures but wasn't entirely successful. Margolis, next door in the bomb shelter, had no such problem. He had come to Anchorage from West Virginia where his family had worked in the coal mines for generations. During the construction season (May through September in those days) he worked ten hours a day, seven days a week on military construction. He made a lot of money, and drew unemployment pay the rest of the year. His justification for living in Alaska was easy. He was obviously better off, even underground, and would eventually have his own house. He had never been out of Anchorage, except for one hunting trip with a friend down on the Kenai, and couldn't care less about the wilderness or anything else about Alaska, except continued military construction contracts, of course. He had money for the first time in his life.

Anchorage had, even more, that air of commerce about it that we noticed in '54. In the late '50s money in Alaska was government sent. Then the U.S. Government (there was no state government bureaucracy yet) employed one out of every three Alaskans and supplied 71 per cent of the dollars in the economy. Since Anchorage had half of the Territory's population, most of those dollars went there.

It wasn't until mid June that the birch and aspen were green and poppies were blooming along sheltered south-facing walls. The fireweed blooms were just beginning their climb to the sky. I always used these ubiquitous magenta flowers as harbingers of fall. In June the blooms were at the bottom of the flower, by July about halfway up, by August at the top and by late August the whole thing would go to wind-blown seed. Then it would be September and summer would be over. As I came to realize just how short Alaskan summers were, I would mentally try to slow the fireweed clock, but it was relentless.

Jill was out surveying the vegetable garden—to come.

'A chocolate cake for supper if you dig up those old plants for me.'

The mosquitoes lashed at my bare sweaty back as I spaded the sandy loam, but by evening it was finished. As I leaned on my shovel, sipping a beer, a Super Cub roared over the birch at fifty feet, showered Raspberry Road, and me, with insecticide and flew on. Jill appeared at the back door, brought out by the noise of the low flying aircraft.

'The Residents Association tried to collect for it this afternoon, but I wouldn't contribute,' she answered my questioning look. A local residents' association (as we were outside Anchorage city limits) had paid the pilot to spray for mosquitoes and the practice was to be repeated several times during the mosquito season in June and July. The spraying program eventually died when it became known that the insecticide killed everything else, too.

Anchorage was hot that bright June evening. At 6 p.m. the sun had $3\frac{1}{2}$ hours to go before it set. The KFQD radio announcer gave the temperature as 74°F—the reading had just passed the all-time record for the day. Over the top of the natives' trailer I could see the green Chugach, finally almost bare of snow.

Jill had her seed packets and held them out for me to see.

'Zucchini, radishes, carrots and pumpkins. The pumpkins are for Halloween.'

'No tomatoes?'

'Don't be ridiculous. In this climate?'

As spring merged into summer, dust clouds rose from passing traffic on Raspberry Road. I tried to keep the dust at bay by wetting down the road with the garden hose. The matter was solved by another collection effort and a man with a tank truck appeared who then proceeded to spray the road with old crankcase oil. It stopped the dust, but the VW was black with oil from then on.

Our budget was in trouble. Even though I received a 25 per cent cost-of-living bonus we barely scraped through each month. Jill looked up from her green covered 'Family Financial Record'. It was June 30, 1958.

'Without any extras, we've spent $615 this month, and the Weather Bureau has paid you $620. That leaves us $5 for this evening, how about Peggy's, since you get paid tomorrow.'

'Okay.' But I was uneasy about the money.

Peggy's Airport Cafe had hamburger steak for a dollar. The place was on East 5th and overlooked a row of hangars along the runway at Merrill Field.

That June evening Merrill Field seemed like a honey pot, to which all the light aircraft in Alaska had come. It was the general aviation airport for Anchorage, supplementing the float plane base at Lake Hood beside which we had camped in '54. Everyone with a light aircraft seemed to be flying it this glorious June evening. Take-offs were at one minute intervals and the Cessnas, Super Cubs and myriad other types buzzed down the runway, turned right and disappeared toward the sun. In five minutes they would be over the wilderness. That was one way to escape from Anchorage. But it took money, lots of it. I cut into my hamburger steak. I felt trapped.

There are a few public benches in front of the Anchorage city hall. Down among the flower beds and the flags, near the log cabin built for the tourists, and facing the heavy traffic on Fourth Avenue, they are usually occupied by natives, occasionally by tourists, but rarely by anyone else. I sat down next to him, the July sun warm on my back. 'Hello.' He stared back, but didn't say a word. I turned toward the traffic filled street. Thus we sat for a while. He was tired. Tired of that bench and that town. Tired of doing nothing. 'Where are you from?', I asked, but didn't catch the name of the village. He seemed resentful, or angry. Perhaps he was angry at me, first for trying to take his picture as though he was odd, or something, then for patronizing him by asking questions, even though they seemed innocent to me. Perhaps he had been asked too many questions, by too many white men, and he was tired of the white man's society. Perhaps his mind wasn't in Anchorage at all, but up on the edge of the Chukchi Sea, with his rifle in his hand. Perhaps he remembered how he had braced himself in the bow of the *umiak*, and waited for the seal to surface. Those were good times, he thought. The memories of hardship had faded, only those of freedom remained.

I looked around the busy cafe for solace in a kindred face but found none. Those people, mostly pilots from the airfield across the road, didn't have my problem. They had solved their dilemma by flying; with their light aircraft they spun webs of communication across Alaska. To them it was a matter of an hour's flight to visit a friend on a remote homestead, and through this communication learn something of what that friend had found in the wilderness.

I envied them their understanding of what life in Alaska implied. The problem was one of communication. For my life in Alaska to be the true experience I wanted it to be, I had come to realize that links between the different areas of the state would have to be established. Living in Anchorage, I needed a connection with the wilderness, with friends in Fairbanks. I would have to make contact with those areas of Alaskan life of which I so far had no experience: the Arctic and the sea. My idealized concept of life there was changing. To live in Alaska would have to be a more active experience than I thought. Merely to have a job in Anchorage wouldn't produce the new life we were after. The country was big and demanding and Jill and I would have to go out to meet it.

We climbed in the VW to drive back home. The neon signs of the 4th Avenue bars were already burning brightly, though at 9 p.m. the sun was still above the northwest horizon. There were fifty bars in Anchorage then, one for every 1000 of the population.

We stopped by a brightly fluorescent-lit Rexall Drug on 5th Avenue to buy a paper. 'Senate passes Statehood Bill' blurted the overlarge headline in the *Anchorage Times*, one of the two newspapers in town. Anchorage was one of the last cities in the U.S. to boast two independent newspapers. Only in 1974 were the seeds of a merger sown. The headline meant that Alaska's days as a Territory were nearly over. At that time Alaska was administered with bureaucratic ineptitude from Washington D.C., 6000 miles away. I showed Jill the paper.

'I don't know, I like the sound of "Territory" better, more frontier-like. "Oregon Territory" covered wagons and all that. But we need representation in Washington. You know we can't even vote in national elections now!'

Jill was beginning to discover that in Alaska, with its small population, she as an individual could actually have an effect on government. In the years to come she would find herself face to face with senators and representatives and would be able to voice her own feelings on the issues that would burden the fledgling state. It was a privilege denied citizens of more populous states, and one which was to make Alaska such an exciting place for her to live in.

By 10 p.m. Anchorage's streets were almost deserted; a few traffic lights blinked unnecessarily down empty streets. As we drove along Sand Lake Road we could see McKinley 140 miles away, black against the yellow sky where the sun had just set. Beyond it Camp Denali had opened for the summer.

'I miss those people,' her eyes were moist.

I stopped the VW on the edge of the road and looked at Jill. The yellow glow of the sky was reflected in her eyes.

'But we're meeting people here.'

'Yes, I suppose that it's just that it all began there and what I really miss is the small beginning. When I worked there, there were just a few of us. We could get close to each other. I guess I thought that's the way it would be here. But it's harder. Everybody is busy. We are busy. I wonder sometimes if I should get so involved in things. I can't seem to do less in this place. People in Anchorage don't have time for each other, and we are just as guilty as everyone else.'

'It seems to be the way of a big town. We had the same problem in Los Angeles, but I certainly didn't expect it here.'

'It's a shame. We are all losing.'

Chapter 6

Summer 1959

On January 3, 1959, President Eisenhower signed the Alaska Statehood Bill and Alaska became the forty-ninth state of the Union. At the time of statehood Alaska had a population of 226,000 of whom 43,000 were natives. Only a million acres of the state's total of three hundred and seventy-five million acres had been taken by private individuals.

The first major gas field in Alaska was dicovered on the Kenai Peninsula, near the Swanson River oil field.

Over the upper Fortymile valley the otherwise clear July morning sky was marred by fluffy white cumulus. They floated gently over the spruce and birch covered hills near the Canadian border, casting slowly moving shadows on the empty green land. By noon the shadows had merged, while overhead the cumulus formed anvil tops on the edge of the stratosphere at 27,000 feet. The calm waters of a cut-off meander of the Fortymile River about twenty miles south of Chicken were disturbed by the first drops of rain. At 3 p.m. the now black sky was rent by a brilliant flash of lightning that left a smouldering scar down the side of a large spruce. At the base of the spruce some dry needles, protected from the rain by the large tree above, began to burn.

Two days later in Anchorage my phone rang. It was Stan Abbott of the *Anchorage Daily News*. I had done some photographic stories for the paper over the past year. My camera was allowing me to break out of my Anchorage trap, but slowly. Perhaps this call would mean a further release.

Summer 1959

'Big fire up near Chicken, Jon, 45,000 acres so far. Can you be at Merrill at 5 tomorrow morning?'

Fortunately I had the next two days off.

'I'm lucky this time, Stan, yes.'

The DC-3 under charter to the Bureau of Land Management (a Federal agency charged with fire control over 222 million acres of Alaska) stuck its tail in the air, finally lifted its aged wheels off the runway and we were airborne. I was away. Peggy's cafe was off the dipping right wing as we turned northeast. At last I had joined that buzzing fleet of airplanes that I had seen over my hamburger steak the previous summer. I was spinning my first aerial thread over Alaska.

The roaring, sound-filled fuselage was lined with native fire fighters, hired in Anchorage to supplement those four hundred from villages all over interior Alaska who were already on the fire. The fire season (May 15 to August 15) provided employment for Indian and Eskimo men and temporarily took them away from the boredom of village life in the summer. The shoulder to shoulder line opposite us had fallen asleep, hard hats pulled over their eyes. I nudged Stan to ask him the flying time to Tanacross, but he was asleep too.

The DC-3 seemed to struggle just to stay aloft, though it was probably running fine, for a thirty-year-old airplane. I craned my neck to catch glimpses of peak and glacier but saw mostly the top of the wing. Finally, we left the mountains behind and flew over the gently rolling green waves of the Interior. As we landed at Tanacross I could see that one of the hills ahead had erupted into a gray-black mushroom cloud, that towered toward the stratsophere looking like the thundercloud that had caused it. The fire.

Firefighting in Alaska requires an arsenal of Army and Air Force hardware. Lightning-caused fires (one out of three) are usually far from a road and a fleet of helicopters and aircraft are brought in to transport the hundreds of natives, who lash at the fire perimeter with picks, shovels, bulldozers and chain saws. Over them the sky is filled with DC-6, B-25, and other World War II vintage aircraft that fly low over the edge of the advancing flames and bomb them with fire retardant materials (mixed with fertilizer to promote later growth). Between the ground pounders and the bomber pilots are the helicopter pilots who are kept busy ferrying fire bosses, operations chiefs, line bosses, crew bosses, Forest Service personnel, injured firefighters, food and equipment and bothersome journalists and photographers around. In spite of all this activity an average of 402 fires burn up 825,000 acres of Alaska each year.

The BLM is considering a 'let burn' policy. Should acres of black spruce with no commercial value be saved at enormous expense? Is 'commercial value' the correct criterion by which to assess a wilderness? The natural, wild state of the land is for it to be burned by lightning strikes. Is man right to try to prevent this spectacular cleansing of the earth?

As our helicopter flapped toward the column of smoke I looked below at the blackened smoking trail of destruction left by the flames. How many animals had been burned, how many nests incinerated, how long would it be before the trees grew

89

They had been out there on the Fortymile fire for several days, along with the rest of the Indian contingent from Tanacross, when Curly and I flapped down in his helicopter for a look. The day was cloudy and the fire huddled down in the tundra. The Indians were almost exhausted, dirty and hot, and they felt that they weren't getting anywhere with the fire. Without the help of a Cat they had built several fire breaks and the flames had jumped them all. The only time they thought they were making headway was when the weather pushed down the fire, as it had today. 'Any chance of getting a Cat up here?', one of them asked Curly. 'I doubt it. We've got all four over on the north side where the fire's headed for Chicken. Don't have any extras for down here. But you guys keep at it. I'll see what I can do. Might get a plane to drop some retardant in here.' We walked over to their camp. About a dozen men, some wearing bright metal hard hats, sat around a smoky campfire. A fuel can full of water, suspended from a spruce pole, was heating over the fire. Some of the men seemed too old for this sort of thing, but all of them, old and young, looked as though the fire had nearly beaten them. Curly called them together for a pep talk. 'I know you think you are forgotten down here in this corner of the fire, but I can tell you that you aren't.' The men looked at him without expression. 'It is just that we have our hands full with the Chicken thing. Damn thing almost took the town yesterday.' One old Indian, gray-haired, his face a mass of wrinkles, ignored Curly and bent over a log he was carving into the shape of a woman. The air was full of a smoky haze, the black spruce stood around like sentinels. The forest was gray everywhere, there was hardly a wind, and, except for Curly's voice, not a sound. 'Just hang on here for a couple more days and we'll have this thing licked. Keep in touch on the radio.' Curly seemed to have trouble with his words; it all sounded too formal for the situation. He felt uncomfortable with the Indians.

We climbed back into the helicopter, and the pilot pulled us out of the burnt clearing, scattering ashes and dust toward the Indian camp. Ahead of us the fire flared up again, fingers of flame were crawling across the Indians' newly cleared break. Curly was on the radio. 'Tanacross base! Get up to Bravo ridge. Fire's cutting your break!' The distance produced by the radio seemed to have loosened Curly's tongue. We hovered near the flareup so the Indians would be able to find it. They tramped out of their camp in a long line, working their way through the brush, not fast, but slow and plodding. Curly peered through the plexiglass at the line of men. 'Christ, those guys are tired. We'll have to get them out of there.'

again in this land of slow growth? My instincts were against the fire. It should be put out. It seemed wrong. But if I was to be consistent in my thinking of Alaska as a true wilderness, surely this baptism of flame was an integral part of it. A fiery expression of nature's irrationality.

But man wanted this land, his land, for himself, for whatever use, and this vast armada was being used to prevent its loss. I wanted them to win.

The helicopter settled into the tundra on a ridge ten miles west of the orange flames that had crowned through a grove of large spruce. The base camp site was piled high with Army C-rations, bed rolls, tents and assorted equipment. Curly Brown, operations chief, was staring at his radio.

'East? Those weather boys in Anchorage promised me it would stay north!' he yelled at the electronic marvel a few inches from his lips. He looked over the top of the radio at the flames, as they leapt from spruce to spruce with a roar that easily spanned the distance.

'It's coming this way,' he said to no-one in particular. 'Damn wind's changed! Call Fairbanks, send down a B-25,' he said into the radio.

The radio was his link with everyone on the fire and he controlled the mammoth operation as a general would his army.

'Bring that Tanacross native crew out of there, tell them chopper'll be there in five minutes.'

The blades hadn't stopped on the helicopter that had brought us when they accelerated to take off RPM. We were whipped by the wash as the chopper headed for the group of nineteen Tanacross Indians now caught in the path of the flames. Half an hour later it was back with the first load of hard-hatted, blackened and exhausted men. Their eyes closed as soon as they found a bed roll on which to collapse. They had been fighting the beast for two days and now the wind change had caused the fire to jump their prepared breach, nullifying their efforts.

Curly was impatient.

'Where in hell is that fucking B-25?'

'Takes about an hour from Fairbanks, Curly,' pacified a crew boss.

The B-25 finally called in.

'Get the western edge, just below us,' said Curly, calmer now that the tardy plane had arrived. The two-engined modified former Air Force aircraft seemed to fly directly into the flames, Icarus style, as it dumped hundreds of pounds of red colored chemicals onto the trees just ahead of the fire.

'Great.' Curly was pleased. 'Let's have another one.'

The evening brought coolness, a calming of the winds and higher humidity. The fire relaxed its hot grip on the trees and descended to smoulder in the tundra.

By mid-morning next day the fire was crowning again, but headed south this time. Curly resumed his dialogue with his men.

We helicoptered back to Tanacross and caught the relief DC-3 back to Anchorage. We had stories and pictures. Curly would have five more days of battle ahead of him and in the end the fire was put out by rain. But it had burned 100,000 acres by the time the drops fell.

Summer 1959

I walked in the warm evening light down Raspberry Road. Ahead of me was a plywood building built on pilings to prevent it from sinking into the mushy swamp at the end of the road. A scattering of black spruce surrounded the small building and formed a background for it. 'Come in', a gruff voice answered my knock.

He felt the shape grow against the skin of his fingers. His hands, gray with caked clay, moved delicately over the emerging pot as it turned under them. Gradually the shape became useful. The clay ceased to be inert, and slowly assumed form. Alex Combs withdrew his large sensitive hands from the pot.

'Want some wine?'

We had met Alex and Muriel a few months after we had moved into the house on Raspberry Road. He was about forty then; bald and bearded, his face expressed a confidence in the direction his life and art were going that I envied. In 1955 he had broken with a rigid administration at Temple university in Philadelphia and had come to Alaska with his family. The place offered him a freedom of expression denied in the south.

The wine gurgled into a ceramic cup.

Both Alex and Bill Berry used Alaska for material but in opposite ways. Bill painted every detail (with his knowledge of animal anatomy and plant and tree construction and his obsession for accuracy it was probably impossible for him to do otherwise) and insisted that we draw our own conclusions of the beauty and meaning in the landscape. There were probably several meanings in each picture, but the primary impression was of reality, of having been there—on an arctic plain with a lonely wolf that cringed against swirling stinging snow. The realism was immediate and convincing, not like a photograph which would appear distant and plastic, removed from reality by layers of film, lens and technology.

During long summers away from his job as art consultant with the Anchorage school system, Alex wet his hands with the salt water of Kachemak Bay and Cook Inlet as a commercial fisherman. His ceramic forms reflected the sea and its forms of wave and spray. Though he came from a realistic background in art, his use of the Alaska scene was an inspiration for abstraction: he simplified that environment into color and form that was as vital as the land.

'Refill?'

'Thanks.' I gulped the wine.

'Jon, why don't you mount up some of your photographs and try to sell them. I don't like photographs, but somebody might.' Alex was always helpful. 'And another thing, don't you think what you've just written is a little overdone? "Hands wet with salt water!" I just went fishing to earn some money, and to get some fish.'

'Best I can do, Alex. Do you have any more wine?'

'Yep. I think you need it.'

'But I like your work and I might even go on.'

'God!'

I always felt that art in Alaska was a victim of the country itself. The stupendous mountains, vast skies and distances had dominated the art for years. Artists, amateur and professional, merely stood in awe of what was before them and then transferred

93

that scene to canvas as best they could within the limits of their ability. Alaska dominated their artistic senses, prevented rational interpretation and suppressed inspiration. For years Alaskan art consisted of endless scenes of log cabins, spruce trees and snowy mountains, done in unimaginative representational straightforward style without real knowledge or understanding of the land or its people.

Sydney Lawrence, a pioneer Alaskan artist, managed to come to terms with the problem by romanticizing the landscape into his own concept of what it should look like. I think he succeeded to a certain extent, especially in his use of low angle sunlight. The long shadows, even in summer, the long periods of time when the sun is just above the horizon, are important elements of the Alaskan light environment, but are frequently forgotten or misused.

Much early native Alaskan art shows this understanding. The native people of Alaska lived intimately with the land and with each other. Their masks, the decorative art of the Indians of Southeast Alaska, and the carvings of the Eskimos, derive from long association and knowledge of the subjects. Native art had a genuine interpretive quality that was severely lacking in white man's art at that time. Early and even recent white man came to Alaska and painted what he saw, not what was actually there. Artists like Bill Berry and Alex Combs, though their art appears dissimilar, have managed through intimate knowledge to look into the mountains, the seas and the people and have brought the essence of Alaska to canvas and clay.

As I walked back up Raspberry Road that late August day in 1959, I began to think of Anchorage more as a home and less as an adversary.

Anchorage hospitality wasn't a myth and we exchanged evenings with more new friends as the months passed. But the city wouldn't give any of us a chance to develop those relationships beyond a superficial level. There were too many forces impinging on us in the bursting sophisticated environment of Anchorage life for us to have the time.

In an effort to involve ourselves more in the city's life, we joined: folk dancing, discussion groups, voter groups. We discussed non-gods with the Unitarians. I think both our new friends in Anchorage and we were after the same thing—a closer relationship with each other. But as usually happens in a large city, we purposely put obstacles, in the form of things to do, between ourselves. We made person to person relationships, more and more important as a city grows, increasingly difficult to achieve. We found the more we tried to find each other in the city, through staged meetings at book clubs and the like, the less we succeeded. The city, as it grew, tightened its grip on our time and pulled us apart. It was a sad consequence of Anchorage's growth that its people would lose the very closeness they had hoped to achieve by going to Alaska.

Chapter 7

Autumn 1959

In 1960 the Swanson River field came on production, at 30,000 barrels a day. The total field reserve was set at 175 million barrels. A refinery was built near Port Nikiski on Cook Inlet, and shipments began to West Coast ports.

Toward the end of September, when the last birch and aspen leaves had fluttered to the ground and the first snows covered the rocky peaks of the Chugach, a long period of semi-hibernation began. Cars were winterized, home fuel tanks filled. Winter would begin in October and last until March. It is the longest and most important season in Alaska.

But first the brief autumn. It was both a time of separation and of coming together. Ties between friends across Alaska were gradually loosened, for both driving on the limited road system, and flying would become more difficult in the months ahead. The population slowly settled into immobility. A social drawing together took place, and communication between nearby friends increased. Small towns became smaller, smaller towns became villages. But the communication was nearly always between friends, most of them new. Almost no-one had any relatives in Alaska, and this need to make new friends was daunting to some at first.

In Anchorage, the snows come late and light, but a sense of the closing in of a wilderness of cold enveloped even this largest town. In its quest for a separate identity, Anchorage tried to ignore this Alaskan inconvenience, but it came upon it, nevertheless.

The entrance to Halibut Cove, across Kachemak Bay from Homer at the lower end of the Kenai Peninsula. Kachemak is from an Aleut dialect word meaning 'Smoke' from the coal smoke that used to come from burning coal seams that still lie exposed on sea cliffs near Homer. Local residents can pick up lumps of coal on the beach to supplement their fuel supply.

Homer itself, a town of 3000, has suddenly found itself swamped by weekenders from Anchorage, less than a day's drive up the Sterling Highway. These two keep their boat in the small boat harbor built into the end of the five mile long spit of gravel jutting out from Homer into the bay. This late July evening they are fishing for halibut, and as the evening wears on they will probably cruise to the left about five miles, tie up, and surf fish for salmon along a wide gravel beach called Glacier Spit. Tucked into these trees on the lower slopes of the Kenai Mountains are many cabins, empty during the week, but filled with weekenders in the summer. When unoccupied they are frequently vandalized by people who come across the bay in boats. The cabins are virtually indefensible, and the rapidly increasing crimes of housebreaking and squatting are turning cabins in the wilderness into liabilities. One family I know returned to their cabin to find it occupied by a family of squatters who refused to move, and even pulled a gun on the angry owners. Another found his cabin cleaned out.

These mountains, about 5000 feet high, reflect the more temperate climate of this part of Alaska. Here the climate is modified by warm seas, rain and snowfall is high, cloud cover great, and winter temperatures rarely fall below 10°F. Rain can occur in any winter month. This type of landscape extends all along the coastal arc from Kodiak Island through Southeast Alaska.

An Eskimo *umiak* sails in on a light afternoon breeze toward the beach at Gambell on St Lawrence Island in 1959. The *umiak* is a skin covered hunting boat, still used by the Alaskan Eskimos, about 25 feet long and 5 feet wide. The frame is of wooden stringers nailed, lashed and bolted together, and covered with six or seven skins of the bearded seal. Up to the 50s, sail power was dominant, in spite of the fact that outboard motors have been available to the Alaskan Eskimos since the 20s. But even the sail on this *umiak* has been supplemented by a 15 hp outboard, though it is not in use at the moment. Nowadays, every Eskimo boat owner has at least one outboard, and probably several. If he breaks down at sea, or among the devious channels of the polar ice pack while on a seal or walrus hunt, he has a spare motor to get him home.

Today, Eskimos commonly have light aluminum skiffs on which they put 20 to 25 hp outboards. They use these more fragile runabouts mainly in the summer for fishing trips or seal hunts. I joined one of the latter at Kaktovik one summer evening when the Arctic Ocean was calm, the sky clear, but the air bitter cold in the wind created by our full throttle dash toward the ice pack a few miles offshore. As we left the beach at the village we were joined by a second skiff and the two boats raced in close formation while a shouted conversation was carried on between the four or five men and women in each. Our speed slackened only slightly as we entered the steadily thickening mass of floating ice that stretched across the northern horizon. Suddenly the motors were cut and we glided in silence into a small bay ringed with ice. The dark shape of a seal broke the glassy surface of the water ahead, but disappeared before a rifle could be brought to bear on it. But no matter. The excursion was a lark anyway, and we spent the next hour dodging ice floes and each other on our way back to the village.

But Gambell in the 50s was a more gentle place, and when this *umiak* settled against the beach, its crew assisted by the wife of the man in the bow who waits to throw her the line, there was no sound of internal combustion. Only a low conversation, the sound of the keel, first on the gravel of the beach, then on the shore ice, and after, the sucking sound of the knife as it cut into the flesh of the seal.

October, before the snows came to cover the gone-to-seed fireweed and last summer's leaves, was a time of depression. A time when personal insecurity and the problems of human relationships were compounded by the anticipation of darkness and cold. The light went out of the sky and seemed to go out of our lives at the same time. In Alaska, the climate and the movement of the sun became an integral part of our way of life, and our emotions (and those of many of the people we knew) moved inexorably with the seasons. I'm sure this emotional tie with the movement of the sun is real and is found all over the north. Alcoholism and psychological problems of all sorts reach a maximum during the dark cold days of winter in Scandinavia as well as Alaska. This fact probably underlaid unexplained differences and loss of communication between Jill and me that autumn. The sap that rose in the spring fell in the fall.

Our first winter had been a time of newness, of anticipation and looking forward. Of a perverse excitement of a day with only $5\frac{1}{2}$ hours of sunlight, of a sensation of cold far beyond any we had experienced before. It had been an exciting time when each snowstorm brought a new delight in the beauty of the landscape. But in this the beginning of our second winter, especially in this strange time when the cold had come but not the snow, we felt drawn apart.

I withdrew into my photography, which only made the communication between us more difficult, and the ego-beast was gnawing at my heels. I tramped around the country I could reach, toward Talkeetna, down to the Kenai in my search for pictures, and through them, recognition. I fought the beast off, but it was a self-centered fight and Jill was not allowed to participate.

Looking back, I realize how narrow-minded I was, not to have included her more in my search for fulfilment, but I was typical of a large number of men who end up in places like Alaska.

I knew many, who because Alaska offered them the opportunities, flew across her wilderness, hunted for days on end for moose they didn't need, climbed her mountains or floated on her rivers in *their* single-minded searches for identity or ego or personal fulfilment without their wives, as though the pioneering demands of Alaska justified the sacrifice of a relationship.

Much of the cause of the extremely high divorce rate in Alaska, I think, stems from this very fact. Some men, when they come to Alaska, seem to shed the civilized art of personal relationship and use the land as an excuse for a release of male aggressiveness to the exclusion of their womenfolk. The latter, left at home, say, in Anchorage surburbia, feel rejected and unneeded, and look around for someone else, preferably someone who is still in town.

I know now that I was guilty of this, and I was about to make matters worse by taking up flying again. I thought at the time that by feeling more fulfilled in Alaska, I would be able to bring more to our relationship, but that sort of happiness must come from within the pairing, not be externally imposed.

And so I flew. The Air National Guard, which in Alaska was really the state government airline, offered me a part-time job flying their two-engined C-47s all over the state. I would be released from my Anchorage trap.

Autumn 1959

About this same time, Jill received an offer of a summer job at Camp Denali. She accepted. She obviously had a few aggressive instincts of her own and wasn't going to be left out.

The C-47 (the military version of the DC-3) was a marvellous old airplane that was built like a truck, and flew low and slow. It gave me the feeling it would fly forever. Its electronics were minimal, and its landing gear retraction system sounded like a flushing toilet.

On a cold late November day with the temperature at 10 above and a light snow beginning to fall, Jim Rhodes and I went through the pre-take-off check on the end of runway 24 at Anchorage International. Jim took the left seat for the first leg to Bethel. I would fly it to Nome and Gambell. Jim worked at an insurance agency in Anchorage; he was anxious to get out of town this Saturday morning too.

'Air Guard 971 cleared for take-off.'

At 1000 ft we entered the base of the overcast and turned right to the Bethel heading. In the aircraft with us were used books for the school at Gambell and barrels of oil for heating in the Eskimo village on the north-west tip of St Lawrence Island.

About an hour out of Anchorage the enveloping gray of the clouds suddenly parted and we were thrust into a crystal of orange and blue. The sun was low in the south and its golden rays streamed across the flat snow-covered land like streaks of paint. The dome of deep blue over us was of space itself. We were suspended in this world as though motionless; the distance to the horizon was infinite. I felt the same oneness with Alaska that I had experienced on McKinley. I settled back in my seat, calm and at peace.

After three hours, Bethel appeared as a few black dots along the bank of the frozen Kuskokwim River. It was the largest Eskimo village in the Yukon—Kuskokwim delta area—but it looked insignificant in the vastness of the snowy plain.

The wheels settled on the snowpacked runway and we taxied up to a delapidated building that housed the fuel supply. As Jim cut the engines I looked at the outside air temperature gauge: 32°F below zero.

'We'll have to preheat the engines if we stay very long,' I said.

'Won't be long. I hate Bethel. It's a real dump.'

The cold snow squeaked beneath my boots as I walked into the town. The irregular 'street' of snow was lined with tar-paper shacks and leaning houses, made from the boxes used to ship gasoline and patched by the gasoline cans themselves. Smoke from stovepipes rose straight up into the cold blue air. At 3:30 p.m. the sun was already below the horizon.

The town was apparently empty. Of the 1700 Eskimos who lived there hardly any were visible. There was no reason to be out; there was nothing to do. One of the biggest problems in Bethel was boredom and the usual solution to the problem was alcohol. Bethel had the highest proportion of people living below the poverty line of any town in the U.S. and almost 80 per cent unemployment, but the liquor store did a booming trade. The town had grown as a result of an inflow of people from over fifty surrounding villages. Those people had survived on a subsistence economy, but there just wasn't enough fish or game around Bethel to support such a large population, and no work

99

Two Athabascan Indian kids try to make a toy out of last year's snowmobile at Arctic Village. It is early September, school hasn't started yet, and in a quiet place like Arctic Village there is little for these kids to do. But this can be an advantage, too, for they are never far from home. Native people, generally, love their kids, and have a close relationship with them. The children are usually around when the adults are, not banished to another room. In the summer they stay up as late as the grownups which usually means well past midnight, but this is compensated for by long sleeps in the winter. This snowmobile may be only a year or so old, but they don't last long these days. 'When they first came out they would go and go. Not any more,' I was told. Under the streamlined hood is the gasoline engine that drives a cleated belt over the bogie wheels now resting on the ground. The handle bars are used to steer the skis at the front and the whole thing can whiz over the snow at 30 miles per hour or more. But, unlike the dog teams it has replaced, a snowmobile can suddenly break down miles from anywhere and then it is a long, cold trek back to the village. Most cabins in Arctic Village have at least one old snowmobile rusting in the yard and I saw one place with three. Fuel must be flown in, the expense is high, but these noisy mechanized dog teams are here to stay, no matter what the cost. 'They don't eat in the summer, do they?'

The logs for this cabin, and for most of the buildings in the village, were brought down the East Fork of the Chandalar from a grove of spruce about five miles up-stream. The trees are small and taper rapidly. Unlike many native villages in the far north, Arctic Village lies in a beautiful valley of trees, lakes, meadows and rivers, ringed by the craggy peaks of the Brooks Range.

for cash either. The answer to a life on welfare was vodka. The place was a sad dump, a victim of the disaster that takes place when two opposite worlds come together. The white world of cash for work done and the Eskimo world of fish to eat. The Eskimos in Bethel couldn't decide which they were in and hence ended up in limbo and drunk. (In an effort to come to grips with the problem the people of Bethel voted to make the community dry in October 1973 and again in February 1976.)

We took off northward in the deepening twilight toward Nome. Around us the world became bare and blue. Snow plains and sky. Though scattered over the treeless plain between the Kuskokwim and Yukon Rivers were dozens of Eskimo villages, I could see not a light, not a track or road. The moon rose, full, and cast a white other-worldly light across the vacant land.

The C-47 droned on in the blue-black sky toward Nome. We hardly said a word—words seemed irrelevant to the beauty of the night. But an Eskimo on the ground, looking up at the sound of our engines, would find his sky marred by an ungainly—and to him irrelevant—aluminium bird. Our presence in his sky continued a slow process of change, of sophistication, started by the first airplane he or his father saw, which could lead to a gradual frustration with his way of life. Eventually he might leave his small village and move to a place like Bethel.

A few areas of new sea ice glowed dully in the moonlight along the shore of Norton Sound; then there was the blackness of the sea. After an hour a tiny group of lights sparkled in the clear air where the sea met the white land of Seward Peninsula. Nome.

By 9 a.m. next morning the southeastern sky was red-orange, colored by a yet invisible sun. I stood on a pile of snow and ice-covered boulders that formed part of a sea wall, built in an attempt to keep the Bering Sea from Nome's Front Street. That cold November morning the heaving dark sea was beginning its winter freeze up. Slush ice formed out at sea had been brought to shore by the south wind. This morning the slush along the beach extended 30 feet out to sea. By spring, the beach would be lined with huge blocks of ice that would form a wall of their own.

The sands of the beach had spelt the end of the fabulous Klondike. In one week in August in 1899, 8000 people left Dawson City for the golden beaches of Nome. They packed steamers like the *Casca* in which we had slept in Whitehorse, and floated down the Yukon for the new El Dorado. By 1903 the tents and cabins stretched for twenty miles along the beach and 25,000 feverish, greedy men dug for their fortunes.

The Klondike gold rush lasted three years from the day Cormack and Henderson met at the point where the Klondike River flowed into the Yukon. Their discovery of gold in those Yukon creeks in 1897 caused a worldwide gold fever that infected over a million people. The finds on the Nome beaches continued this obsession with easy wealth for another few years, but eventually all the surface gold was taken back aboard the steamers to Seattle and San Francisco and the deeper gold was left to the dredges and the mines. Nome's reason for existence ceased in the mid 30s when the price of gold fell. The town remains as an epitaph to the white man's greed.

A few Victorian-style houses on Front Street just caught the first rays of the sun as it inched coldly over the Bering Sea. They looked alien to the wild sea and land around Nome. Their designs had been carried in the minds of the gold seekers from the streets of San Francisco. Erected in this wilderness to replace the tents and cabins on the beach, they now housed the few descendants of the gold diggers that were left in Nome. Seventy per cent of the 2200 people in Nome were Eskimo, and most of them lived in poor shacks on the east end. Nome was another Alaskan town that lived on government payrolls, and for the Eskimos it was another life between two worlds. Here, too, the answer to their dilemma was alcohol.

Ahead of the C-47, St Lawrence Island rose like a great white whale from the ice-dotted blue of the Bering Sea. Its snowy treeless shape stretched across our southern horizon, while ahead and to the right were the hazy snow mountains of Siberia, forty miles away. Just below us now a large headland met the sea in a narrow beach. Clustered in the snow on the edge of the beach was the village of Gambell.

I landed the C-47 on the snowy strip on the edge of the sea; most of the runway consisted of steel mats from World War II. As soon as I taxied to a stop at the edge of the village, the airplane was surrounded by dozens of parka-clad kids and adults who were joined by more from the rapidly emptying village. I cut the still idling engines, but the running and dancing people seemed used to the danger from the whirling propellers.

The boxes of books were loaded on to dog sleds and taken into the village. A larger sled awaited the fuel and while the unloading took place, I walked along the short path to the village.

The buildings were mostly small frame houses, with a few Quonset buildings also from World War II. Here and there was a skin boat inverted on a rack of poles. An American flag fluttered from the roof of the elementary school, while across the sea I could see the snowy Siberian mountains. There had been intermarriage and frequent contact between the St Lawrence Island people and the Siberian Eskimos until the first part of this century when the Soviets ended it. A village store and a couple of churches completed the village, and I continued on down to the beach.

Seated on a small hummock overlooking the sea were a woman and her child. I sat down beside them.

'Hello,' I said, hesitantly.

She didn't reply, but continued to stare out to sea. I followed her gaze and saw a pale white sail above a long skin boat that was finding a path through the ice.

She said something in Suk, a Siberian dialect of Yupik, the Eskimo language of southwestern Alaska. Her face broke into a broad smile that closed her eyes to thin slits and she pointed to the boat.

As the skin boat came closer I could make out five men on board, heavily clad in skin parkas. Harpoons leaned against the gunwale; on the stern an outboard motor gave the wind some help.

The woman, who now had put the child in a pouch on her back, pulled on the line thrown to her, and soon the men were on the beach. Out of the boat they dragged a dead seal.

They immediately cut the seal open, skinned it, gutted it and cut up the meat. The white snow was red with the seal's blood and a stream of it flowed back into the clear sea, turning the water purple.

The men and the woman were soon joined by others from the village and the seal meat was taken away, leaving behind only the blood-stained snow.

Here was a part of Alaska where people still lived off what the land and the sea could provide. But these Eskimos were changing too. Already their children from the eighth grade on went to school in Nome and only came back to Gambell for a few months in the summer. Eventually, they might not come back at all. The outboard was replacing the wind, and would require fuel. Snowmobiles were coming.

But I was wrong to try to think of these people as artifacts to be preserved. They were human beings like me, and if I used sophisticated tools, why shouldn't they? But I had been brought up with them. I not only knew how to work the tools, but how to put them aside as well. It may be the last step in man's sophistication to learn to put his tools down and return to the land.

For these Eskimos, the whole process would be accelerated. Culture began on St Lawrence Island about 400 BC when the people believed that all living things belonged to a spirit world. Since then the lives of the Islanders had been in harmony with the wildlife around them which provided their necessities. Their lives were simple and their minds were able to cope with whatever problems of survival came along.

Now we have presented them with an embarrassment of tools: tools that they can use (Eskimos are good mechanics) but whose use not only produces a disharmony with their environment, but a psychological disharmony with their culture. The industrial revolution took us 150 years to understand and even now we have doubts as to our ability to cope with its complexities. No wonder that twentieth-century technology, advancing over Alaska with exponential rapidity, has forced many of the natives into an alcoholic escape.

The sled of fuel drums, surrounded by most of the village people, was on its way up the path from the airstrip. Ropes tied to the sled were over the shoulders of four big men, while the back of the sled was covered with a mosaic of sealskin mittens. Jim ran up the path to meet me.

'We better get going, Jon, I don't like the looks of this visibility.'

I was reluctant to leave this peaceful corner of the Arctic, but already a fog had moved in off the sea onto the beach, and the light from the low sun was becoming diffused and indistinct.

The little group around the sled waved as we roared over them on our take-off. The fuel would help them through the winter ahead, but dependence on it would bring them closer to the white man's energy-consuming world. Their independence would gradually end, their culture merge with his.

Chapter 8
Winter 1961

Natural gas from the Swanson River field was piped to Anchorage by mid 1961. Offshore exploration for oil began in Cook Inlet. By 1962 the first drilling platform was built in the difficult tidal waters of the inlet. In 1963 a group including Shell, Richfield and Standard of California struck oil on Middle Ground Shoal about sixty miles southwest of Anchorage.

In Anchorage, by early December, about a foot or two of snow covered the ground, daytime temperatures were in the twenties and traffic moved gingerly. A night of freezing fog would cover the bare branches of the birch with crystals that glowed a dull red-orange in the low sunlight. The two junked cars next door were masked by the snow and the city took on the mantle of winter like an ugly woman putting on a mink coat.

The snow deadened the sounds of both the airplanes and the cars, and seemed to bring the city together in a unified condition of white. The excesses of Anchorage were softened and its eyesores covered, most of them to be forgotten until revealed by the melting snows of spring. Jill and I moved closer to the new friends we had made there. Both they and we seemed to have more time for each other in the winter, though each contact still had a time-bound feeling; we seemed to have only a limited amount of it to give each other. Anchorage had infested us all with its temporal illness; the city took away all the lulls in our lives.

Bill Nancarrow had invited us to Deneki Lakes for Christmas. Liz and Bill Berry with their son Mark were living there for the winter while Bill wrote and illustrated a book. We would be able to discard the time-disease of Anchorage for two weeks and return to the area that had given us our first flowering of love for the Alaskan wilderness. This time we would be able to experience it in the company of close friends who had shared our discovery during that summer. But Ginny Nan wouldn't be there; she had died of cancer the previous summer. Ginny Wood wrote of the last days of her friend for the Camp Denali newspaper:

An operation in Fairbanks in January revealed that Ginny Nan, as she was affectionately called, had cancer—probably incurable. She was sent to Seattle for treatment.

'I'll be back in the spring,' she announced gaily as she boarded a jet for the States.

When we saw her in the hospital in April, it was apparent even to Ginny herself that she would not return. The doctors gave her only a few more weeks.

'I guess I won't be seeing you at Deneki Lakes when you come through to camp,' she said wistfully.

I had said goodbye and was to fly back to Alaska the next day when the thought struck me. By hook or by crook I was going to take Ginny Nan with me. The end would not come alone, far away from her beloved Alaska. It took a bit of doing. The doctors predicted it might hasten the end, but it wouldn't matter. The flight now took only three hours by jet, and the airline would take her if she could sit up.

Woody wheeled Ginny Nan aboard in a wheelchair. As the big plane soared into the air toward the north, Ginny Nan's spirits soared with it. She was going home.

The effect was miraculous. When the plane landed at Anchorage, Ginny Nan insisted on walking down the ramp to meet Bill. At the end of the week in a rest home she was dressing for meals, taking rides with friends, and was ready to go back to Deneki Lakes. Her letters, at first with shaky handwriting, then in her firm neat script, were full of the joy of living. She was doing the dishes. Today she picked up bark from the place where Bill was peeling logs. She took a two-mile walk. The birds were returning and the big new log home was almost completed.

The Fairbanks doctors were amazed. The cancer was still there—the end inevitable; but there had been an unexplainable lull in its onslaught. When I arrived with the loaded Travelall en route to camp in early June, it was hard to believe that life at Deneki Lakes would be any different.

When the end came it was merciful and fast. A week of weakness and discomfort; only two days of real distress. She died where she wanted to be—at home at her beloved Deneki Lakes with Bill, and her close friend, Liz Berry, nearby.

Alaska perhaps is one of the few places under the American flag where one is permitted to have a dignified burial, devoid of the middlemen, commercialization or barbarity that customarily goes with undertakers, funerals and cemeteries. Ginny Nan was laid to rest in the evening after her death in a grave dug by friends in a clearing in the spruce that she had chosen herself. Bill had fashioned the coffin—a privilege denied to husbands in modern times. We flew in from camp to join her other McKinley Park friends in saying goodbye. On the lake a moose appeared for his evening feeding, while nearby swam Ginny Nan's beloved grebes with their new brood.

The lake was empty. I stood on the dock and looked south toward the place where the sun would appear from behind Carlo Mountain. The smooth snow-covered surface of Deneki Lake was broken only by a few ptarmigan tracks. The temperature was 15°F below zero, but the air was still and the smoke from Bill Nan's cabin rose straight up into a deep blue sky. On this December 22 the sun rose at about 8:45 a.m., but now at noon it still hadn't shone on the Lakes.

At 12:10 p.m. the sun appeared, barely a hand's breadth above the southern horizon, its highest position for the day. In southern Alaska the winter sun never rises far enough above the southern horizon to release its light and warmth. The ending of a long sunrise, at noon, is followed by an afternoon of sunset. By late February this spell is broken and the higher sun at noon shines white in the clear air, its warmth felt on the face. It is the first sign of spring in the far north. In mid winter the sun's effect is only psychological. The yellow-orange light which colored everything it touched gave the appearance of life and warmth where there was none. It was the shortest day of the year.

The golden rays outlined the west ridge of Carlo Mountain and caught the tops of the snow-covered spruce on the eastern side of the lake in a frosty glow. From the south shore, blue fingers of spruce shadows fed across the lake toward me to be lost in a burnished carpet of snow.

By 2:30 p.m. the sun disappeared again behind the hills of Windy Pass and the lakes were left in a cold blue shadow that soon deepened to night. At 4:00 p.m. the first stars appeared.

By the next morning the temperature was 35°F below zero, and that evening, 42°F below zero. The air became more still, the purple haze, characteristic of cold weather in the north, blended distant mountains into the early night. On Christmas Eve the temperature fell to 52°F below zero.

The cabin was bursting that Christmas Eve with a joyous sound of talk and laughter, composed of our voices and those of Bill Nan's neighbors in McKinley Park who had come to be with him on this first Christmas without Ginny Nan. We tried to ignore the cold, but its presence around us made the group closer. The warmth from the hot stove created an island of heat in the wilderness of cold. The cold was never far away. Whenever the door was opened, a cloud of condensation rushed across the floor, to dissipate reluctantly in the heat of the room. Layers of ice built up on the inside of the windows, obscuring the night and isolating us even more from the alien cold.

Every time I went out, to the outhouse (where the visits were brief) or for more wood, I was made conscious of the fragility of my body without the protection of the stove's heat, or layers of clothing. My cheeks would begin to smart after a short time, my hands, without gloves, took minutes of painful thawing after only a minute of exposure. The human body is pathetically vulnerable to cold.

Bill Berry recounted his tales of Windy Pass. He made up vast stories of mythical people who, he said, lived at Windy Pass, just down the road toward Cantwell. They spent their cold winter nights in Bacchanalian orgies, emptied vats of wine, and rolled naked in the snow after roasting themselves in steaming saunas. They solved all the problems of humanity while at the same time they created new and insoluble ones. To hear about their sexual excesses was a delight, and we egged Bill on far into Christmas morning. I had never spent a Christmas Eve like it before. The closeness of the people, the cold and the warmth, the stories and the wilderness around combined to reinforce my love for the place and the people in it.

Jill and I, bundled against the cold with down parkas, Eskimo mukluks (boots made from caribou skin) and multiple layers of sweaters, set out at noon on Christmas Day for a walk across the lake. It was 50°F below and the air itself felt solid. The sun had just made its brief appearance, but today its intensity was dimmed by something we hadn't seen for days, thin cirrus clouds.

'Maybe we're in for a change,' I postulated.

Jill's face was almost invisible behind the fur ruff of her parka. 'I hope so. This cold is beginning to get on my nerves. It was interesting at first, but now I find it a bit frightening the way it goes on and on. And I'm afraid to let Takla play outside with Mark. If she lost a mitten, her fingers would freeze.'

We were following a moose trail along the edge of the lake, though there was no sign of the moose that had made it. A piping chickadee flew by, its body so tiny it could conserve its warmth under a covering of down. But the red squirrels, voles and other small animals had burrowed into the moss and snow beneath the trees where the temperature was a comfortable (to them) 25°F above zero. The powder-dry snow settled behind us in little clouds of gold dust. After a short time we were in the blue twilight of the spruce forest.

We stopped. There was absolute silence. The trees stood around us like hooded white ghosts, their branches high with carefully balanced stacks of snow that had fallen straight down through the calm air, crystal on crystal, flake on flake. I puffed a a breath at one branch and it was emptied in a trice; its burden sifted down through the still air to settle invisibly on the snow carpet below.

'It seems a shame to speak.'

'Let's not.' We hugged each other in the silent forest, absorbing the quiet and peace.

I thought back to the summer of '54. It seemed noisy and busy compared to this winter wood. No wonder Bill Nan preferred the winter, when he could renew his independence. But this winter he would be alone.

I pulled Jill closer and kissed her.

Halfway back across the lake I looked up and noticed that a gray covering of cloud had replaced the blue void of the sky. The smoke from the cabin was now bent to the north just above the level of the trees. The air below the trees remained calm, but just above them there must be a wind from the south. The cold would be broken.

Winter 1961

When Jill and I reached the cabin again the thermometer stood at 30°F below zero. It had warmed twenty degrees in two hours. I looked back at the forest we had just left. Suddenly, the laden trees exploded in clouds of snow as a gale of warm air from the south burst through Windy Pass and hit them with its full fury. The path of the wind was marked by tree after tree as they were shaken by its force. Then I felt it on my face. I looked at the thermometer, nailed to the log cabin. Zero! Thirty degrees in a few minutes!

'Isn't that amaz . . . ,' Jill's exclamation was left unfinished when we were both submerged under a cascade of snow from a large spruce over our heads. 'I'm going in,' she gulped.

But I was transfixed by the spectacle of change that was being played out before me, and walked down to the edge of the lake. The overcast lowered rapidly and a few flakes of snow began to be carried along on the wind.

Bill Berry appeared from his cabin, still clutching his sketching pencils.

'I guess the Bacchanal down at Windy Pass is still in full swing. Perhaps they are trying to wish us a Merry Christmas with a bit of warmth,' Bill said, shivering in the 30°F above 'warmth'. 'Come on inside, there is still some of last night's cheer left in the bottle.'

We left Bill Nan and the Berrys in early January, and the Alaska Railroad took us south through Windy Pass. I looked, but couldn't find any of Bill's mythical beasts frolicking in the snow.

Chapter 9

Good Friday, 1964

With the birth of Kari at Providence Hospital in Anchorage in 1962, we came of age in Alaska. Jill and I had at last come to terms with living in Anchorage. It wasn't an ideal life and Raspberry Road wasn't our ideal world, but we were reasonably happy within the framework we had built there. Many of the friends we had made soon after our arrival had left for the Lower 48. Such is the transient nature of Anchorage that friends just made are soon gone and those remaining behind are left wondering if their decision to stay was the right one. But others stayed with us, and those people, many of them Alaskans long before us, helped us adjust to a more mature concept of life in Alaska.

Anchorage was growing and maturing with us, and by this time we felt a kinship for the place in spite of its obvious disadvantages. For better or worse it was our town and our state and Jill and I wanted to be part of its evolution. She, much more than I, pushed for laws she thought were for the good of Alaska. She talked to legislators, the governor, and businessmen in an attempt to affect the course of the new state. In Alaska, then, we felt we *could* affect it. At that time Alaska had just realized that as a state she would have a difficult path ahead. The heady euphoria of statehood had long since worn off, and the state was faced by the knowledge that the social needs of both the native and non-native people, would have to be met largely from the slender resources of a population of only 235,000.

If Anchorage was to be the city of Alaska it should be a good one. Part of its maturity would have to be control. There were now too many people living too close together for each to retain the independence he wanted. Junkyards would have to be fenced (but the owners protested this law to the end). Sewers would have to be built, plans for the future made. All this went against the grain of the early Anchorage residents who had built their town from scratch. The new laws restricted freedom, but they were a necessary result of more and more people living closer together.

Music was coming. Orchestras passing through on Europe-Tokyo flights would stop for a night to earn more cash, and we Anchorageites would flock at great expense to hear them in the high school auditorium. A music festival was held each June. The Anchorage Symphony was formed of local amateurs who fiddled and blew themselves a passable noise.

I flew across Alaska in my aged C-47, climbed more mountains, explored more valleys and skied. In this way I tried to achieve a balance in my Alaskan life between the wilderness I came for and the city I got. Together Jill and I were almost happy, but our lives lacked real fulfilment. I submerged myself again in photography, but this time not to the exclusion of Jill. We worked together to build the photographic business that would eventually free me from the confining work at the Weather Bureau, and it was beginning to prosper.

In my newly finished basement darkroom I bent over the developer tray to watch the image appear. It was the first in a new series of prints I would sell in an Anchorage shop. The developer moved just perceptibly in the yellow safe light and then stopped. The vibration began again almost immediately. An earthquake. Another one. We had many small ones in Anchorage, situated as it was in a maze of major faults. It would stop soon.

But the developer slopped out of the tray, the vibration increased rapidly. A jar of chemicals fell from a shelf and smashed near my feet. I tried to push the now jumping bottles back on the shelves, but I couldn't keep up and they crashed around me in a shower of glass. The door of the darkroom flew open and I was knocked to the floor, unable to stand on the rocking surface. The lights in the basement dimmed to brown, and before they went out I could see the concrete floor heave up and down several feet as the earthquake waves moved rapidly through it. The concrete block walls of the basement bent in and out as though made of rubber. Finally I was plunged into darkness, huddled in a corner, with the contents of the darkroom raining about me. A loud crash was the enlarger smashing to bits on the floor. The noise was deafening and interminable.

I was lost in an earth gone mad. It pushed me from one side to another in a frenzy of movement. With my head between my knees I froze in terror at the terrible force running through my body. For five minutes the earthquake rushed through the earth in wave after wave until, its primordial energy spent, it stopped.

I lifted my head. There was silence in the blackness. I picked my way through the debris to the stairway and struggled unsteadily upward. Jill was huddled in a corner of the living room with Kari in her arms. Takla was on a chair in the center. They were all uninjured.

'I picked Kari up from the floor just before that big bookcase fell,' said Jill, her voice trembling. The heavy bookcase, with its books scattered across the floor, could easily have killed the two-year-old.

The tallest building in Anchorage at the time of the earthquake was the 14-story Westward Hotel, the one on the left with the orange roof. But 'new building techniques' have allowed builders to erect higher structures on this earthquake-prone bluff in defiance of a natural event that, they say, won't happen again for 50 years. But they said that in 1964; now in 1976, there are only 38 years to go. Next to the Westward is a television transmitter, and farther to the right are a bank, complete with a sign on the roof that rotates and changes color with the weather, and another hotel. The group of houses below the downtown buildings are some of the oldest in town and are bordered by the Alaska Railroad track as it enters Anchorage from Seward. It is almost high tide in Knik Arm, and a few boats, tethered to buoys, are afloat. The Arm is a dangerous place for small boats like these with 30-foot tides that produce vicious currents. The Chugach is in a midsummer coat of green with only a patch of last winter's snow left in a gully. By late August that peak could be white.

Anchorage high school football players practice in a park on the site of homes destroyed in the earthquake.

Anchorage, 5th Avenue, westbound.

The Union Oil Building on 9th Avenue in Anchorage. Most major oil companies have offices, if not full scale buildings in Anchorage, and the oil men have been instrumental in increasing the height of the Anchorage skyline. BP built an edifice in the apparent wilderness of Arctic Boulevard a few years ago and now it is surrounded by a cluster of sister buildings. All of these new buildings must be built to the highest earthquake standards, and probably will not actually fall down if another 8.4 shudder should come along. This particular block of glass has been built a block or two away from the section of downtown Anchorage that shifted twelve feet toward Knik Arm. But that moving earth has now sprouted an assortment of hotels, office buildings and even a court house, constructed on the remains of those buildings destroyed in the earthquake. Economics being what they are, it is unlikely that the valuable vacant land would have remained so for long. After all, Los Angeles and San Francisco are constructing towers over 40 stories now and it is likely that they are nearer to a major earthquake than is Anchorage.

The afternoon sun reflected in the glass has been partially dimmed by a sheet of clouds, spreading over the western sky from behind the Aleutian Range that lies across Cook Inlet from Anchorage. By the next morning the sky would be overcast and a heavy rain falling, but for now this August Sunday is mild and dry. I stroll over to the Park Strip, just to the right, where a few families are picnicking and catching the last of the sun. Down at the lower end of the Park, near P Street, a religious group has set up a battery of loudspeakers, and a man is extolling the virtues of virtue and pointing out the sin of sinning. About a hundred people listen to him, and those on the edge of the group hand out leaflets to passers-by, including me. 'Have you been saved?' I am asked. As I leave, stuffing the paper into my pocket, the group bursts into a gospel hymn, led by the muted guitars of a rock band and the man who had been speaking of sin.

I quickly checked the house, but the structure appeared to be intact. Nothing remained on any shelf, and everything breakable had been broken. Outside the frozen ground around the house had heaved and cracked. I sensed an odd silence as I looked toward Anchorage. Normally at this time of day, the evening rush hour, the gentle roar of home-bound traffic would signal the departure of workers from their jobs. But this evening the city was quiet, as though it had ceased to exist.

We collapsed in shock in the shambles of the living room for several minutes. The very earth we had learned to trust had hit us with an incredible force, had rent our house, and had almost killed Kari. From a storm there is shelter, from a flood there is high ground, but when the earth itself seethes and turns there is no escape. We had received a terrible psychological jolt as well as a physical one, and our deepest most primitive mental chords had first been struck, then shattered.

We were brought back to life by the sound of car wheels on the gravel beside the house. A drawn, bearded face appeared at the door. It was Burt Bollenbach with whom I worked at the airport Weather Bureau office.

'The tower collapsed and killed one guy. The airport building is a mess, concrete blocks all over the place. But I heard that Turnagain is gone, and Amy said that she would either be here or visiting the Marstons there.'

'She isn't here.' I helped him through the door. 'Have some coffee. We'll get out the camp stove.'

'No thanks. I want to get to the Marstons.' Burt turned back toward his car. I went for my parka. 'Wait, Burt, I'll come along. You might need help.'

The ride along Sand Lake Road was one of awful anticipation. As we reached Spenard Road several police and ambulance cars sped past with lights flashing. Although a darkening twilight had fallen over the city, there were no lights in the houses. Only darting flashlights, car headlights or lanterns lit the gloom.

Halfway down Turnagain Parkway we were stopped by large cracks across the road. A group of people and cars blocked the way ahead. A woman separated herself from the group. It was Amy.

'Burt!' She ran up to us, bursting with news. 'The Marstons' house has been destroyed. In fact the whole bluff has fallen into the inlet. Everybody got out, as far as I know, but there must be a lot of houses wrecked.'

'Do they need us to help?'

'No. Everybody seems to have been taken care of for now. We can come back in the morning when it is light.'

As we drove home Amy recounted her experiences of the previous hour, and it became obvious to us that a disaster of enormous magnitude had befallen our city. The car radio crackled to life with warnings of possible tidal waves.

Later that night Jill managed to heat a pot of soup with our camp stove, but sleep didn't come easily. The bed was rocked every hour or so by aftershocks, every one of which we expected to grow into another terrible earthquake. The house was cold without heat, but at least we had a house. I thought of my friends on the Turnagain bluff, their homes swallowed by the grasping earth. At first light I would do what I could to help them.

Good Friday, 1964

But as a dim light spread into the bedroom the next morning the phone rang. I was told to report for duty at the Weather Bureau.

In the four minutes from 5:36 p.m. to 5:40 p.m. Anchorage lost nine of its citizens, 215 houses and 157 commercial buildings. Damage totalled $200,000,000. Seventy-five per cent of the property in Anchorage was either in ruins or needed extensive repair.

Elsewhere in Alaska it was water, not heaving land that shattered the lives of its people.

In Prince William Sound twenty-five of the seventy-two people in the native village of Chenega were drowned when the tidal wave (tsunami) generated by the earthquake swamped much of the island.

On Kodiak Island, fifteen blocks of the town of 2,500 people were levelled by the wave; one hundred fishing boats and three out of five canneries were demolished.

In Valdez the tragedy was extreme. The 400-ft Alaska Steamship *Chena* was unloading at the city's dock. Twenty-eight of the twelve hundred people who lived in Valdez were on the dock, helping or watching the unloading, men, women and children.

The earthquake and tidal wave struck together in one screaming cataclysm. The people on the dock tried to run for shore, but it disintegrated beneath their running feet and disappeared under the thrashing wave.

The *Chena* itself hit bottom several times, but the skipper got the ship under way and it rode the wave like a tossing cork.

By nightfall the waterfront was ablaze as one after another of the oil storage tanks ignited. The townspeople fled the apocalyptic scene and spent the cold night on a hill behind their wrecked town.

In Seward, the town on Resurrection Bay where we had boarded the *Aleutian* ten years before, the dock with almost all of the waterfront and eight fuel storage tanks slid into the bay, thirty seconds after the earthquake started. The remaining storage tanks broke open and poured burning fuel on the water of the bay.

As soon as the earthquake ended the tidal waves came. The mountain of surging water picked up the flaming fuel and other floating debris and hurled it into Seward. Dozens of homes were crushed or set on fire. The wall of flame then swept around the north end of the town and crossed the only road into Seward, clearing it of those fleeing people who had managed to get into their cars. When the water fell away, Seward's means of livelihood, its waterfront, was destroyed. The town was without power, heat or water. Flames flared at the low hanging clouds and cast a flickering orange glow upon the faces of its terrified people. They were isolated. The only road, the road we had travelled so happily with Jim the fisherman, was blocked. All the bridges between Anchorage and Seward had collapsed or were rendered impassable.

Alaska's Governor at the time, William Egan, was from Valdez. He said, 'Along with so many thousands of others, I shed tears unashamed at what my eyes saw in a land of love . . . .'

One hundred and fourteen Alaskans died that Good Friday, half of them Indians, Eskimos and Alents. In a land of few people.

115

Chapter 10

A Leaving—1968

Within three months in 1965, three oil fields were discovered in Cook Inlet, near the original Middle Ground Shoal discoveries. By 1968, there were eleven drilling platforms in the inlet, with ninety wells producing a total of 220,000 barrels a day from the inlet and Swanson River fields combined. The Cook Inlet Basin was estimated to contain 1.5 billion barrels of oil. Alaska's economy had become based on fishing, timber—and oil.

Then on March 13, 1968 Atlantic Richfield discovered one of the world's largest oilfields at Prudhoe Bay on the Arctic Coast, with an estimated reserve of at least twenty billion barrels. With this discovery, Alaska, and not just Anchorage, was thrust on a course of sophistication from which there would now be no return.

The earthquake made Anchorage a small town again. A new spirit took over and people found time for each other. Care and concern replaced the old busy preoccupation. In those few minutes a spirit born of the Alaskan wilderness swept through Anchorage and welded its people into a whole.

Many left Alaska after the earthquake. Husbands with work stayed, but wives and children without homes fled Outside. But most eventually came back.

The houses and buildings were rebuilt, shattered lives put back together again. We all helped. Anchorage had one goal: to start again. The town went back to the beginning. Its people stood up, looked at each other, and recognised friends.

Anchorage was in Alaska again. An interchange of people and help moved from the rest of Alaska to the stricken towns in the earthquake area. The waves of unity spread across the state. I think the other towns felt Anchorage had been finally knocked down to size.

Help came from the federal government, from private individuals and agencies. I had never been in a place on the receiving end of aid and it was a humbling feeling to know how much other people gave a damn.

But as the months passed the broken houses were bulldozed down and some of the spirit went with them. Money poured into Alaska and Anchorage. Money to rebuild and new money born of oil.

In time people in Anchorage again looked down their own paths, to their own goals. The busy preoccupation returned. To some the new oil money meant that their goals would come easier, but others saw it as divisive. Anchorage had been given a second chance in the earthquake and for a while the town had worked; the spirit had come back. But now it was losing it again.

The new money made my own goals easier, too. I returned to my own path. More money in Anchorage meant more people would buy my photography. I could see what was happening both to Anchorage and to me. My pictures were selling, many to the new oil men. Anchorage was the center of the growing oil world in Alaska and it revelled in its new glitter.

Around Anchorage a new suburbia grew. Even Raspberry Road felt the influx of people. The spaces between the houses were filled with new ones, trees in the nearby woods were cleared for people who followed the oil money north. On the slopes of the Chugach, the lights of Anchorage climbed higher each year until they reached the tundra above the tree line.

Downtown offices expanded and new buildings were built to house more and more oil companies and the myriad of associated suppliers that follow them everywhere. Even more aggressive men followed those we had found when we arrived and the character of Anchorage became more and more like the cities on the West Coast.

In that environment of spreading suburbia, Jill and I found that we were falling into the same ruts that we had watched our friends dig back in Los Angeles. The quest for a different life in Anchorage was becoming more difficult with each passing year, and the temptation was to fall back into a work/play pattern that was not unlike that found in any American city.

Each morning and evening streams of traffic filled the ever-widening streets of Anchorage with workers to fill the new office buildings. Branches of large U.S. chain stores were welcomed into Anchorage like manna. Their conveniences made them welcome, but each new shopping center stamped a blot of sameness on Anchorage and destroyed more of its special character.

The two roads leading out of Anchorage became choked with wilderness seekers, trying to find that elusive solitude they had been led to expect in a place with so much space. But they found instead other seekers and ended up inviting each other to their campers for beer.

Jill and I came to the painful realization that we were losing the battle for our dream. The migration of more people to the West Coast had led to our move from Los

Angeles; now it seemed, with the discovery of oil, those same people were taking over Anchorage.

When an offer of a well-paid job near London came along, I took it. I took it partly because we felt we needed a change from the growing frustration of life in Anchorage, and partly because our economic situation was getting no better. If I was ever to build up enough capital to start a photographic business, I would never do it under the handicap of the high Anchorage cost of living.

But after several years in England we began to recognize the symptoms. Maps and pictures of Alaska started appearing on our walls, correspondence and visits by our Alaskan friends produced periods of longing and brought back memories. We were undergoing a familiar pattern that I had observed in many of my friends before.

After a number of years in Alaska, the isolation, the long cold, dark winters, the lack of new stimulation from outside Alaska build up and people leave. But once away they look back from their new homes in the complex, crime-ridden society Outside, and realize that the disadvantages of climate and isolation in Alaska are made up for by the relative simplicity of its life. Where Anchorage, for example, was troubled with increasing crime and congestion, the cities Outside were affected much more viciously. So people return, and this time frequently stay. Some Alaskans seem to need this verification by experience, for living in a place like Alaska requires constant justification.

So we, too, began to make plans to return in a year or two. I would be a photographer this time; the experience I had gained in Europe would be invaluable, and we now had the money to strike out on our own. This time there would be no compromise.

But it was not to be; we would never return together. In October, 1971, Jill was crushed to death in a car crash near London.

Chapter 11

A Return

Our lives stopped, too. The impossible had happened. Takla, Kari and I stared in numb silence at each other across an empty room. A black void had opened and our lives and our thoughts fell into it. Only just in time did we catch them and slowly pull them back into the light again.

But it was a long and difficult time. A force in our house had vanished, and now it would be from within us that a new source of strength would have to come. For the time of testing had arrived.

For years Jill and I had planned for the time when I would break away from confining security and become a photographer. That time had come, only I now would have to break the flow of my life without her help. But I had to do it, and I had to do it now.

I sold our house in Anchorage for the capital it would bring. It was painful to sever such a strong link with Alaska, but I knew I could never live in that house again, without Jill.

I became a photographer, but in England. I realized that even if I did return to Alaska, I would have to build up experience in the world. I knew so little of it, and at first felt lost. Gradually I learned.

From England I joined expeditions to Africa and Asia. I discovered wild areas in the Sahara far larger and emptier than the Alaskan ones I had known. I met Tuareg as at one with their desert environment as those Eskimos on St Lawrence Island. But I looked back from a distance to the green and white jewel that is Alaska. To me Alaska still seemed a place of life, of forest and river, of falling snow and browsing

119

caribou. The Sahara was vast, pure and sterile. An abstract place of silence, left behind by ancient rains.

In Scandinavia I found a kindred place. The fireweed blossomed on the mountain slopes of Norway and climbed up their stems to an autumn of their own. The water of the high snows plunged over the rocks above fjords that brought back to me some of the feeling of Southeast Alaska. But Scandinavia didn't have the essential space that was Alaska. Each valley had a road, over the next hill was another valley with a road, and another. There was no beyond.

But in Alaska a road had begun, too. A road that would cut her in half. The long delay after the oil discoveries in the Arctic had ended, the contracts had been let, the bulldozers that had been poised for four years bit their blades into the Arctic gravel for the first time on April 29, 1974, and the construction of the trans-Alaska pipeline began.

The telephone rang. It was my agent in London. 'Alaska, you've been there, haven't you? Oh, you used to live there? Great, even better. We could use an article and some pictures on that pipeline project. Want to go?'

The 707 accelerated down the runway at London Airport, climbed, banked right, and took up a northerly heading for, surprisingly, the great circle route to Anchorage starts north from London. Below was the little village along the Thames that had been our home for the years since Alaska. Kari and Takla would stay with friends this summer while I went back. Back to what I didn't know.

What had Alaska become in those six years? Not long in an established society like England where change comes slowly and with difficulty. But in a place like Alaska six years was a measurable part of its history. Alaska had a reprieve from industrial development after the first discovery of oil in 1968; her economy had trickled along, unsure of the future. Change had been slow, but in this summer of 1974 the dams were about to burst. Below now were the hills of Scotland where I had found some solace from that crowd on the island further south. Eight hours over the top of the world would be a vast and wonderful land. Or would there?

The summer-bare islands of Canada's high Arctic emerged from the trailing edge of the wing as though painted on an unrolling background. Beyond the silver tip of the wing the mosaic of brown-green islands separated by ice-choked channels of blue water merged into a distant hazy horizon. Out of the windows to the right, less than 300 miles away now, was the Pole. The left wing pointed to the rest of the world: distant, crowded and south. The compressed island of Britain might as well have been on Mars. These sterile treeless islands and icy seas were features of another planet. The 707 turned a few degrees south of west; our farthest point north had been reached. The nose now pointed to Alaska.

The burst of oil that Atlantic-Richfield (ARCO) stirred up beneath the Arctic snows in March, 1968 had kindled a fever in Alaska. It was a modern version of '98, only this time instead of individual prospectors struggling their hopeless way over the Chilkoot Pass, these prospectors were the major oil companies of the world. They came to the Arctic by air, for there was no road or trail, or they forced their way among the ice flows of the Arctic Ocean for a few weeks in the summer. But they came, and brought drilling rigs, miles of pipe and seismic wire, and poked holes in the tundra. They set off a charge and listened. And listened. But didn't speak, not yet.

The rush was on. Exploration around ARCO's discovery well went on apace, and in secret. By September, 1969 they were ready. Each company thought they knew where the oil was under the Arctic, but to tell anyone would give the show away. For on September 10, 1969 the State of Alaska held an oil lease sale in Anchorage and auctioned to the highest bidder 451,000 acres of previously unleased land around Prudhoe Bay. The bidding, based on seismic and other geological information, carefully and secretly gathered, was in the form of sealed bids. Beginning at 8 a.m., state officials in the packed Sydney Lawrence Auditorium opened the envelopes and by 5.30 p.m. the State was $900,040,000 richer. For the first time in its history Alaska was out of the red.

So those oil companies, or at least their money, were welcomed into Alaska. They spent a good deal more getting additional rigs to the Arctic tundra. And they did find more oil. Altogether they discovered a potential of at least 9 billion barrels from the Prudhoe Bay field and the state began to wonder if it had been cheated.

The oil companies began to wonder too. They had found the oil, but how to get it to market?

First, the market itself. Barring a spectacular sense of energy conservation developing in the consumptive U.S. conscience, or else some repressive action by the U.S. Government, America will need at least fifteen million barrels of oil a day until world supplies run out, at which time they will have to think of something else. Meanwhile, Alaskan oil, by itself could supply the U.S. for two years, but in reality will only balance out the loss in producing wells occurring year after year in U.S. fields. This would at least preclude America buying that much oil from those dastardly Arabs (who, incidentally, hold thirty times the oil under Prudhoe Bay, just to get things in perspective).

Oil and gas provide 75 per cent of the total energy needs of the U.S. The American way of life consumes 33 per cent of the world's energy so that its 6 per cent of the planet's population can double its GNP every sixteen years. What Americans are going to do with all their national products is to burn more energy which brings us back to that Alaskan oil. And how to get it from the cold Arctic to the thirsty market in the south.

Plan 1: By Sea
This plan was the cheapest, though most companies were sceptical as to whether it would work. The Northwest Passage, those ice-choked channels now below the wing of my 707, would be the route. In mid-December 1968, Humble, ARCO and British Petroleum (BP) chipped in and bought a test tanker. They reinforced the bow, beefed up the engines, stuck a helicopter on top and a covey of scientists inside and sent the *Manhattan* from Pennsylvania to the Canadian Arctic in August 1969. The brave experiment ended in November when the *Manhattan*, proudly displaying the symbolic drum of oil she had picked up at Prudhoe Bay and trying to ignore the big hole in her starboard side she picked up east of Baffin, sailed into New York. She had made the

121

round trip, but only with difficulty and with the essential aid of Canadian ice breakers. It was obvious this was not the way to move nine billion barrels of oil out of Prudhoe Bay. Another forty million dollars into the Arctic and still no oil to market.

Plan 2: A Pipeline

Even before the *Manhattan* sailed the same three oil companies announced plans for their 789-mile oil pipeline from Prudhoe Bay to Valdez. The decision to build it and even its eventual route were made in closed meetings in the company board-rooms, without public consultation or government recommendations. This was in the days when oil companies could drill for and bring out the public's oil without the need to inform or consult anyone about their plans. But times were changing. Not only did the aggressive industry announce their finished plans, but in April, 1969 they even ordered the pipe, from Japan. To their great surprise, the first pipe wasn't laid until 1975.

The pipeline was to be the largest privately financed project in history, if multi-national oil companies, some bigger than some nations, can be considered 'private'. Its length was not unduly long as pipelines go, but the engineering and environmental problems to be surmounted in crossing Alaska were unique. The four-foot tube would cross three mountain ranges at passes of up to 4800 feet, six hundred rivers and streams including the Yukon, and five active earthquake faults. Of the total length, four hundred and nine miles would be buried 'conventionally', but to avoid thawing the permafrost three hundred and eighty-two miles would be elevated. The oil brought up at Prudhoe would be hot, 180°F., and to avoid the whole thing seizing up on a cold winter's night, the oil would be maintained at 130°F. for all of its four-and-a-half day journey to Valdez. When the line was full and delivering its two million barrels a day to the Valdez terminal there would be nine million barrels of oil lying in a long tube across Alaska, or 11,300 barrels in every mile.

At Valdez the pipeline would become intermittent as the oil would then be trans-ferred to a series of 150,000-ton tankers for the last part of the journey to the West Coast and that market. 'Maybe we can finally sell the stuff and get our money back', said an oil man, neatly summing up the point of the project.

Obviously a project like this would portent great dangers to the Alaskan environ-ment and this fact wasn't lost on conservationists both within and without Alaska. One of America's long series of acts of conscience, this time concern for the environ-ment (to be followed by concern for energy), swept the country in the late 60s and early 70s. Unfortunately for the oil companies and their frozen Arctic oil, this cause latched on to the trans-Alaska pipeline as the epitome of big business trying to tear up the wilderness. No sooner had Plan 2 been put into action than it was stopped.

Americans convinced their members in Congress that they really wanted to save what was left of their land, and on January 1, 1970 the National Environmental Policy Act put the passions of the people into law. This was greeted with dismay in the oil offices of Anchorage. It was only a matter of time until the first injunction came. But it came from an unexpected quarter.

A Return

On the banks of the Yukon, a few miles upstream from the proposed crossing of the pipeline, lies a collection of log houses that is the Indian settlement of Stevens Village. About sixty-six people lived there in 1970 and they came to the sudden realization that the pipeline would cross lands which they claimed as aboriginally theirs. Seward, you see, bought from the Russians in 1867, not the land, but only the right to tax and govern it. The land itself still belonged to the original inhabitants, the natives. When Alaska was given a territorial government in 1884 the Act stated that the natives 'shall not be disturbed in the possession of any lands actually in their use or occupancy or now claimed by them'. The people of Stevens Village, noting this generous offer by a then distant and little caring Federal Government, decided to take them up on it. They persuaded a Federal District Judge in Washington D.C. to issue an injunction preventing the pipeline being built across twenty miles of village land.

In fact, the question of native land claims, brought to a head by the knowledge that much of native land had become valuable to the white man in his search for oil, recreation sites, wilderness parks and 'transportation corridors', was not settled until Congress passed a Bill in 1971, giving the Alaskan natives most of what they asked for. Forty million acres, $462 million to be paid by the U.S. over an eleven year period, and $500 million from oil and mineral royalties. The Bill also authorized the U.S. Department of the Interior to select eighty million acres as parks and wildlife areas, evidence of the environmental feeling of the time.

But until the native claims Bill was passed, Alaska's land was legally frozen, preventing the pipeline builders from receiving rights-of-way permits for their big tube.

As if all this wasn't enough, opposition came from the expected quarter. The conservationists. Three Outside national groups: The Wilderness Society, Friends of the Earth and the Environmental Defense Fund convinced the same Federal Judge in Washington to grant an injunction, preventing the issue of a right-of-way permit for the construction of the pipeline haul road from the Yukon to Prudhoe Bay, until it could be shown to conform to the new environmental law.

The newly arrived Japanese pipe was given a coating to prevent rust and stored at Valdez, Fairbanks and Prudhoe Bay. More holes were bored in the permafrost to determine how best to build the line. The pipeline builders (seven oil companies now formed the Alyeska Pipeline Service Company to build the pipeline) invested millions in studies of all kinds. Caribou were counted, grass was seeded and its growth rate measured to see if it could cover up the pipeline scar. Test pipe was buried, and hot air was blown through it to simulate the hot oil. A massive public relations campaign was mounted to convince the people of Alaska that the pipeline would be no more obvious than 'a fine thread down the middle of Manhattan Island. That's the proportionate space it takes up,'—as one oil company president put it.

As time dragged on and the pipeline project continued to languish in the distant courtrooms of Washington, many Alaskans began to weigh their economic situation (equipment and materials ordered in anticipation of a boom were lying idle, businesses were going bankrupt) against the saving of the environment. And then those damn

123

natives. Were they ever going to be happy? Early in the game a delegation of Fairbanks business men met the chief at Stevens Village, but came away without convincing the Indians to back down.

The Sierra Club, that California based conservation group, in its efforts to save Alaska from itself, became more and more unpopular as the prospect of oil money receded into the future. By September, 1971, it has been said, 85 per cent of Alaskans wanted the pipeline to be built. But I question figures like this. I suspect it may represent a fair representation of Fairbanks and Anchorage businessmen, but few others. (I don't personally know anyone wholeheartedly in favor of the pipeline.) The total for the state, including remote villages, and people living away from population centers was probably nearer 50 per cent. But Alaskan opinion surveys are notoriously difficult to get. Most people, of course, were and are ambivalent; they would like the money but not the turmoil that generates it. What was true was that Outside interests were not welcome, no matter how well-intentioned they might be. Alaskans had for too long been under the remote bureaucracy of Washington.

The oil industry, while not at all pleased that they couldn't go ahead with their project, did use the delay to improve its design. It is now admitted that if they had gone ahead in 1970, disastrous, and for them expensive mistakes would have been made. The pressure of the environmentalists, in the form of new laws, caused the companies to look more closely at what they were doing in the Arctic. Some, though not by any means all, of their early mistakes stemmed from ignorance of the fragile nature of the country in which they were working. They were forced to learn.

Finally, on November 16, 1973, President Nixon signed a bill which swept away the last obstacle to the project—a 1920 Mineral Leasing Law that restricted right-of-way widths of pipelines, for this one needed more room. Congress, reacting to short term 'shortages' in the U.S. of petroleum products, caused, as it turned out, by poor distribution and also collusion within the oil industry itself, and the new 'cause' of the U.S., energy independence, gave the bill the go ahead. Incidentally, Congress was so anxious that the pipeline be built, that it included in the bill a provision prohibiting further court action on environmental matters connected with it.

There was never any real doubt that the pipeline would be built. The pressures brought to bear by the oil industry to build the line and thus regain some of the money they had spent in searching the Arctic for oil were enormous. Congress was lobbied, massive public relations campaigns launched, the Alaska state government prodded, and men bribed. The oil was there and in corporate thinking, that meant a resource to be exploited. The fact that the oil companies didn't actually own the oil, which underlay public lands and belonged to the American people, didn't hinder them in their thinking. Thinking which probably went as follows: What method of oil delivery provides the greatest flexibility in marketing, and hence the greatest profit potential? Tankers. What is the most accessible ice-free port on the coast of Alaska at which these tankers could call? Valdez. What is the cheapest and quickest way to get the oil from Prudhoe Bay to Valdez? A pipeline. End of conference. Let's have lunch.

Oil companies are businesses. Businesses must make profits to survive, and survival,

124

even corporate survival, is a basic human instinct. The oil companies have had every intention of surviving their Alaskan experience; now that they have found the means, the oil, they will. It is important that Alaskans and others concerned with Alaska and its environment realize this. Early suggestions by the Sierra Club and others that the oil pipeline should be routed eastward from Prudhoe Bay and around the Arctic Wildlife Range and then through central Canada to the Midwest, would fall on unreceptive ears at the oil companies. Their market would be restricted to the U.S. and the possibility of selling oil to Japan or other lucrative markets would be denied them. Hence, this plan, no matter how efficient it might be from the point of view of environmental impact or North American energy policy, would be regarded as being against the interests of the corporate profit-making policies. To force the oil companies to build pipelines against their corporate interests requires Government control and regulation, and the Government itself, while not actually controlled by Big Oil, is strongly influenced by it in its decision-making process. The oil industry is represented on 132 federal advisory boards. Oil-dominated companies receive one-half of all federal government funds for coal research.

The assorted annoying impediments brought against the construction of the pipeline between the time the decision to build it was made, in 1968, and the beginning of construction in 1974, were dealt with in the most expeditious manner possible by the oil companies. They encouraged the passage of the Native Land Claims Bill so they could deal with the (hopefully) less sophisticated regional native corporations. They sent their lobbyists to Washington and Juneau where they twisted arms in the time-honored fashion.

But all of this took time. Meanwhile, in Anchorage and Fairbanks, oil company staffs were reduced, machinery positioned along the pipeline route was mothballed, secondary suppliers were told to wait. Alaska sank into its own economic recession as the great gifts of oil were withheld from the gasping population. The gifts that Alaska eventually received were to prove incalculable in magnitude and devastating to its tenuous life style.

Below the wing was Alaska now, green with early summer leaves, the meandering Yukon a silver ribbon through a velvet carpet. Villages, trails, even roads were scattered over the land, but I couldn't see them. Did that thin thread of a pipeline really matter so much?

We started our descent toward Anchorage; features on the ground began to emerge. The new Fairbanks-Anchorage road paralleled the Alaska Railroad into McKinley Park and on past Deneki Lakes. At that moment a truck sped by on the yet unpaved section and smothered Bill Nan's house in a pall of dust. It had no sooner settled when another lumbered by in the opposite direction. Deneki Lakes had lost its isolation.

The aircraft circled over an Anchorage that spread virtually unbroken from Knik Arm to the Chugach foothills. Downtown, new concrete and glass buildings had grown in the empty spaces left by the earthquake, spaces which I had been told by geologists were unsafe to build on. The plane dipped a wing toward Raspberry Road as it lined up on Runway 24. The advancing walkway of the new jet-age terminal building fastened itself leech-like to the side of the fuselage and I was back. The whine of the jet engines died away as they drank the last of the 15,300 gallons of fuel it took to get me there.

Chapter 12

Another Anchorage

Many Alaskans, including political leaders think of themselves as heroes in a TV western. In the northern version of the last frontier, as in the western version, wilderness is to be despoiled and destroyed as valueless, a nuisance or a threat . . . . Unfortunately, many Alaskans hold this view without realizing it, or recognizing it.

George Rogers, Professor of Economics,
University of Alaska

Those who want to leave one great wilderness for future generations are going to starve those who have made Alaska what it is.

Anchorage banker

Nobody gives a damn who your grandfather was or what he did.

Anchorage resident

And they don't either. The Anchorage of the '50s or of the earthquake was gone. In its place was that beast that most people feared would come—a Los Angeles of the north. The population had climbed to 150,000; the roads were wider but still choked with cars. A helicopter hovered over commuter routes advising by radio of alternative ways to work.

Anchorage struck me as a vast flat anthill on which someone had stepped, causing

A strong southwest breeze bends the grass of the churchyard of a Russian Orthodox church, high on a sea bluff overlooking the small fishing village of Ninilchik on the Kenai Peninsula south of Anchorage. Beyond the church stretch the gray waters of Cook Inlet, on the far shore of which rise the volcanoes of Mount Iliamna, to the left of the church, and Mount Redoubt, both about 10,000 feet.

Ninilchik was founded by free Russian colonial citizens about 1835, and the village of log houses interspersed with newer wooden ones still harbors people who speak Russian as a first language. The village is now officially a native village belonging to the native corporation, called Cook Inlet Region, Inc. set up under the Alaska Native Land Claims Act.

In 1861, seventy-five years after the Russian merchant Shelikhov founded the first colony in what was called Russian America, these onion domes showed above 43 villages, and the Orthodox church served 12,000 people, many of them natives.

Also in 1861, the Russian capital, New Archangel in Southeast Alaska had a population of some 2500, public libraries, a theater, public gardens, two scientific institutes and four hospitals. The children of the town were schooled to the age of seventeen, and a number of diseases were subdued by a program of inoculations.

At three o'clock in the afternoon of October 18, 1867, a few months after the Americans finally paid the $7,200,000 bill owed the Russians for the purchase of what would now be called Alaska, the Russian flag was hauled down, the stars and stripes was run up, and the name of the capital changed to Sitka. Within ten years Sitka was a ghost town, most of the Russians having departed for home, pressured out by the American military government that took over the colony. Finally, the detachment of soldiers left, too, to fight an Indian war in Idaho, taking with them the last of the American settlers who had tried to carry on where the Russians had left off. Alaska was left to its aboriginal inhabitants, the Eskimos, the Aleuts, and the Indians.

A row of houses in Nome, about 1960.

Today Nome's 2500 people are mostly native, many in from the surrounding villages on the Seward Peninsula, including the entire population transferred from the isolated rock of King Island south of the Bering Strait. The climate and position of Nome doesn't seem strange to them, but it seems odd to visiting white men. The place is accessible only by air, or by a brief barge service in the summer. Or, if you have a dog team, it is the finish line of a race along the Iditarod Trail from Anchorage to Nome each spring, reliving the days when mail was brought along the trail to Nome by dog team. But otherwise Nome is isolated.

Its location was, of course, dictated by the presence of gold in the beach, and by the end of the summer of 1900 there were 30,000 gold seekers grubbing in the sand. There were no natives in Nome then. They were scattered in the surrounding villages from Gambell on St Lawrence Island to Wales on the Bering Straits. Today the high school for these villages is in Nome, and it has become the largest native village in the area. But the white man is coming back. The native corporations set up under the Land Claims Act are leasing their land for oil exploration, and men are coming back for the new form of gold, at the pleasure of the natives.

The local natives are used to the adversity of the Arctic weather that plagues the town, and causes most white people to remain only as long as necessary. In November 1974 a Bering Sea storm battered down the sea wall of boulders that had been built to protect Front Street and flooded the streets of Nome with blocks of ice and sea water. The natives took this whim of the weather in their stride. A Nome city official remarked: 'The native people aren't going to scream for help . . . they won't ask for help, we have to ask them what's wrong.' They weren't as surprised as the white man that the Bering Sea invaded this crazy town on the beach.

the ants to run in all directions at once. The hurry and bustle of the place was at least up to a medium-sized city on the West Coast, but in contrast to the recession-plagued South 48, there was now money at the end of the trail in Anchorage.

The boom had hit Anchorage in the form of thousands of new people, most of them from Oklahoma, Texas and other Southwest States where oil companies have their headquarters, though more recent arrivals came from high unemployment areas on the West Coast. The people coming to Anchorage for the money were rootless, like the miners of '98, but these new prospectors brought their families too. Rootless or not, they needed a place to live and the houses (5000 new ones a year) march up the Chugach foothills.

But once settled the new people have only each other, probably no friends and certainly no relatives. It is the experience that Jill and I had, but multipled a hundred-fold. 'Nobody gives a damn who your grandfather was . . . ,' or who *you* are. The new and insecure Anchorage resident, with his new wealth reaches out for 'things'. 'Things' you can trust; they won't let you down like your wife who just went to live with that man in College Park. So Anchorage has become a place of 'things', the exact opposite of the wilderness around it. Cars, boats, snowmobiles, airplanes, skis, summer and winter cabins, shopping centers to make purchase easier. What will happen when they run out of things to buy?

For most of these people (certainly for their wives and children) life in Alaska is life in Anchorage, and that has become more and more like a city anywhere in the U.S. The oil boom has homogenized Anchorage into an all-purpose U.S. city.

Alaska attracts people in flight. People who have had a past they want to forget and a future that will never come. In a place like Anchorage they can now find freedom in familiar American commercial surroundings. No mother-in-laws, no mothers. They have the freedom to fling themselves into an unrestricted social environment, but one with a Safeway down the road.

But freedom means a lack of stability, except for what can be found in those 'things'. There are 15,200 alcoholics in Alaska. Drug use and juvenile crime are high. Some Anchorage schools are almost impossible to teach in. The suicide rate in Alaska is now 34 per cent higher than the national average, and youths aged 16 to 19 are among the highest incidence. I know of one family who take their kids out of Anchorage every summer to get them away from the atmosphere of aimlessness among the young. Forty per cent of the Anchorage telephone book changes every year.

What has oil to do with this? Everything. While oil is not responsible for the entire population increase in Alaska, it was the catalyst that triggered off the boom. The new people and the money the industry brought into the state have caused a rapid increase in local and state government payrolls, as government services were geared up to cope with the new social situation. Without oil Alaska would have become a pauper state, a victim of decreasing military spending and diminishing revenues from fishing and other traditional revenue sources. (The Bristol Bay salmon catch in '74 was a disaster. Fishing in that area has dropped 98 per cent over the past few years, because of heavy salmon fishing on the high seas by the Japanese and the Russians.) The state would have found itself relying on timber and pulp sales to the

Another Anchorage

Japanese. The money from oil has brought life to the economy of the state, but the swarms of new people now finding the road to the north are eroding and will eventually destroy its spirit.

There is a strong and increasing core of people in Anchorage, many of whom are refugees from the plastic horrors of West Coast cities, who are trying to make a better place of Anchorage, in spite of oil. Through their efforts a State Park has been established in the Chugach above the city; bicycle paths are fighting their way through the city. Junk cars and other eyesores are disappearing slowly (though Bill Margolis' were still in his front yard on Raspberry Road).

But many of these people have given up the unequal struggle and are fleeing Anchorage the way we fled Los Angeles. To cabins along the new road to Fairbanks, to Homer and the Kenai Peninsula. To the wilderness itself. A friend of mine, John, has built a cabin six miles up Moose Creek from Camp Denali. There he lives with his wife on virtually a subsistence level. He told me he didn't have any particular project. He said he didn't want to write or study lichens; he just wanted to slow down. He spends his time existing; chopping wood to keep warm, trapping to supplement the stock of food from Fairbanks. After a month or so he found he *had* slowed down. He said that he sometimes has trouble following the conversation of their infrequent visitors. He has escaped. One group of ten has brought a farm in the Matanuska Valley. The new young in Alaska are using Anchorage (and Fairbanks) as stopping points before they find their own way into the wilderness, there to build cabins and at least try to live a simpler life. Most will return to the cities when either their money or their will runs out, but in the meantime they will have discovered a bit more about themselves. Others will stay. A group I know have been living, Eskimo-style, near Ambler, a tiny village on the Kobuk River in northwestern Alaska since the early '60s. Some years they don't visit Fairbanks at all.

Then there is the story of the three Anchorage boys who followed the gold rush trail over the Chilkoot Pass, built a raft and sailed down the Yukon. Along the river they built a cabin and stayed a winter. The possibilities are there, but they are decreasing.

To climb McKinley these days has become a problem in crowd avoidance. During the summer of 1975 over three hundred people climbed the South Peak, most of them by the West Buttress route, on the opposite side of the mountain to our route up the Muldrow. At any one time during the summer one could find between six and a dozen parties on the twenty miles of the route. In 1974 the U.S. Army hauled out two tons of trash and used equipment from the 7000 foot to the 14,500 foot area of the route, and in 1975 one ton. From the 5000 or so people who visited McKinley Park during a typical summer in the 50s the numbers have increased to 350,000. Private cars are now prohibited in the Park except in special circumstances and the wildlife must be viewed from a bus. Even Ginny Wood and Celia Hunter have felt the pressures. After a quarter of a century of running Camp Denali, they counted 1975 as their last and sold it to friends in McKinley Park.

As I walked around a strangely deserted Anchorage downtown one Saturday afternoon the effects of oil seemed temporarily to recede. Most of the population had fled the city to their boats and cabins, leaving downtown to aged tourists with blue-

131

Ship Creek never was much for fishing, except, perhaps, years ago when Anchorage was a small town. It flows along the edge of Elmendorf Air Force Base and then through the Alaska Railroad, where it empties into the mud of Knik Arm near the Port of Anchorage. But it is close, and kids like to sit along its muddy banks and try for the few salmon and trout that survive the creek's industrial journey. Nowadays there are fewer fish than ever and these kids have come empty-handed from their fishing in the city. For them to get out into the wilds, or at least down to Bird Creek along the Seward Highway, would require the use of Dad and his car. The trouble is that with only two roads leading out of Anchorage, most of the good fishing spots are fished out now, and it is necessary to drive farther and farther. Everybody, of course, has the same idea, and the result is a common one in modern society: too many people over-using limited resources. Limited? Fishing in Alaska? But there is limited access to the fishing for the average Alaskan. To realize the full potential of Alaska requires a combination of money, time and the use of an airplane. Most people can't afford enough of any of these. These kids could have come from the vast number of people in Anchorage who are not rich, are not benefitting from the oil boom, and whose parents may even have to work weekends and nights to pay for the escalating rents and food prices. No flights across the wilderness for them, no experience on a clear stream far from anyone else. Their life in Anchorage is almost like life anywhere, and their fishing will continue to be in Ship Creek.

haired wives, a few drunks (white and native), and a beautiful girl selling flowers in front of the Post Office.

A few new downtown buildings did show imagination, but most followed the familiar Alaskan pattern of architectural design, that of maximum rentable floor space for the least possible cost. An era of plentiful money would seem to me the time to bend this rule. Union Oil tried, with their building, but unfortunately the color of its walls of reflecting glass has caused it to be dubbed the 'vertical oil slick'. Over on 3rd Avenue the Westward Hotel had found itself a twenty-two story erection next to the fourteen story bore that survived the earthquake. The new structure now takes over from its neighbor as the tallest building in Alaska, or, at least, the tallest building built on the site of an 8.4 grade earthquake.

I pushed open the door of Woolworth's on 4th Avenue, intent on a chocolate milk shake unattainable in England, and there already bent over the counter was one of Alaska's two Senators in Congress, Mike Gravel. The double-decker cone was already in his grasp when he turned to me.

'Mike, Jon Gardey. Remember? Unitarian Fellowship. Twelve years ago. You taught my daughter Takla in Sunday School'.

'Hello . . . Jon . . . Must run . . . have a TV interview at one. Good to see you again.'

He swept out into 4th Avenue, preoccupied with the upcoming primary election in August. (He won.) I don't think he really remembered me, but I wonder how many Senators can be found in the local Woolworth's buying an ice cream. Some Alaskan qualities could still be found.

Outside, the light-colored buildings separated by nearly empty streets took on an abstract quality in the brilliant sunlight. It was as though the city had been built but had yet to be occupied by its citizens. It was only a weekend reprieve; by Monday the streets would be full again.

In the late afternoon I drove out to Raspberry Road along the route Jill and I had followed in our desperate search for a house. The potato field across which we had gazed at the Chugach had now sprouted a bumper crop of houses and even one particularly fertile patch had turned into a church. Raspberry Road itself, strangely, still wasn't paved, but the dust was now settled by an outfit called 'Alaska Pollution Control, Inc'. (Raspberry Road was finally paved in September 1975.) Our house stood much as we had left it, though the present owners had taken down a fence I had spent weeks erecting. Perhaps it rotted. I didn't go in. I couldn't.

Chapter 13

Valdez

If there has to be a villain in the piece, I suppose it must be Alyeska Pipeline Service Company, the consortium of oil companies responsible for the construction and operation of the pipeline, though to picture conservation interests as white shiny knights is as distorted as to paint Alyeska and the oil companies as all black. In the continuing skirmishes, each side is out for itself first, understandably, held in check by the efforts of its opponents and its own conscience. I believe Aleyska would have tried to build the pipeline with a fraction of the environmental studies they finally completed had it not been for conservation pressure. Equally, had the pipeline been a smaller project I doubt if it would have stirred up the national interest necessary to bring about the environmental laws that control its construction and that of succeeding pipelines across Alaska.

As Robert Miller, Manager of Public Affairs for Alyeska wrote to Jim Kowalsky, Alaska representative of Friends of the Earth, in August, 1974: '. . . keep watching us . . . and be assured we're watching you.'

The bumper sticker on the car ahead of me as I drove up Bragaw Street toward the Alyeska office read 'Let the Bastards Freeze in the Dark', a reference to Sierra Club efforts to stop the pipeline. (The opposition had come back, I thought rather weakly, with 'Freezing in the Dark Builds Character'. And so it goes.)

I fully expected the car with the bumper sticker to turn into the Alyeska parking lot, but it continued on down Bragaw. Such are the preconceived ideas generated in the heat of battle.

As I entered the busy, brightly lit office I had the feeling I was walking into the lion's

The rain that had fallen on Valdez all night had finally stopped, but the tops of the sharp mountain around the soggy town still poked into the base of a gray woolly mass of cloud that swirled up from Valdez Arm. I left Gene to try to find a rowboat for fishing and, negotiating enormous water-filled potholes, followed the road to the city dock. Huge trucks, loaded with more prefabricated buildings brought in from Anchorage to add even more clutter and dismal plastic to the temporary town that Valdez had become, splashed muddy water in my direction. Across the water, Alyeska was creating a miniature smog with a trash-burning fire, a smog that spread up the green slopes behind the rising storage tanks of the pipeline terminal. I reached the dock. Halfway across the water a speeding boat cut the glassy surface of Port Valdez as it headed for my side of the few-mile-wide channel.

At the end of the dock a group of white-hatted terminal workers waited for the ferry that would take them over to the construction site. Until the road was finished, this ferry would provide transportation from the housing area near Valdez to the site. As I approached the men a security cop motioned me to stop, but after his back was turned a young girl walked past me and edged her way along the railing toward the men. She went unnoticed as the boat had just arrived and the shift was changing. The girl didn't seem to know any of the men. Who were these white hats? She moved closer. The cop turned and glared at her. She stopped.

To the girl the white hats looked like an invading force, as, in fact, they were. Her isolated Valdez, caught in its mountain ring, had been swamped by these white hats and she wanted a closer look at them. They had moved in on the small town in such force that they had filled all the seats at the soda fountain and had taken all the food from the shelves in the grocery store. Next fall their kids would pack her classrooms. The old shift came up the gangway from the boat. 'Move back!' the cop bellowed. The girl backed up without looking around, and then stopped again. The number of white hats doubled as the two shifts combined, and her figure was temporarily lost in the mass of fat men. Finally, the new shift boarded the boat, taking the cop with them, and the others drove away in a school bus. The dock was empty and the girl moved to the edge to watch the boat roar to the other side.

For her, Valdez had become a city under attack. Her small place of few people who had lived through the horrors of the earthquake had become a bursting place of new men, aggressive and heavy. Her home was changing before her very eyes. I wondered if, when she grew up, she would remember what it was like before they came.

Sound. The sound of many things. Cats, trucks, cars, helicopters, people, boats, machines, saws, explosions, airplanes. Around Liam the air is filled with sound. He looks up from time to time, wondering about the sound, but he is more concerned with the building of his fort. The construction isn't going well. There are too many rocks along the shore here and he will soon move. Liam lifts his head. A new, louder sound. From behind the dark spruce a float plane appears, the sound of its engine whining across the calm lake. Then the engine dies, and the plane's floats cut the glassy water into fragments. The silver intruder crunches onto the shore near Liam, its waves demolish his fort. At the same time a large station wagon arrives at the parking lot on the edge of the lake in a cloud of dust. Two men jump out and greet the pilot. 'Hiya, Bill! You see anything when you came in?' 'Yeah, saw two moose up the valley near the river. We can land right near them, couple of lakes there. No problem. Get your gear in and we'll go get 'em.' The two men load rifles and packs into the plane and climb in. The last one in pushes the float plane off the beach and boards the seat next to the pilot. The engine is restarted and the pilot turns the nose down the lake. The wash from the takeoff pelts Liam with water and stones, and he is forced to huddle down near the ground. In a few moments the intruder is gone and the surface of the lake resumes its reflection. But the old sound is still there.

Just down the road from Liam, Alyeska is building its pipeline terminal near Valdez, and it is the sound from this construction that fills the air around him. A sound that has filled the valley between the mountains like a noisy smog since the construction began.

den. The impression was further enhanced by a large security officer blocking the door beyond the receptionist. She buzzed the door behind him and I was admitted to the inner sanctum. I thought I would find a group of ogres, their hands dripping with oil. Instead I was greeted by a friendly, pretty girl who plied me with eye-catching Press kits, brochures, maps and charts to make the eye boggle. I staggered out past the cop under a load of glossy paper that could only have been published by someone with either a lot to say, or, perhaps, something to hide.

Armed with Alyeska's version, oil company handouts, conservation literature of all sorts and my own prejudices I was ready to tackle the pipeline. I proposed to travel from Valdez to Prudhoe Bay along the route of the pipeline-to-be, to see for myself the first effects of this technological invasion of Alaska.

The ferry *Bartlett* crept through Valdez Narrows in a July fog so thick that I had trouble making out the sides of the 3000-ft-wide channel. Through this narrow passage Alyeska proposed to move twenty-one 150,000 ton tankers a week, over a period of at least twenty years, the approximate life of the pipeline. That is almost 22,000 tankers. The possibility of a catastrophe must surely exist, with daily oil spills almost unavoidable. The recent Government decision not to require double bottoms on the new tankers further increases the likelihood of disaster. The tanker flow can never stop, once started; it must be as continuous as the pipeline, indeed it is an integral part of it.

As I waited for the *Bartlett* to inch its way up Port Valdez I searched through my pile of glossy handouts to see what Alyeska had in store for the former cannery of Dayville, the terminal site opposite the town of Valdez.

> . . . the terminal site covers 1000 acres . . . 18 tanks . . . 250 feet in diameter and 62 feet high with a capacity of 510,000 barrels of oil . . . each with containment dikes equal to 110 per cent of the capacity of the total volume of the tanks . . . 4 berths will permit simultaneous loading of 4 tankers . . . up to 150,000 tons. . . . oily ballast will be pumped from tankers into onshore storage tanks . . . no ballast will be pumped directly into the sound . . . The ballast will settle for a minimum of six hours . . . passed through a . . . flotation treatment unit until it can be discharged at less than 8 parts of oil per million.

In spite of all that, the fishermen at Cordova, a small fishing community just around the corner from Valdez, have strongly opposed the pipeline. They fear that their fishing and hence their livelihood could become the victim of oil spills. Though it is true that over the past five years non-oil-industry sources have spilled more oil in Cook Inlet than the oil industry, the sheer scale of the Alyeska operation means that a significantly higher amount of oil could find its way into the nearly closed waters of Prince William Sound. Initially, Alyeska, brightly lit in the public eye, will probably spill hardly a drop. But what will happen after, say, five years of increasingly routine operation? By that time 3,650,000,000 barrels of oil will have passed over Port Valdez and Prince William Sound. I believe that this interface between the pipeline and the tankers could be a great danger to the environment, and one that will be the most difficult to control once the line is operating, in spite of an intensive monitoring program.

As the *Bartlett* nestled up to the Valdez dock I could just make out the white beard of Gene Wescott. Gene had grown up with me in Los Angeles and was now a Professor at the University of Alaska. He had offered to drive me to Fairbanks.

In his deep voice—which sounds ominous to those who don't know him—he greeted me with a complaint.

'I tried to rent a rowboat this afternoon to do some fishing and the guy wanted $40. Last year it was $10. How about that for "impact"?' Gene is a dedicated fisherman; he could see his leisure activity threatened.

As a result of the new environmental laws, government agencies who propose to build—or allow to be built—pipelines or roads, or any construction that will affect the environment, must assess the 'impact' or effect the new construction will have on that environment, and the people who live in the area, and then supply a written statement. Thus the word 'impact' has taken on a sinister meaning in Alaska.

We drove through the rain and fog, past a new town of temporary housing near the airport, to the campground. During the night the rain threatened to beat the tent to the ground, but by dawn the sky had cleared and the spectacular setting of Valdez was revealed. All around mountains rose from the pale blue waters of Port Valdez to peaks splashed with patches of late snow. From the dock at the new town site of Valdez I looked across at Alyeska's pipeline terminal, though I didn't have the dime required by the telescope that they had thoughtfully provided.

Bulldozers were busy on the side of the hill, preparing bases for the 510,000-barrel tanks to hold pipeline oil until it could be loaded on the tankers. A shuttle of high speed boats ferried workers from Valdez to the terminal site. Smoke from a fire at the site spread up and down Port Valdez.

Valdez itself was all new. Relocated to a better site after the earthquake disaster, its new grid of streets still hadn't been filled in with buildings. The original plan to build all buildings as Swiss-type chalets went by the board with the arrival of the pipeline and its pressure for housing.

'The worst thing that ever happened to us was the earthquake,' said one bearded resident. 'The second worst is the pipeline.' The town was inundated with workers building the terminal across the bay. Its original population of 1,100 was up to 4,500 by the time Gene and I were picking our way through the water-filled potholes in its unfinished streets. We stopped in the local supermarket to buy food for our trip north to Fairbanks.

'Sorry. We don't have any,' was the reply to our request for bread, milk, eggs, tea, butter, etc., etc. The shelves were virtually bare. A housewife to whom I gave a questioning look threw up her hands.

'It's been like this ever since they came to build that terminal.'

Along with the influx of men have come the prostitutes, but instead of standing on street corners, they cruise around in Winnebago campers. Contacts are made in bars and then the pair go for a ride.

Illegal casinos have blossomed in Valdez since the arrival of the pipeline, and the local police, consisting of only three troopers between Valdez and Glennallen 115 miles away, are helpless in the face of rapidly escalating gambling and crime. The head of the trooper detachment in Valdez alleges that he was approached by the Cosa Nostra several times but refused to be bought out. He pleaded for help in his unequal fight with the powerful forces of crime that had descended on his town.

Valdez had changed forever. As we drove past the piles of Japanese pipe waiting near the levelled site of old Valdez to be laid end to end towards Fairbanks, I wondered whether the realities of the statistics found in government impact statements had ever dawned on the pipeline planners. Prostitutes, bare grocery shelves and $40 rowboats were tangible examples of the changes occurring in the lifestyle of the small town. They are changes over which the people of Valdez now have no control whatsoever. If they don't like what is happening their only option is to leave. A number have.

We stopped by the 40-ft-high piles of pipe that had been there since 1971.

'Listen,' said Gene, rolling down the car window.

The valley was filled with a roar. A roar of dozens of Cats, trucks and cars. A roar that smothered the former peace of the beautiful place. Overhead a helicopter flapped toward Thompson Pass with a load of steel girders.

From Valdez the pipeline route parallels the Richardson Highway, one of the most beautiful drives in Alaska. Fortunately, most of this section will be underground, but a long section across the Copper River Basin near Gulkana will have to be on raised supports to prevent thawing of the permafrost. Besides representing an ugly visual scar across 80 miles of forest and tundra, the pipe would have presented a barrier to free migration of the Nelchina caribou herd. To counter this Alyeska was forced, in a section near Sourdough, to bury seven miles of the line in the frozen soil. To prevent the thing sinking into an ever-increasing pool of mud, electric motors will pump brine around the pipe to keep the ground near it frozen.

Studies of caribou migration occupied considerable time and controversy during the early stages of the pipeline planning. In the summers of 1971 and 1972, the Alaska Cooperative Wildlife Research Unit at the University of Alaska, under the direction of Dr David Klein, in a project partially paid for by Alyeska, erected a simulated snow fence and burlap pipeline across caribou migration paths near Prudhoe Bay. The purpose of the project was to find out if the caribou, of which Alaska has 450,000 in 13 major herds, would cross a pipeline. Ramps, raised sections and other devices were built to encourage the animals across. Only 23 per cent availed themselves of the ramps and underpasses, but 42 per cent went around the ends of the 2-mile barrier. Alyeska contends that the project was for planning purposes and showed that caribou, which can migrate 20 to 40 miles a day, could easily skip the raised portions of their pipeline and cross the buried sections. This is probably true, but it is beyond question that the pipeline or pipelines across Alaska will have long-term effects on caribou. The route of the trans-Alaska pipeline is fortunate in that it approximately divides the *present* ranges of the two major herds—the Arctic and Porcupine. But caribou change their migration patterns over the years, and barriers such as pipelines represent new obstacles to their free movement, however well designed. As more pipelines and roads are built the herds will eventually decrease in size, as a result of the cumulative effects of man's incursions into the Alaskan wilderness.

At Paxson, 185 miles north of Valdez, we turned left on to the Denali Highway. This road, opened in 1957, was for Jill and me the route from Anchorage to McKinley Park. In summers past, those long drives had brought us briefly back to our beginnings in Alaska. Twenty miles out Gene stopped his VW at Tangle Lakes.

'See if I can get a few grayling for supper.' He collected his fishing gear and disappeared down toward the lakes.

The parking lot was full of campers and cars as well as the people that had come in them, and I wandered off over the soft tundra to get away. The northern horizon was serrated with the big snow peaks of the Alaska Range, and as I sank down on a hill I felt for the first time a coming home. The parking lot and its incursive people were away somewhere. Beyond my outstretched boots was the wilderness again; its longed-for familiarity overwhelmed me with peace. I drank in its space and was suffused with a happiness I had found nowhere else.

After a while Gene came up over the hill.

'Better go.' We piled in and drove back to the Richardson Highway at Paxson.

The road skirted the edge of Summit Lake as it crossed the divide of the Alaska Range and began its descent into the Tanana Valley.

'Alyeska tried to put their construction camp right on Summit Lake, but the State surveillance people made them move it. You got to watch those guys,' Gene said as we left the lake and began our descent toward the Delta River.

(Alyeska's work in the field is monitored on the spot by a State-Federal team of inspectors, who cruise up and down the route in helicopters and light aircraft. Permits for actual work must be approved by this team.)

The camp for 1100 people was now located around the corner and hopefully wouldn't affect the beautiful lake. But the influx of workers is bound to attract development.

Some idea of the stringent stipulations under which Alyeska must operate can be gleaned from entries in an Environmental Assessment Atlas prepared by the Bureau of Land Management and the Alaska State Division of Pipeline:

> A grizzly bear concentration occurs during the salmon spawning period in the area between Paxson and Summit Lakes . . . Bears may become a nuisance and a hazard if attracted when improper garbage disposal practices are used.
>
> Fish Creek, Gunn Creek and (Upper) Gulkana River. Streams are exceptionally sensitive fish spawning habitat. No siltation. As directed by Authorized Officer [the surveillance team], activities adjacent to or crossing . . . may be limited to period from mid-August through about mid-May. Reference Stipulations 1.3.4, 2.3.3.3, 2.5.1, 2.5.2, 2.5.3, 2.8 and 2.11.
>
> Proposed pipeline route is considered to be subject to the following maximum probable earthquakes:
> 2. Paxson north to Donnelly Dome, Richter Magnitude 8.0.

And so on. For 800 miles.

The Richardson roadhouse, 69 miles from Fairbanks and 1451 miles from Dawson Creek. It is one of the oldest roadhouses in Alaska, dating from the early part of the century. In those days Alaskans walked or took dog teams from Valdez to Fairbanks, and the travellers came to roadhouses like this about every 50 miles. Today, most tourists travel by self-contained camper and many Alaskan roadhouses, like this one, are for sale. It is a shame to see places like this go, because without the contact with people a stay in one of these inns produces, much of the point of travel is lost. It is not replaced by conversations with other tourists in campgrounds, tourists who are also on the move, are strangers to the land, and can bring no new knowledge of the country. Just up the road, beyond the roadhouse is Banner Creek, a stream once rich in gold, but now run out. A pick, shovel and gold pan, no longer used, grace the front of the roadhouse up among the antlers and the Schlitz sign. It has just rained. A violent thunderstorm lashed the ground less than an hour earlier, but has now passed to the east, where, behind me, the setting sun has formed a rainbow on the retreating shower. All around the trees drip the recent rain to the ground in the quiet of a late evening.

A native woman and child in Fairbanks.

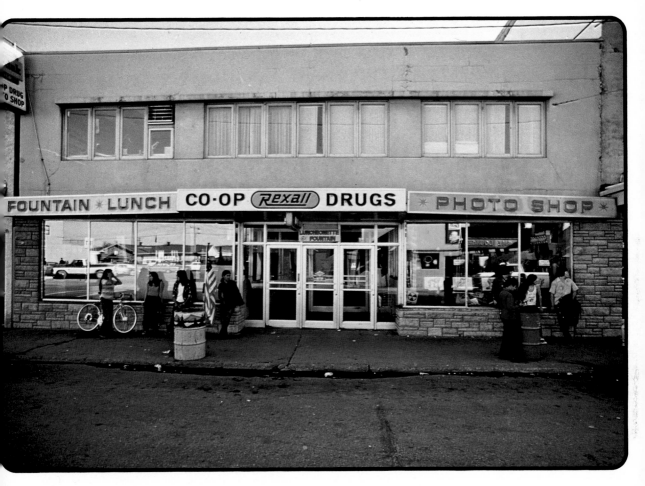

The Co-op Drug, 2nd Avenue, Fairbanks.

Fairbanks, First Avenue and Cushman Street, a Sunday evening in July, 1974. Out of the picture to the left is the Chena River, and the log cabin put up by the Chamber of Commerce for the tourists. There attendants will extol the virtues of the 'Golden Heart of Alaska', and hand you brochures about trips down the river on a paddle boat, and tours of the Prudhoe Bay oilfields. Just above the girl's elbow is the French Quarter, an offshoot of the Flame Lounge on Second Avenue, but a little farther on is the Arctic Pancake House which balances the street a bit. The antennas of Fairbank's two commercial TV stations rise into the clear summer sky. In addition to these two, there is a commercial-free Public Broadcasting station at the University of Alaska and five radio stations. Most of the radio stations, with the exception of the one emanating from the University, transmit rock music or country and western, and the TV stations use mostly film or taped programs from the Lower 48.

Interior Alaska has short, warm and usually dry summers, and the days are long. The sun settles behind the green hills to the north of the town for only a couple of hours around midnight, which gives plenty of time for it to bring the afternoon temperatures into the 80s and 90s. Fairbanks summer evenings, like this one, are glorious for being outdoors and act as some compensation for the days of darkness and cold and fog that smother the town during the winter and cause the inhabitants to sleep late, read a lot, hold frequent parties and drink. On a cold winter afternoon, with full darkness and dense ice fog at 3 p.m., even the French Quarter might look inviting.

Chapter 14

Fairbanks

Gene lives with his two small sons in an A-frame house he built himself, 3000 feet up on Ester Dome, a hill just west of Fairbanks. From his windows stretches an unbroken sweep of the Alaskan Range from Mount Hayes in the east to McKinley. That summer evening the peaks were pink in the glow from a sun just edging into the northern horizon. The savory smells of the Tangle Lakes grayling filled the angular room. On the walls were a collection of his wood block prints. We ate in a silence that is characteristic of time spent with Gene. I think we have known eath other so long that our thoughts must travel back and forth without the need for verbalization. Gene's oldest son switched on the TV. Lincoln was being assassinated, again, in living color this time.

I suggested to Gene that we take a walk.

'This place isn't what it was,' he began as we made our way along one of the trails he had marked in the spruce forest. 'People are coming in droves. You should see the lines at Safeway these days. And they run out of everything, too. Last week I tried to buy a battery for my radio in the Co-op. Day before Alyeska had come in and bought all they had, 37 batteries.'

'I bet the ice fog will be bad next winter with the increased population.'

'It was bad enough last winter. Even then it spread to places it had never been before.'

Ice fog is an insidious northern phenomenon that plagues Fairbanks every winter. It is a fog of ice crystals that forms in very cold temperatures, usually below minus 30°F, when a thin layer of air near the ground becomes saturated with pollution. The usual pollutants are car exhaust and heating fumes. The density of the fog is a function of both the temperature and the amount of pollution. Fairbanks, in a basin with little or no air circulation in winter, is uniquely prone to the dreary gray blanket that can last for days.

The increased population and traffic associated with the pipeline had already, in the winter of '73–'74, caused the fog to form at higher temperatures and hence to last longer. By the winter of '74–'75 the level of pollution was such that on 72 per cent of winter days the carbon monoxide level exceeded U.S. standards for air quality. (The Fairbanks level of lead pollution is the highest in the U.S.) Alyeska, then, in an attempt to mitigate the impact its project had had on Fairbanks' air, restricted the use of their vehicles on days when the pollution reached certain levels. But by then the situation had become almost intolerable and Fairbanks was becoming virtually uninhabitable on cold winter days.

The lane into the birch and aspen woods was the same as it had been that September evening twenty years before, when Jill and I in the first flush of our Alaskan experiences walked down it to the Woods' cabin. The patterns of light and shadow, the peace and the beautiful greens and yellows were as distant as ever from Fairbanks and its pipeline problems.

Bucky Wilson had a new house, a large log building with a long eave that overhung a porch smothered in a profusion of flowers. The house was carefully placed among the aspen trees and seemed to grow out of the forest. Along the drive to the house was the tiny cabin he first built and where he had given Jill and me our farewell party so long ago.

For Bucky, his wife Judy and their two children, life in the aspen woods, near close friends, had a unique combination of community and individuality that is difficult to achieve. All Bucky's neighbors had at least five acres. Their log houses were far enough apart not to be visible from each other, yet close enough to be in walking or skiing contact, even on the coldest winter days. Their houses formed an oasis of tranquility in the building momentum of Fairbanks.

'Jon! How are you!' Bucky greeted me as I walked up the drive. 'I hope you are going to stay a while this time.'

As I settled down in the cosy living room, I began to wonder if I should come back to stay. Judy plied us with coffee and cakes and the three of us brought back memories in each other, some easy and some very hard. Our collective past in Alaska was telescoped into bright summers, good climbs and cold winter evenings of warmth. The pipeline and all it implied receded into its rightful place as a damnable incursion into an Alaska of few people, space and peace.

That evening Bucky and I went to an open sauna at the log homestead house of the Koponens, a Quaker family who lived on Chena Ridge. I had been to saunas before (many Alaskans have them tucked in corners of their houses) but never one open to all comers. This one had been going for fifteen years, every Sunday, and by the time we arrived there was already a line of naked bodies, of both sexes and all ages, waiting to roast in the tiny wood-fired sauna.

After duly sweating my cares away, sandwiched between two beautiful girls and a

147

60-year-old insurance agent, I staggered out to the porch and sat down steaming in a group of naked cooling conversationalists.

In the fleshy circle were several professors, a lawyer or two, a couple of hippies in for their weekly bath and an intense young man running for the state legislature in the upcoming August primary election.

The pipeline and what it meant to the Alaskan way of life was the main topic. Most of the circle agreed that the state needed the money from the damn thing, but deplored the damage it was doing.

The candidate wondered why Alyeska was going so fast—were they trying to cover something up?

No, said one of the lawyers, they just want to get their money back.

'There are both state and federal surveillance teams watching their every move,' I commented.

'Good luck to them,' said the candidate. 'The pipeline is 800 miles long and by next summer Alyeska will have 20,000 people working on it. As of now there are only 26 surveillance people.'

Inside the house a telephone rang.

'At least theirs works,' muttered a professor. 'Mine quit a week ago. Can't even get a dial tone now. Telephone company claims that the system is overloaded with all the pipeline contractors.' Little did he realise that by the winter of '74–'75 the Fairbanks telephone system would break down almost completely. Emergency numbers were impossible to dial, the prospect of a reduction in 8-party service laughable. At 50 below the lack of telephone communication is a major hazard, and was compounded by frequent power failure in the overloaded electricity system. On one 50 below night in December '74, the struggling system failed over a large area around Fairbanks. Electrically heated houses soon cooled in the extreme cold and their water pipes froze and burst.

Bucky arrived, dripping, from his sauna, treble recorder in hand, and proceeded to cheer us up with some Baroque trills. The conversation turned to happier things such as the fact that we were all sitting out there without a stitch on and there were no mosquitoes.

Fairbanks, as the center of supply for the pipeline, has received more than its share of 'impact'. Shipments of basics such as building materials and staple foods are in short supply. (Fairbanks had on hand that summer only a fourteen-day reserve of food.) The Alaska Railroad and the trucking industry have devoted their carrying capacity to the lucrative and insatiable demands of the pipeline. For example, each month the workers consume twenty railcars of canned goods and 5,400 prime steers. A combination of scarcity and plentiful money has sent Fairbanks' prices soaring, especially rents.

By September 1974 five out of Fairbanks' fourteen schools went on double shift to cope with an increase in students from 8000 to 12,000. As Bucky's son Aron said, 'You can always tell the pipeline kids. They wear suspenders and have shiny shoes.'

On a bright July day, a few days after the sauna, I walked over the Chena River bridge and down 2nd Avenue. The area had changed little from the last time I had

Fairbanks

seen it in the late '60s. There was the same collection of disoriented natives and down and out whites. There were a number of spruced up, fresh from the Slope oil men, but most of them take their leaves in Dallas, courtesy of the oil companies and not among the dubious delights of downtown Fairbanks. Some of the bars had taken on new and more up-to-date names such as 'The Roustabout', 'The Pipeliner'. A bank advertised 'Pipeliner Accounts'. Presumably your cash is stashed in a length of Alyeska's pipe. The streets were crowded with traffic, much of it yellow pickups with the fateful Alyeska code numbers on their sides.

But the old section of Fairbanks, with its log and clapboard houses, away from the frenzy of the new freeways and hectic activity of the outskirts to the east and west, was an oasis of calm. I have always been surprised by the appearance of this section of shaded streets, and seemingly out of place mid-west style houses—built in one of Fairbanks' previous booms, by long-forgotten men, who in their day were after the money that Alaska gave them from its golden streams. Now the oilmen have come and I wonder about the Fairbanks they will leave behind when they, too, are gone.

'Hey, look, that guy is taking our picture!'
'Yeah, probably some tourist.'
I pushed my camera back into its bag and walked into a bar for a beer.

After the bright sun of Second Avenue, Fairbanks, the dark bar was like a cave. As my eyes adjusted, figures emerged from the gloom. They were mostly men, a few women and girls, some natives. They all looked unhappy and stared at their cans of beer or gripped their glasses of booze as though they were on a ship in a storm. 'What do you want, mister?' The fat bartender demanded as he rearranged the spilled beer on the top of the bar with a sodden rag. 'A Bud, please.' 'Yeah.' He reached for a can in the cooler below the bar, flipped the pull top off and plunked the can on the beery bar. 'That'll be a buck.' I handed him a dollar, put the frozen can to my lips and guzzled the glacial beer. A girl who looked like a native, but in the dark I couldn't tell, sidled up to me. 'Wanna come home with me?' 'No, thanks.' I finished the beer and walked out of the smelly bar into the bright sunlight of Second Avenue.

I headed for the Co-op Drug across the street, trying to avoid the two guys with the hats who were still eyeing me suspiciously. The front of the Co-op was lined with native teenagers, listlessly leaning against the windows, waiting for something to happen. They hardly spoke to each other, but just stared at the passing traffic, waiting, killing time. An oil barrel on the sidewalk with a scene of mountains, spruce trees and lakes painted on it served as a trash can, but it was nearly empty while the concrete around it was covered with ice cream wrappers, cigarette packs and tourist film cartons. Through the second of the Co-op's double doors and I was nearly overwhelmed by a warm, moist smell of perfume, popcorn, hamburgers and onions. The Co-op sold everything from motor oil to Leicas. The waitress smiled. She was from McGrath down on the Kuskokwim, a native girl who figured she had a pretty good job working in the Co-op. But it was only temporary, she said. As soon as she could get her union card she would be up on the pipeline. 'Driving a bus, or, maybe working in a kitchen.' She was very pretty. Her oriental eyes smiled easily, her full lips looked soft. 'Hamburger and milkshake, please.' 'Chocolate?' 'Yes, please.' She didn't ask me to come home with her. I might have.

This portable offspring of the parent station down the road at North Pole was set up one summer at the Alaska State Fair at Fairbanks. The station call letters, KJNP, the man inside the trailer told me, stand for King Jesus North Pole, and he went on to point out that the station, run by a missionary outfit, broadcasts in Russian, Athabascan Indian, Inupiat Eskimo and English. With its 50,000 watts of power it easily reaches the hitherto unenlightened inhabitants of the wilderness around Fairbanks. As one avid listener, Jasper Heath, put it in a poem he wrote in appreciation of the arrival of the station's transmissions:

GOD'S LONESOME TRAPPER

The coffee pot is empty
The candle's burning low
My bible's wet with tears
But my heart is all aglow.

It's cold in this little log cabin
The Yukon stove is out
But praise the Lord, for full salvation
Now I can sing and shout.

I can listen to the radio
And tune to KJNP
And hear them singing praises
And it cheers the heart of me.

'The Gospel Station at the Top of the Nation', otherwise known as 'Your Singspiration Information with Inspiration Station' is run from a collection of log houses at North Pole, a place 14 miles south of Fairbanks that also boasts a Trading Post with a plywood Santa Claus and his team of reindeer permanently galloping across the roof. But to get back to that Gospel station. With sixty churches in the Fairbanks area it is not surprising that a missionary station such as this should spring up. Fundamentalist religions have a strong hold on the people of Alaska, many of whom have come to the state from the strongly Baptist areas of the U.S. south and southwest. Virtually every town and village in Alaska has a fundamentalist church and the native villages are not excepted.

I started to pick up some of the material arranged on the table on the porch of the trailer. The announcer emerged. 'Help yourself, it's all free.' He was dressed in a black suit with a white shirt and a narrow black tie. He looked like an undertaker, but a friendly one. 'I hope you listen to us,' he said.

Fifty thousand people went to the Alaska State Fair in Fairbanks in August of 1974. There they saw giant vegetables, candidates running for state and federal office, home made pies, a lady with a lynx, paintings, pottery, a TV crew filming the lady with the lynx, a man trying to light a lamp by pedalling a bicycle, a ferris wheel, a lady doing a strange oriental dance, cotton candy, hot dogs, a man who claimed that 'human potential' and not oil was Alaska's greatest natural resource, but that it could only be tapped through transcendental meditation, a high school band that played a selection of songs from Carousel and the Alaska Flag Song, a U.S. Senator from Alaska, more giant vegetables, the Lieutenant Governor of Alaska, a section of Alyeska's pipe, an exhibit of cakes, a horse jumping competition, a radio announcer doing a remote broadcast from the fair, an exhibit of children's paintings from local schools, an exhibit of the children's parent's paintings done in evening class, a man selling vacuum cleaners, a cake made into the shape of a typewriter, a parade to celebrate the fiftieth anniversary of the fair, a horse show, a 'battle of the bands', over 6000 entrants in the Competitive Exhibit Division, showing things Alaskans had 'made, grown, prepared, sewed, or designed themselves', the *Imaginary Invalid*, by Molière, produced by the Fairbanks Drama Association at the fairgrounds, in the open air, weather permitting (two of the more recent productions of this group were *Oil Can Annie* and *Pipeline Fanny*, which were produced in the hold of the river boat *Nenana* now in drydock on the south bank of the Chena), walls of paintings of snowy mountains, spruce trees and lakes, a cake in the shape of a spruce tree, an exhibit by the Fairbanks Pipeline Impact Group that showed what it was like to be impacted by a pipeline, the Harvest Queen Pageant, and each other.

Chapter 15

North

From Fairbanks a road leads north to the old gold dredging area around Fox, then bends northwest to Livengood 73 miles away. The road then runs back southwest to Manley Hot Springs on the Tanana River. Livengood was once a town of 3500 gold seekers, but is now inhabited only by two prospectors who put threatening 'No Trespassing' signs on all available trees, adding one every time the price of gold goes up $10. I suppose that, in the summer of 1975, with the gold price sinking, they took them down again. Livengood was the farthest north point on this route; beyond for 400 miles to the Arctic coast, was a wilderness. It was peopled only by a couple of native villages, a few never-give-up prospectors at Wiseman, 170 miles north of Livengood, and Sam Wright, who used to be the Unitarian minister in Anchorage, and who lives with his wife on Big Lake, just east of the pipeline route. This land of few people has been invaded.

While I was visiting Bucky, a means of seeing the changes in the north showed up in the person of Karl Francis, an old friend of ours who had just taken a job as the environmental man for Alaskan Arctic Gas. This company was the Alaskan portion of a 19-member consortium proposing to build a buried gas pipeline from Prudhoe Bay eastward to the Mackenzie River, and thence south to Calgary to connect with the existing gas distribution system. I had known Karl in the early '60s when he was a student at the University of Alaska, and at first I was alarmed to find he had joined the 'opposition'. But then I realized that there were few better places for an environmentally aware person to be. I believe there is too much of a 'them and us' attitude between conservationists and oil people in Alaska. More might be accomplished by infusing the oil industry with good workable environmental ideas: the present system of confrontation only serves to harden their attitudes and make it more difficult for them to back down over an issue, until forced to do so by law. The oil companies have seen the logic in this by hiring people who might otherwise act against them. But this is two-edged. These same people are bringing an environmental thinking to the center of decision making within organizations like Alyeska. The difficulty, of course, lies in getting this thinking accepted in the face of the economic needs of the company.

Karl was about to make his first inspection trip to Arctic Gas' grizzly bear research project, based at the old oil camp of Sagwon north of the Brooks Range.

'Why not come along, Jon, maybe you will see something to photograph.'

Our chartered Piper Aztec buzzed down the runway at Fairbanks, following a Hercules humping a load to the Arctic. At 48,000 lb. a time, these freight aircraft were leaving Fairbanks at the rate of one an hour at the height of the airlift to the oil fields around 1970.

Between the Yukon and Prudhoe Bay, Alyeska had built twelve construction camps since work on the pipeline began on April 29, 1974. By October a gravel road 360 miles long lay where none had been before.

The Cats, trucks and huge Euclid loaders scurrying from the gravel pit to the growing ends of the road below our wing illustrated the sudden urgency of the project. The pressure pent up over the four-year delay had finally burst upon the land, and the land was reeling under the shock. Those 3000 men below, moving 200,000 cubic yards of gravel a day, were the spearhead of the force that was cutting Alaska in half.

By October the cut was complete.

Coldfoot, Old Man, Prospect, Happy Valley. Names that evoked the days of gold were strung like nerve centers along the route. That August day the fibers between the new centers were visibly growing, stretching gravelly tentacles toward each other until they met when two Cat blades kissed.

Near Liverpool the gravel food for the fibers came from gold tailings, as the leavings of one rush acted as fuel for another. Elsewhere the 85 million cubic yards of gravel needed for the project would have to come from stream beds and from borrow pits carved out of the forests and the tundra.

There is a great potential danger to fish in this vast excavation of their spawning streams. Alyeska is prohibited from interfering with the streams themselves and must take its gravel from the edges. But it is the man actually driving the Cat who must be monitored. By clouding the stream, or diverting its course, he could destroy its spawning potential.

Below us a Hercules left a trail of dust as it rose from Coldfoot airstrip and headed back to Fairbanks. A helicopter felt its way along the new road, just above treetop level. In the Aztec the radio crackled with traffic. Skip, the pilot, broke in.

'Chandalar, this is Charlie 8427. What is your weather, please?'

'Charlie 8427, Chandalar. Weather. Sky clear, temperature 58, wind 030 at 20. Altimeter 002.'

Chandalar was the last camp before Dietrich Pass, at 4800 feet the highest on the pipeline. The report meant that the pass was open. The way to the Arctic was clear.

Wiseman, a tiny gold mining town, appeared from beneath the right wing. When Alyeska's road builders tried to build their road past Wiseman earlier in the summer, they were confronted by Henry Leonard and John Bullock, two wizened Wiseman miners. They stood astride their tractor, parked in Alyeska's hard-won right-of-way, six shooters strapped to their hips, and refused to move.

'Your goddamned road crosses our claims' shouted Harry at the astounded Alyeska Cat skinner.

Alyeska called up reinforcement in the person of a State Trooper, flown in from Fairbanks, who convinced the irate miners to take their case to court.

Earlier in the year Alyeska managed to work their way around another obstacle, this time one thrown in their path by the Eskimos at Anaktuvuk Pass. This is a village in a pass through the Brooks Range, the range of mountains that separates the North Slope from the rest of Alaska, about 100 miles west of the pipeline corridor over Dietrich Pass. Early in the spring of 1974, while the ground was still frozen, Alyeska packed tons of material on trucks and sleds for their coming construction season on the Slope, and set off from the Livengood road over a previously gouged scar called the Hickel Highway. This track, named derisively after a former governor of Alaska, was made by the state government to encourage the oil companies into the Arctic. The track is a travesty against the environment, breaking all the rules of Arctic road engineering. It was merely dug into the tundra by a Cat with its blade down. By the first spring breakup after its construction it became impassable. It had been in use only six weeks, though it was later revived at great state expense. Alyeska trundled their supplies up this road, which incidentally was outside the corridor to which their permit applies, until they reached the Eskimos at Anaktuvuk Pass. Then Alyeska found itself in the court the Wiseman miners had bypassed.

> . . . Defendants' trespass will disrupt Plaintiffs' trapping, hunting, and fishing activities and will destroy plaintiffs' interest in an unspoiled homeland . . . Defendants' trespass will cause Plaintiffs irreparable injury by wholly denigrating their constitutional rights to due process of law, equal protection of the laws, and to property. Plaintiffs have no speedy or adequate remedy at law . . .
>
> From: Plaintiff Brief in Rhoda Ahgook et al vs Alyeska Pipeline Service Company et al.

The extent of the U.S. obsession with energy, and its own dwindling reserves in the spring of 1974, was evident in the decision:

> . . . Defendants' most forceful allegation of relative hardship is the high probability that seeking an alternative route through Dietrich Pass would require a vastly larger expenditure of time, money and effort . . . Plaintiffs' Counsel makes light of the critical national interest here involved . . . Not only would there be an indeterminate delay in the construction of the Trans-Alaska Pipeline, but a devastating impact on the thousands of persons directly or indirectly affected

by such a delay could result . . . Therefore it is ordered:
1. That Plaintiff's motion for a preliminary injunction is denied . . .

From: Memorandum and Order in the case of
Rhoda Ahgook et al vs Alyeska Pipeline
Service Company. U.S. District Court,
James Van der Heydt presiding.

The Eskimos first appealed against the Court's decision, but then in a generous gesture, settled with Alyeska out of court.

It now becomes in the national interest to trammel over native lands. Not only that but the dangerous precedent is set that the *pipeline* is in the national interest and not the country or people that it displaces. The steel snake is tightening its grip on Alaska.

On the slope below Dietrich Pass was the wreckage of a De Havilland Beaver that had crashed only a few days before, trying to negotiate the pass in bad weather. Three Alyeska men and the pilot were killed.

Our own wings seemed to scrape the bare rock walls of the Brooks Range as we climbed through the pass. Below us on the crest, Cats were making the first cuts in the previously undisturbed rocks of this Arctic pass. Ahead, the craggy mountains gradually melted into a broad plain that disappeared into the northern distance. The Arctic Slope. Below that treeless plain was the oil.

The Eskimo village of Kaktovik on Barter Island (so named because it was one of the four great trading centers of the northern aboriginal Eskimos). It is nearly midnight in mid summer, the sun is approaching its lowest point for the night. Beyond the village is the airstrip, built and maintained by the military who operate the DEW-line site, whose two hundred foot high antennas are just out of the picture to the left. The airstrip is used by the F27s of Wien Air Alaska for their twice weekly air service, weather permitting. Beyond the airstrip is Bernard Spit and the calm water of the Beaufort Sea. The polar ice pack begins in the broken floes a few miles offshore, but thickens rapidly beyond ten miles to the nearly solid sheet that surrounds the pole.

The red building on the left in the village is the church, and to its right is the large white building of the school with its two silver colored fuel tanks. Beyond an empty area lies the Quonset that is the village meeting hall, and to the upper right of the hall is the modular building of the post office. The group of new houses to the right of the post office were financed by grants and loans from the Alaska State Housing Authority, with the practical assistance of Inupiat Builders, Inc., a native company. At the extreme right, next to the house with the silver colored roof, are the blackened remains of a house that recently burnt to the ground. Fire is the greatest hazard in the Arctic; once started, a house fire will usually consume the building.

Although the village looks quiet, nearly everybody is awake. People are strolling up and down the single street, three wheeled Hondas are scurrying along the road to the airstrip and back, and Harold Kavelook, who is building his new house (the light tan one at the extreme left), is taking advantage of the good weather to get a few more roof joists up. Bright summer days like this one occur rarely in Kaktovik and no one is going to be caught sleeping through what could be one of the half dozen good summer days. Or nights.

The Athabascan Indian village of Arctic Village on the upper East Fork of the Chandalar River. The village is sited in the center of a broad valley that narrows and disappears into the gray peaks of the Brooks Range in the background. Although it is early September, the day is mild, the afternoon sun warm, the air still. The village is silent, and our feet crunch loudly as we walk on the gravel of the village street.

Walter is heading for his afternoon nap. His house is the one on the right with the aluminum roof and the curtains in the window. I bid him a good sleep and walk on, past the falling down church, that has been replaced by a new one about a quarter of a mile behind me, and climb down the hill behind the church to the Chandalar. The river here is slow moving and muddy, and pulled up on the bank are about ten flat bottomed, outboard powered river boats that the villagers use to bring down moose and caribou they have shot, or to catch fish.

There isn't much to do in Arctic Village, aside from building cabins. Since liquor and drugs were prohibited by village ordinance and a strict control kept at the airport, which lies about a mile to the left, the place has been even quieter. Most of the people exist on welfare payments from the state of Alaska or the Federal government, though a few have gone off to work on the pipeline. A new sewage plant under construction has given some work to local people, and has caused a small center of activity along the road to the airport. But most summer afternoons are like this one, the silence broken only by the sounds of children at play.

Chapter 16

An Arctic Village

I stepped down from the wing to join Karl as he greeted the six inhabitants of Sagwon –the six members of the research team who had spent the spring and summer at this abandoned oil exploration base, studying the roamings of grizzlies, caribou and sheep and, it seemed, every other wild animal and bird between the Sagavanirktok River and the Canadian border 200 miles to the east. Harry Reynolds, a moustached Alaska Fish and Wildlife man, Jim Curatolo and Gregg Moore, who represented an outfit with the trendy name of Renewable Resources Consulting Services, were the scientific core of the group, supported by Lee Peet who flew a Super Cub that bristled with direction-finding antennae, Steve Lindsey who flew the Jet Ranger helicopter and Harry's wife, Pat, who cooked the meals and thus kept the whole thing going. But before Karl and I could join this happy group for a beer we had to load Skip's Aztec with their accumulated garbage, including carefully packaged sewage, to be flown back to Fairbanks.

'Got to fly it all out,' explained Harry, 'Can't clutter up the Arctic, you know, and besides, I think Fairbanks needs it.'

The Aztec banked south and disappeared toward the Brooks Range that stretched across our southern horizon, its highest peaks dusted with an early September snow. Over us the sky was clear, the wind blew lightly from the northeast and the evening air had the nip of coming frost. Over to the left the control tower gazed with vacant glass eyes over a ramshackle collection of prefabricated housing units and work shops, the door of one creaking gently in the breeze. Surrounding the camp were a scattering of oil drums. The place represented the old days in the search for Arctic oil when restrictions were few and usually went unheeded anyway. When the frenzied search for oil pushed aside all consideration of the environment, Sagwon stood as a stark reminder of what greedy men can do when they think nobody is watching.

The research group had taken over one of the abandoned buildings that had been a kitchen and had turned it into their office and dining room. One wall was covered by a map bristling with colored pins that marked the location of caribou and grizzly sightings. The other walls were lined with books and an assortment of bones, feathers and rocks that no doubt had some scientific significance. In the center of the room an ancient oil heater made ominous thumping noises but didn't actually explode.

'Number 69 today,' said Jim.

'69 what?' I asked.

'69 grizzlies tagged, 12 with radios,' he answered. 'We find them with Steve's helicopter, shoot them with a muscle relaxant drug and when they settle down on the tundra we slip either a radio collar or one with colored tapes over their heads. After an hour or so they wander off again a bit unsteady, but they soon recover.'

'What do they say to you with their new radios?' I cut in.

'Then Lee and Gregg fly around in the Super Cub and when they pick up a signal they plot it on a map.' It's difficult to put a scientist off his track.

Hence the map on the wall with the colored pins. Once the migration patterns of the caribou and the wanderings of the grizzlies are known, the effect of a pipeline through their midst can be better assessed. The oil industry, and particularly Arctic Gas, have spent millions on this type of environmental research in the Arctic. Most of this work has been new, and with adequate financing for the first time, it has opened up new areas of knowledge in this little-known land. Researchers are not asked whether a pipeline or other industrial activity should take place, but, rather, how its effect on the environment can be minimized. While this is a worthy aim, and one that the Alaskan experience with industrial development has brought into sharp focus for the first time, it is a compromise and should be recognized as such. Obviously, the oil industry is not going to spend its money on research to prove that its project is environmentally unworkable. In the framework of preliminary environmental information, economic factors, energy potential of the resource and other data, a decision to build a project is made. Then, usually in good faith, but with corporate interests at heart, attempts are made to tailor the project, with information gained from the research, to the environmental concerns of conservationists. Industrial development in the Arctic is not done to benefit its environment, but rather the consumer and the company that supplies him. The environment must always lose. At least here, with some prodding, industry is trying to lessen that loss.

The helicopter hunted its way up the bare river valley. The whirring rotors above me blurred the view of the craggy Arctic peaks that lined the sides of the valley. Below, the willow-bordered stream spread over its wide sand and rock bed and flowed with the clarity of liquid glass. Black shapes of arctic char darted toward each other in the deep pools formed in the eddies of the stream.

Steve squinted through his sunglasses against the unexpected glare of a September sun in the Arctic.

'Nothing yet.'

Harry sat in the left seat beside Steve, a shotgun across his lap. 'Let's try the Marsh Fork,' he said, fingering the trigger.

Steve banked the helicopter to the right and we entered a long valley that penetrated deeply into the rugged frost-splintered mountains. Ahead of us brown-red tundra spread up the slopes until it merged with the gray talus thrown down by the rocky peaks. Beside me Jim opened a metal case and began to load dart cartridges.

'There's one!' Steve put the helicopter into a tight bank that forced me into my seat and pointed the rotors at a clump of willows almost directly below. Suddenly, out of the bushes bounded a grizzly, her tan coat rippling in the sun as she ran furiously through the willows on the edge of the river.

Jim handed a loaded cartridge to Harry who inserted it into the chamber and gently but firmly closed the breech. He leaned out of the window, braced against his seat belt. The shotgun was brought up to his shoulder and he pointed the barrel just ahead of the helicopter's landing skid. Steve brought the helicopter up behind the running bear which was now crashing headlong through the willows and low bushes, sending a flurry of branches and leaves to each side.

BANG! The first dart hit the bear in the thick fat of her rump.

'Got her! But she's bigger than usual. Load me another, Jim.' Harry sighed, put the shotgun on his lap and studied the bear through his binoculars. Steve hovered to allow the still running bear to calm down.

Another loaded cartridge was placed in the chamber. The helicopter gained on the bear which had stopped to look back at us. As we approached she resumed her bounding run along the river.

BANG! 'That should do it.' Harry handed the gun to me over the back of the seat. 'Let's wait over there, Steve.' Harry pointed to a red tundra-covered hill beside the river, ahead of the galloping bear. The helicopter settled on the hill, scattering red bearberry leaves in all directions in the rotor downwash. We waited ten minutes while the bear, the drug beginning to take effect, slowed to a walk.

'She's headed for the river!' Harry shouted as he clambered back into his seat from his observation perch on the landing skid. We lifted off in a steep bank, back toward the river. Steve flew a few feet over the water, its surface churned into a turmoil by the downwash. The bear turned away from the river in which she could have drowned, weakened by the drug.

'She's going down, I think,' said Jim, peering through his binoculars, 'Beautiful creature, it's a shame we have to treat her this way. Hope she realizes the trouble we are going to over her.'

The bear began to stagger as the muscle-relaxant drug took effect. The proud beast became a pathetic cripple, if only temporarily, as her hind legs collapsed beneath her. She struggled up again only to have her front legs fail. Finally she gave up. Propped weakly on her front feet and gasping for breath through her open jaws, she swiveled her head toward us and gazed stupefied at our noisy flapping machine. We landed about 100 yards away and Steve cut the engine. When the rotors stopped and hung

An Arctic Village

limply over us, an Arctic silence descended on the valley, a silence so brutally shattered by our intrusive presence.

I stepped out onto the spongy tundra. We had landed in the long afternoon shadow of a dark mountain and the air had the feel of the coming Arctic cold. The vastness of the deep blue sky gave the valley of rock and tundra a remoteness born of another world. Below us the bear, an innocent victim of this onrush of twentieth-century technology, directed a drugged gaze at us.

'She's okay now, but we better hurry. The drug will only last an hour or so.' Harry spoke over his shoulder as he approached the bear, cautiously, backed up by Jim with a 30.06 rifle.

As we came up to the bear she sagged to her side, but her eyes were still open; their tiny pupils followed us.

'She wants to get at us but can't. Must be frustrating.' Harry ran his fingers gently through her thick golden fur.

Jim made a note on a form on his clipboard. 'Number 1070.'

Bear 1070 turned out to be a sow, *Ursus arctos horribilis*, 14 years old, 39 inches high at the shoulder and 71 inches in length. Her two cubs were hiding in a clump of willows across the river. This grizzly was near the northern limit of the range of her species, susceptible to the rigors of a difficult life on the edge of the polar sea.

'Do you have the radio?'

Jim handed Harry a radio transmitter and battery fixed to a collar and it was placed around the bear's neck. The grizzly began to stir as the final blood tests were taken and the number 1070 tatooed on her inner lower lip with an electric tatooer.

It took all of us to roll her over on to the net slung beneath a tubular tripod that Steve had set up. Harry winched her up to the scale. '270 pounds.' Jim made a note on his form.

She was up on her legs again as we lifted off for camp. Her two cubs emerged from the willows and were making their way across the river to their now catalogued mother.

After the long warm evening of coffee and conversation back at the camp, I walked down to the edge of the river. The moonlight sparkled on the clear arctic stream, picking out highlights on wet rocks and turning the quiet eddies into quicksilver. I looked up and was suddenly awed by a shower of cosmic rays that lit up the blue-black sky in an arc from the black serrations of the Brooks Range to the flat horizon to the north-west. The aurora. The green-white waves rippled fiercely to and fro along the arc as though unsure of their direction. Darting streamers from space lit the high atmosphere into a frenzy of eerie space-light, then died away to blackness. Suddenly they were back, brighter than before, seemingly closer, reaching out for the arctic landscape below. But there was no sound. The mad display went on in a silent theatre of space, a visitation from another world.

The first frost of a new winter covered the morning grass as I walked to breakfast. Pat was already at work at the stove.

'I think Lee is going to Arctic Village today, you might try to get a ride. It's a good day for a flight. Best weather we've had all summer.'

165

In the summer of 1974, this pile of gravel on the tundra was the new road from the Yukon River to Prudhoe Bay. The gravel for the 360 mile road was laid in a matter of months, slicing a previously uncut wilderness. The road was built by Alyeska to provide access to the country to make possible construction of the pipeline, and to provide a land-link to the oilfields at Prudhoe Bay. The road will be turned over to the state of Alaska when the pipeline is finished, and will become part of the state road system. The pickup in this picture was one of the first vehicles over this section, 16 miles north of Happy Valley Camp, and 65 miles south of Prudhoe Bay, built only a few days earlier. To construct the road on permafrost, at least five feet of gravel base is used as insulation, so that the heat of the road, generated by traffic, or by the sun, will not melt the ice of the permafrost and cause the road to sink into a watery grave. Thousands of cubic yards of gravel were used for the road and for the parallel pad that runs the length of the pipeline itself, scooped from river beds that border or cross the pipeline route, or from borrow pits. A last minute change in alignment has caused the road to bend to the left at the top of the picture, thus taking it and its traffic away from a nesting area of the peregrine falcon on cliffs above the Sagavanirk-tok River off the right of the picture.

My cameras and I just managed to squeeze into the back seat of Lee's Super Cub; by the time he got into the front seat it seemed as if we were wearing the thing rather than riding in it. I had always had an affection for Super Cubs since I did my first solo in one in Florida, and then proceeded to ground loop it on my first landing. Lee's had enormous tires that enabled him to land almost anywhere, whether there was an airstrip or not. A modification to the wing gave it a bat-like appearance and a low stalling speed.

The familiar hollow roar of the engine vibrated through the fabric as we bounced down the long gravel runway and out over the river. Just over the bluff beyond the river I could see the new pipeline road. It emerged from the foothills of the Brooks Range, passed under us, and then struck out towards Prudhoe Bay, 65 miles north. A straight white line against the autumn-red tundra. A lone yellow Cat crawled towards the north, dragging a compactor behind it.

Lee spoke over the roar of the engine, 'If Harry hadn't been here, Alyeska would have put their road right through some peregrine falcon nests on the edge of that bluff. He alerted the state surveillance people and Alyeska realigned the road. They just connected with the road coming south from Prudhoe last week.'

Over the edge of the bluff that overlooked the isolated slum of Sagwon, a lone falcon circled in a thermal created on the slope of the bluff by the surprisingly warm sun. Lee turned the nose east and we levelled out at about 1000 feet over the rolling red tundra. To the south I could make out a drilling rig, the first I had seen; a road led from it to an airstrip along the river. Immediately across the river was another strip and from that another road led to a collection of white prefabricated buildings that was Alyeska's Happy Valley camp.

'Why the hell are there two airstrips?'

'The Forest Oil rig is a tight one. They don't want anybody to know how they're doing. Shades of '69. There is no contact at all between the two camps even though they're only a few miles apart. Damn waste of gravel if you ask me.' Lee threw up his hands.

We flew east, parallel to the Brooks Range, over an undulating country of small lakes, crossed by large braided rivers that flowed from the Range to the Arctic Ocean, now visible from our altitude as a thin blue line along the northern horizon. On the Ivishak bar a group of caribou sought refuge from insects on some overflow ice in the middle of the stream. This ice, left over from the previous winter and unlikely to melt before the next, forms in layers during the winter. The still liquid stream flows through cracks and spreads over already frozen portions of the river, where it freezes, adding to the existing ice. The bit below looked to be more than four feet thick.

The vast gravel bar of the Canning River stretched across our flight path, marking the western boundary of the Arctic National Wildlife Range. This 13,000 square mile official wilderness, the largest wildlife refuge in the United States, was established in 1960 by edict of the Secretary of the Interior. It could just as easily vanish under the pen of a successor. Conservationists want to see it preserved along with nine new national parks, three new national forests, four wild and scenic rivers, and eight new wildlife refuges to be selected from the 80 million acres set aside for the purpose under

168

the Native Land Claims Act. Most of the planning for these potential legalized wild areas will come from within Alaska, through the Joint Federal-State Land Use Planning Commission, of which Celia Hunter is a member. Celia's job isn't easy. As a banker in Fairbanks said recently, 'How the hell can you do anything with this country if they are going to lock it all up?'

'You should have been here in the spring, Jon.' Lee twisted around and at the same time banked the Super Cub steeply. 'See that white rock down there? I was flying up here looking for bears when I saw that rock moving up the hill. I circled and looked closer and then realized that the ground was completely covered with thousands of caribou, flowing like a river around the rock. You want a shot of Schrader Lake?'

We circled low over a jade-blue lake that reflected the high peaks of the Brooks Range, glaciers hanging from their snowy summits. There was no sign of life below. The lake was a jewel set in a wilderness of tundra and peak.

Lee's left hand pushed the throttle forward and we climbed.

'Better go up a little if we want to get over the top.'

We entered the V-shaped valley of the Okpilak between Mount Michelson and Mount Hubley, both just under 9000 feet. The walls of the peaks on either side plunged in a series of battlements beneath our wings, until they met at the silver river. Ahead the valley was blocked by a glacier, smoothed by summer melt into a flow of ice that looked as though it had been applied with a giant brush. We crested the divide with enough but not too much to spare and throttled back to coast down the valley of the Sheenjek River. Suddenly spruce trees began to appear along the edge of the river and scattered themselves among the jade lakes. We had crossed the northern treeline.

The Sheenjek turned southeast, but we headed southwest. The runway and log houses of Arctic Village soon appeared among the spruce and small lakes along the east fork of the Chandalar River. Lee throttled back and we settled on to the village's gravel strip.

'Goddam, there's Walter. I thought he was working on the pipeline.'

A native with hornrimmed glasses, nylon jacket and pressed trousers climbed out of an orange Datsun pickup and came toward us.

'What's the matter, Walter, Alyeska work you too hard?'

'Damn right, Lee. Ten hours a day, a half an hour for lunch. You try it for a month and see how you like it! I can make almost as much on unemployment anyway. But I guess I'll go back. Boring here.'

Walter drove us the mile into the village. On the left as we entered the scattering of log houses was a new sewage treatment plant. The present system was to put the honey buckets on the nearest frozen lake during the winter. When spring came they conveniently sank out of sight and mind. Walter and Lee disappeared into Walter's log house for coffee. (Not beer. A large sign at the entrance to the village announced that liquor and drugs were prohibited, by order of the village elders, and even threatened to search incoming visitors for contraband bottles.)

I strolled down the deserted gravel road toward what appeared to be the older section of the village. The spire of a log chapel had fallen in, though a new chapel had been built to replace it farther up the road. I learned that the Episcopal services, conducted in the local language, Athabascan, were well attended. Arctic Village is a 'good' village, almost the exact opposite of the Bethel I had seen, and the people I met seemed happier and friendlier. Across a small stream the white school-teacher, her whistle at the ready, was directing her pupils across the parallel bars with regimental precision. Tied up at the village river landing was a small flotilla of flat bottom boats, their Johnsons and Evinrudes at the ready.

It was deathly quiet. The few people moved silently from house to house, even a couple of kids playing on a snowmobile hardly made a sound. The village seemed to take on the quiet and solitude of the wilderness that surrounded it.

It is no wonder that villages like Arctic Village are strongly protesting government efforts to connect them all with roads. Not only would the carve-up of the country destroy their subsistence economy, but the influx of tourists with campers, kids and rifles would obliterate the essence of village life. Indeed, some natives in villages that have already been pushed violently into the American cash economy, such as Barrow, have fled back to the wilderness and subsistence living again. Five hundred natives from Barrow recently set up tents on the tundra some distance from the village, and are returning to traditional lifestyles. The natives and the whites both seem to be escaping Alaskan cities, when they can.

But the old life isn't easy. As Mitch Demientieff, president of the Tanana Chiefs Conference, the regional native association for the Interior, put it, 'It's not all beautiful skies and scenic rivers. Rolling out of the sack at 5:30 a.m. in 60 degrees below zero and putting on the snowshoes; or cutting fish all day in the summer with the sun so hot and mosquitoes so thick you can hardly stand it; sleeping three or four hours a day because the fish are running and must be put up. This is genuine hard work.'

He went on, 'Alaska must learn to respect the rural native existence. Planners and leaders must learn not to try to urbanize or westernize him.'

'Good village,' said Lee as we climbed over the winding Chandalar and headed toward the Brooks Range again. 'You know there was a guy, Peter Stern, a while back, who came to Arctic Village to work for them. He wrote letters for those who couldn't write, built houses and helped everybody. The elders wanted him to stay so they said he should marry Katine, the school teacher, thinking that would encourage him. But he didn't.'

Below, a string of caribou formed a light brown line across the blue water of the upper Chandalar as they began their migration back to the Porcupine flats to the south.

Chapter 17

Prudhoe

Maro Queen was very pretty, with long brown hair, and she was completely unexpected. She squeezed her attractive form between two roughnecks wearing Texan hats and bulky ruff parkas.

'You must be Jon Gardey. I recognize the cameras and the lost look. I'm Maro Queen. I'm supposed to show you around BP. How did you get here?'

'Friend brought me up from Sagwon in his Super Cub.'

Deadhorse Airport, the airport for the Prudhoe Bay oilfields, was named after the construction company that built it, for, as far as I know, there have never been any horses, in any condition, at Prudhoe. That afternoon Lee Peet had dropped me on the ramp next to Wien's Boeing 737 jet, and had taken off again for Sagwon. The arrival of the Anchorage flight had packed the tiny building with men whose tour was up, and with new arrivals beginning a highly paid incarceration in the oilfields.

In contrast to my preconceived idea of oil men as big, brawny and blustery, this crowd could have been seen on any city street. There was a sprinkling of bearded university students, a liberal assortment of men wearing knitted Alaskan sweaters and short haircuts, a few who, obviously on their way south, were dressed to go into immediate action with the girls as soon as they landed in Dallas. There were even a couple of women looking like misplaced housewives. The men were all overweight.

Some of the younger men sat, without speaking, in the few chairs, or leaned against the walls plastered with posters procaliming pipeliner flights to the South 48. Their minds seemed miles away and I suspect had already arrived home and were in bed with a girlfriend.

171

The BP Operations Center at Prudhoe Bay, built between 1972 and 1974 at a cost of 21 million dollars. It is an interesting exercise in Arctic engineering. The building was prefabricated in Seattle, barged to Prudhoe Bay in the summer of 1973 and assembled on the spot. This three-story main building provides living accomodation for 140 men and women, a swimming pool, sauna, an Astroturfed recreation area 200 feet long, a small forest and assorted offices, including a large room to house the computer that will control the flow of oil from BP's western half of the Prudhoe Bay field. The bedrooms are for single occupancy and have individually controlled heating, even their windows can be opened. The interior is reminiscent of a slightly austere, quality hotel, and no muddy boots are allowed; they have to be left in a color-coded locker room. In fact, the whole place is color-coded, and inside looks something like a child's playroom. The numbers designating each floor are five feet high, huge stars adorn the dining area, and colors everywhere are bright and garish, they say, to counter the depressing psychological effects of the dark blue and white landscape outside during the long winter. The structure is built on bright red steel pilings sunk 30 feet into the permafrost. These allow cold air to circulate between the building and the ground, preventing heat transfer from the warm building to the frozen ground. There is a second building, almost as big, that houses the services necessary to maintain the center.

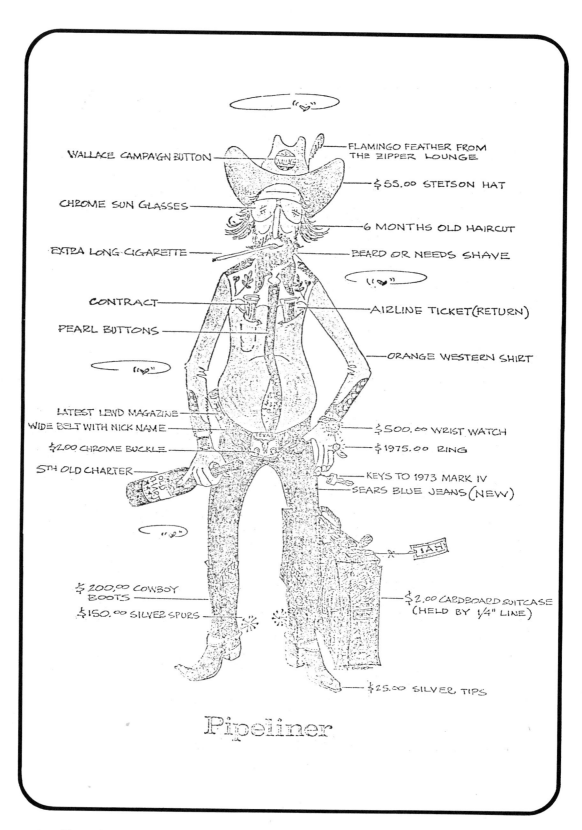

Pipeliner

Found on a wall of a pipeline camp.

Prudhoe

Maro threaded the BP/SOHIO pickup through a helter-skelter mess of trucks and pickups behind the terminal building, and we headed off on a raised gravel road past a large shallow lake. A flight of white-fronted geese took off as we passed.

'I didn't expect to be met by a pretty girl. I thought this was supposed to be a wild place of roustabouts and roughnecks. Are there many like you?'

'I don't exactly change drill bits. About ten of us work at BP's center, mostly as accountants and secretaries.'

'What happens when 120 men and ten women get together?'

'One of each is getting married, to each other, next week. That's what happens.'

The gravel road wound around lakes, past a few low buildings, but otherwise the place seemed almost deserted. My vision of Prudhoe Bay as a field of derricks, all busily pumping oil, admittedly based on California oil fields, was rapidly being demolished. There wasn't an oil well to be seen, or much of anything else.

'Where are all the oil wells?'

Maro's brown eyes were fixed on an advancing truck bearing an enormous steel tank. We just managed to squeeze by, and were then enveloped in dust. 'ARCO has one over by the port, but that's the only one up at the moment. Ours is down, being moved. They take the rigs down when the well is drilled and move them to the next spot on the pad. All they leave up are Chistmas trees.'

'In September?'

'Wise guy. See that thing over there with all the valves and thingamebobs sticking out of it? A Christmas tree. A capped well.'

'Oh, thank you.' You don't want to rile a liberated woman, especially not in Prudhoe Bay.

We passed a large dish antenna, next to a group of buildings under construction.

'Does NASA have a satellite station here?'

'Those buildings are Pump Station 1, the beginning of the pipeline. The antenna points to a satellite over the equator somewhere I think. There is another one at Valdez and a couple of other places. They will use them for backup communications on the pipeline. How do you like our hotel? The whole thing came up by barge from Seattle last summer.'

Ahead, looking like a space station set on the tundra, was BP's operations center. Perched on a forest of bright orange steel pilings, to insulate them from the permafrost, were a pair of large metal buildings painted brown. Rising four stories from the ground, they broke the flat expanse of the lake-dotted tundra with a vengeance.

Maro pulled the pickup under a large sign on the side of the building with SOHIO and BP symbols.

'You look hungry.'

It was like walking into a Hilton. Carpets cushioned my feet, Muzak assailed my ears. The place had the hushed feeling of something very expensive ($21 million).

Why, when presented with twenty-one different beverages, I chose coffee, I don't know. Too many choices causes a retreat to something familiar, I guess. I did stock up on a few of the multitude of multi-vitamins strategically located at the end of the serving line, though. I think I needed them.

175

Mile 204, the trans Alaska Pipeline, summer 1974.

A year earlier there was only a survey line through this valley in the southern Brooks Range, 204 miles south of Prudhoe Bay and 694 miles north of Valdez. A few years before that there were only a few animal trails and perhaps some trap lines put out by a trapper who lived at Wiseman, a few cabins near a mine about 20 miles south. Two weeks before I took the picture there was no road. Today the pipeline itself is being laid down the cleared line to the left of the road, and the wilderness that once filled this valley of the Middle Fork of the Koyukuk has been banished. The 4500-foot peak in the picture has no name and neither does the lake at its foot. I will quote from the *Environmental Assessment Atlas, Trans Alaska Pipeline System*, a book of restrictions laid down for the pipeline builders by the U.S. Bureau of Land Management and the Alaska State Office, Division of Pipeline, from the portion that deals with the section of road and pipeline visible in the picture:

> Caribou are a common winter migrant through the valley . . . the animals migrate northerly along the pipeline right of way from mid March to June 1 and southerly from early August to early December . . . ground and low level aerial activities shall be conducted to assure free movement and passage and to avoid harrassment or harm.
>
> Black and grizzly bears are also common residents through the area . . . eliminate all . . . human food sources that are accessible to bears.
>
> . . . Dall sheep are common residents above the 2500 foot elevation . . .
>
> Raptor habitat area . . . activities restricted from April through August during the nesting season.
>
> . . . highway and pipeline are in close proximity . . . protect buffer zone between pipeline and highway rights of way . . .
>
> High to moderately productive fish streams . . . crossing or other pipeline and highway activities in or adjacent to the rivers may be limited to the months of July and August and from the first of October to the end of March . . .

. . . and so forth.

But the scar of the pipeline across the wilderness remains in spite of the government attempts to regulate the builders. Just out of the picture at the upper left, at mile 200, is Dietrich Camp, an Alyeska construction camp providing housing for about 2000 workers. When construction is finished, commercial and recreational use will probably be made of both the road and the camp, opening the country on either side of the valley to the people of Alaska. Thus this wilderness will be finally and fully 'used'.

Dietrich Camp, Mile 201 on the trans Alaska pipeline, with its airstrip and the pipeline road, summer, 1974.

Forest Oil Company drilling a new well on the North Slope, near the Sagavanirktok River and about 70 miles north of the Brooks Range in the background.

A shallow tundra lake, just north of Sagwon on the North Slope.

Only the top few inches to few feet of the tundra will thaw during the summer, and below this 'active layer' lies permanently frozen ground, 'permafrost', that can extend 2000 feet down in places. Thus rain and melt water remain on the surface creating thousands of lakes such as this. Farther north, near the shore of the Arctic Ocean, the tundra can be 80 per cent covered with standing water. Dunlin, phalarope, sandpiper and other shorebirds breed on the edges of the lakes, as do common eider, Canada geese, snow geese and other migrating waterfowl, and during the summer the sky can be filled with the shapes of thousands of birds. In the dark ridge in the background are the nests of several peregrine falcons.

In June the vegetation around the shore of the lake emerges from the melting snow cover as a mass of brown and dead looking plants that begin a growing season of only four to five weeks. During this time the plants must complete the complete cycle of growth and reproduction—many Arctic plants reproduce by means of vegetative growth rather than seed production. In the height of summer the grass around the lake is flecked with wildflowers: yellow poppies, saxifrage, windflower, lousewort and many other species, but their days of color are brief. Snow can and often does come at any time during the summer, and already by early September this tundra has received a week of night frosts. The vegetation first turned red, but now it is brown, and within a week the early winter snows will come and the first thin sheet of ice will cover the lake.

The trans Alaska pipeline will cross this lake about thirty feet from the near shore.

Maro and I sat down at a circular table next to a forest.

True it was enclosed by glass and only contained eight trees, but with the exception of a single spruce planted as a gag near Deadhorse Airport, the next forest was 200 miles away, south of the Brooks Range. The terrarium even had a bed of tundra and blueberry bushes, with the highest spruce climbing out of sight toward a distant skylight, and had been built by a nursery in Anchorage.

The other walls of the room were painted with bright bold designs in brilliant colors, presumably to stimulate the workers to better things, and to counteract the black and white environment outside during the three months when the sun fails to surmount the southern horizon. We were joined by Phyllis, a business-like brunette, who it turned out, was the center's accountant.

The dining area was filling up with freshly washed men, just in from their twelve-hour day at one of BP's drilling sites about five miles northwest. Two joined our table, one English and one American. The conversation, as I have also discovered in a similar situation, ended up on a point of language. A very correct looking gentleman with a small gray goatee and a silk cravat sat down next to me. I thought my concept of oil men was completely shattered, but he turned out to be an English artist, living in Italy, who was transferring the man-made delights of Prudhoe Bay to canvas.

I took my coffee to the lounge, furnished in modern Italian. The men sitting around with magazines and papers had the bored look of passengers on the tenth day of an ocean cruise, who would give anything to be in the next port. Outside the day had faded to twilight. Thick fog had moved in off the Arctic Ocean, isolating the center from the world. A ship adrift in a swirling Arctic cloud.

It struck me that BP had accomplished a difficult feat. By mixing men and women and providing them with a comfortable environment, they had normalized the extremely difficult Prudhoe Bay work as much as possible. Whether it was the British way of live and let live or a careful hiring program I don't know, but the atmosphere at BP was considerably more amicable than that at other camps I had heard about. Early in the project, women who had managed to assert their rights and get jobs elsewhere were given menial tasks and treated rudely. But these attitudes changed as more women came to work in the Arctic during the pipeline building. Women now number about 1000 out of the 16,000-strong work force.

'Volley ball?' Maro had arrived. 'Swim? Sauna? Movie? I think it's *The Italian Job*. I've seen it twice.'

'No thanks. Anything to drink?'

'Sure. Coffee, tea, milk, orange juice. Twenty-one of them.' Maro's soft Texas accent blended the drinks together.

'Yeah. 21. What time are you going to wake me up in the morning?'

'Everybody else starts at 6, but I'll meet you for breakfast at eight. You look like you need the sleep.'

'You're lovely.'

Before I went to my single room I stopped by the control center, a room full of radios and computers, to see if perchance the Muzak tape was nearing its end. No luck. The operator had just put on a new one and it was a foot in diameter.

Prudhoe

'Goes all the time,' she said.

The thinning fog fed streamers through the steel framework of the rig lying on its side on Pad N. A towering crane pointed to a dim sun trying to burn through the gray clammy mass. It felt cold in the breeze but probably was about 35° above. Around the prostrate rig were about fifteen hard-hatted men in grimy overalls, busily dismembering it. Exposed by the removal of the rig was a small Christmas tree on top of a pipe in a hole in the gravel pad. The well itself.

About six wells are drilled directionally from each pad, totalling initially about 120 production wells for the 45 mile by 20 mile Prudhoe field. The area covered by the wells, in the producing zone 10,000 feet below the pad, is about two miles by three. From the Christmas tree, flow-lines will carry the oil/gas/water mixture forced up the well by gas pressure on the oil reservoir (no pumps are needed) to flow stations. Here the fluid from the well is separated into gas, water and crude oil. The gas is compressed and reinjected back into the Prudhoe oil pool. Environmental restrictions prohibit flaring, and it will be several years before a pipeline will be built to carry it south. The crude oil is then fed to Alyeska's origin station just down the road from BP's center. From there it's $4\frac{1}{2}$ days to Valdez.

There was a struggle going on in one corner of the prone rig. Three oil-splattered men pulled for all they were worth on a long iron bar, the end of which slowly pried up a steel beam that had pinched a cable.

'Pull, goddam it,' yelled a bespectacled man who wasn't pulling himself.

The cable came out.

'Whew. Oh, look fellas, we're famous again. Do you want us to smile or look busy?'

'Just continue what you are doing. Don't mind me. I'll just click away.' I tried to be inconspicuous.

'You aren't going to make us pry up that beam again, are you? Damn cold isn't it.'

I was freezing in the northeast wind. 'Yes. Must be worse in the winter,' I added stupidly.

'Yeah. Pretty miserable. They always find oil in the assholes of the world.'

'Oh, it isn't so bad, Jim, remember yesterday we saw all those caribou?' one of the others broke in, apparently a misplaced environmentalist.

'He's new here, just up from California. He'll get tired of looking at caribou quick enough.'

A cable from the crane descended through the rig.

'Let's get this thing moved.' I was in the way.

On the way back to Deadhorse Airport Maro took me to ARCO's rig near the port. It was nearly on the beach, drilling out under the Arctic Ocean. The sea looked like lead as it reflected the gray blanket of stratus clouds that had come in on the biting northeast wind. This rig, at least, was vertical. The lower part was closed in against the wind that in the winter blows for days at 30 mph with temperatures of 25 below zero F, though it can be much colder.

A general murmur and the hum of machinery at work issued from the shrouded rig, but as I wandered among the piles of pipe and stacked bags of drilling mud, I could see no one.

179

So technological man had crossed Alaska to the edge of the polar sea. The rig's dark shape thrust above the horizontal landscape in virile defiance of the vast empty sea and tundra that spread limitlessly in all directions.

As I reached Maro's pickup I turned to look back at the rig, but it was gone. A fog had swept in from the Arctic Ocean and had obliterated the alien shape.

Chapter 18

The Tightening Sophistication

'. . . things have changed and they just ain't gonna go back to how they were.'
Arrested Fairbanks gambler, July, 1975

ANCHORAGE
By July 1, 1975 the population of Anchorage had grown to 175,700, double the number of five years earlier. Between 1974 and 1975 hospital admissions were up 79 per cent, psychiatric hospital admissions were up 30 per cent, traffic accidents were up 23 per cent, rape arrests were up 20 per cent, those for murder and hard drugs up 60 per cent and 625 per cent. By 1975 there was just under one car for every person in Anchorage. A rescue center was set up for those forced to leave their homes when they were unable to pay the rent.

A member of the Anchorage Chamber of Commerce, quoted in an Alyeska publication: 'We've got big city problems we never used to have. We're choked. I raised three kids here and we used to go everywhere . . . now there are 20 guys at every one of our fishing holes.'

Down in Juneau Alaska's new governor, Jay Hammond, elected on a controlled growth platform by a majority of a few hundred, seemed discouraged: 'We're programmed along certain inexorable courses . . . we're going to have growth and the impact of that growth, no matter what we do. The idea is to channel that growth and learn from it. It may be a lesser of evils . . . not making things better, but keeping them from being as bad as they might be.'

The cars and campers in the right lane climb a hill on a road east out of Anchorage on a warm summer Friday afternoon, and the great escape is on. They are headed for the road to Palmer, and from that Matanuska Valley town they will branch off either to the Susitna Valley, Talkeetna and the road to Fairbanks, or to the Copper River Basin. Most of the people in the cars are seeking the wilderness, some of which is visible in the hills just above them, of the hoped-for quiet of their weekend cabin on a lake far from the thundering horde. With this many people after the same thing, along the same limited road system, it is doubtful whether they will find what they are looking for. I suspect that in their minds they have already compromised. Caught in such a line of cars, it is hard to think of wilderness solitude, and they have probably resigned themselves to sharing their lake with others. Back in the early 60s a friend of mine built a cabin on a lake near Willow. There were no others there, and the road was almost impassable when it rained. Now the road is paved, the ring of cabins around the lake is complete, and outboards whine long into the late summer nights. My friend could always move farther out, but would he maintain his new-found solitude for long? Looking at this line of cars, I would say no.

FAIRBANKS

In Fairbanks it was worse. There prostitution was up 5000 per cent in 1975 over 1974, rape up 130 per cent, robberies up 160 per cent, assaults on the depleted Fairbanks police up 500 per cent, drug offenses up 171 per cent.

About 30,000 new people came to Alaska in 1975, 13,000 of them to Fairbanks and the north to work on the pipeline, a 23 per cent increase in the area's population in just one year. Of these people 31 per cent came without jobs and 58 per cent came with their wives, most of whom were of childbearing age. The strain on local facilities would be severe.

The pipeline was dragging people apart, away from old jobs and from families. There have been numerous cases of both parents taking off for the high wages to be made on the pipeline, leaving small children to fend for themselves in inadequate housing in Fairbanks. The parents can be gone for weeks, and the children are thrust on the strained welfare agencies of the city.

In spite of the fact that the Fairbanks Police Department was seriously depleted by men leaving for the high wages in pipeline security jobs, four times the number of prostitution arrests were made in 1975 over 1974. It was said that any man walking down 2nd Avenue would be asked, 'Wanna party?' This turned out to be an exaggeration. I wasn't. One hooker from Seattle, after five months in Fairbanks, was taking in 700 dollars a night. 'I'm doing fucking good!' she said with a good choice of words, 'At least I'm keeping them away from the little girls. What do you think the rape figures would look like if I wasn't on the job?'

Out at the airport TV crews arrived from all over the world like vultures descending on a kill. They were soon out the door, cameras and boom mikes at the ready, Alyeska passes pinned to their leather jackets. They floated up and down the pipeline ready to stick a lens in the face of the first minority worker they saw.

The airport lobby at Fairbanks has always seen a rich mixture of people. Situated on the edge of a vast land, the last airport on the end of the road, it attracts a cross section of Alaskans. Native girls with long straight black hair and tinted wire frame glasses, and their men, thumbs in tight jean pockets, aggressive new youths enjoying their new-found power. Hippies or people just in from the bush, which two types are frequently undistinguishable, with their packs and Blazo boxes and broken starter motors. Business men and politicians with suits and Samsonite brief cases, greeting each other with manufactured smiles and hale fellow handshakes. Through this mixture float the tourists like summering birds or the pure WASPS they probably are. The women with blue-white hair and sequined glasses, the men in checkered trousers and white shoes, with matching luggage bearing tour labels. They view Fairbanks as a present-day wild west town, a real one, almost as good as the one back at Disneyland. Thrown into the lobby like misplaced bears are the hard-hatted Boomers on their way to the pipeline camps.

The week before I was there a pipeliner hit the girl behind the Wien Air Alaska counter, knocking her to the floor. He didn't like the fact that she couldn't get him on the next flight to Dallas. Another time a riot occurred on a flight to Deadhorse Airport when the maximum of two drinks was imposed by the cabin staff. The

The Tightening Sophistication

Boomers tore up the seats and pushed the staff around the airplane, injuring some of them.

The dime clicked into the pay telephone near the Alyeska counter. 'I got the job mom!' The slim girl with curly red hair, faded jeans and a tank top spoke excitedly into the mouthpiece on the long-distance line. 'I'll be gone to Coldfoot Camp nine weeks and I think I'll be driving a bus. What? Oh, about eleven fifty an hour. I'll send some money home as soon as I can. Bye.' She hurried out to board the Alaska Airlines milkrun flight up to the pipeline camps.

A cop in a getup that made him look like one of Custer's men who had been too fat to leave the scene, strolled up and down the lobby kicking the feet of the long hairs sleeping on the floor. Two women, one with a micro-skirt and fishnet stockings, the other with a skirt just dense enough to blur the design on her underpants, both carrying white cosmetic cases, were getting their tickets at the Alyeska counter. They were headed for Old Man Camp.

A girl with black hair that hung to her breasts came up to me proffering a cantaloupe wrapped in a soggy copy of the *Fairbanks News-Miner*. 'We can't finish it. Would you like some?'

Downtown at the Union Hall men were filling out forms. It has been said that a few thousand in the right pocket speeds up the forms and helps them get to the right place. Sometimes this is the only way a Hoper—a newcomer looking for pipeline work—can get on the golden pipeline payroll. As the pipeline project progressed, bringing with it the certain promise of an enormous capital outlay for both equipment and wages, the Teamsters Union moved into Alaska in force. This maverick but powerful union, with a dim record of labor relations in the Lower 48, had been an influence upon the Alaska state government for several years; but now, with control of nearly all the pipeline jobs, they threatened to take over. Governor Hammond, quoted in the London *Guardian* of November 27, 1975, alleged that it 'was a matter of urgency to determine who runs the state—the elected government or the Teamsters Union.' The Big Time Operators have arrived in the North.

The project is so big, that large contractors are treated like 'the government' and are ripped off with impunity. Featherbedding is common. Frequently workers spend their highly paid hours sleeping in the shuttle buses, or selling off project material to friends in return for large amounts of money or grass. Powerful unions like the welders wield their weight with ease and demand special treatment. Jesse Carr, the top man in the Teamsters, has the power to shut down all of Alaska through his control of the transportation industry. Alaska's miniscule law enforcement agencies, with only a hundred uniformed troopers to look after the whole state, are further hamstrung by the reluctance of officials to act in the face of strong union threats.

Near the center of Fairbanks, on the edge of a gravel pit lake, screened from the bursting town by a forest of spruce, a group of Alaskans, young and old, had taken off their clothes. Some swam, some drank wine, some smoked the just legalized pot (Alaska and Nepal are the only two places in the world where the possession of marijuana is legal), but most just rested in the warm sun.

Charles Parr's platform. (From a leaflet he gave me at the Alaska State Fair, in Fairbanks, August, 1974.)

'No one in his right mind would live in a place that has 60 below weather, floods and earthquakes, unless it offered something he couldn't find elsewhere. You and I have found it and that's why we're here.
'As your representative in Juneau, my top priority job will be to see that Alaska remains Alaska and that the Great Land remains great.
'Your vote and support will be appreciated.'

A native girl pauses for a cigarette in front of a Fairbanks store.

The Tightening Sophistication

ALYESKA PIPELINE

The first length of pipe on the line was laid ceremoniously in the bed of the Tonsina River on March 27, 1975—for some strange reason, on the eleventh anniversary of the earthquake. To the surprise of the throng of invited onlookers, it rose from the muck like a thing from the dead and had to be forced back into its grave again. The pipeline was on its way. By the end of the summer work was virtually completed on the work pad of gravel almost 800 miles long that paralleled the new road from Fairbanks to the Arctic, and also on the Richardson Highway south to Valdez, which carved a new swath through the wilderness. The 18 work camps were completed and by June were housing over 20,000 workers. At Fairbanks and Valdez 75,000 40-foot lengths of pipe were welded into 80-foot lengths and trundled over the road system to staging areas along the pipeline route. As a result, the State of Alaska was forced to ask 300 million dollars from the Federal government to repair damage to Alaska's highways caused by the Alyeska trucks. Average loading on the roads increased from 4000 tons in 1973 to 32,000 tons in 1975.

Dick Nilsen, whom I met over a Budwieser in the Fairbanks Airport bar where he was about to board a flight to Seattle to visit his parents, told me about his life at Coldfoot Camp. Like many, he has a girlfriend; they both work 12-hour days, but her room mate works nights. 'A damn good arrangement' he commented. Then he told me the story about the 50 cases of beer that someone brought in on his own air-craft, in spite of the Alyeska prohibition against liquor. The 50 cases disappeared in two and a half hours down by the river in a party joined by workers from up and down the line. He told me the fishing is good there too, as long as either the Alyeska manage-ment weren't watching or the state surveillance people weren't around. Alyeska has since tried to clamp down on the booze by checking luggage. Dick said to me, 'They'll be building pipelines up here for 15 years. You watch, when this one is finished we'll be working on another.'

When the pipeline was approved, rigid stipulations were set up for protecting the environment. Enforcement of these regulations, which came about under national environmental legislation, is in the hands of state and federal monitors. These moni-tors are few, the project is big, and it has been declared in the national interest—or to bring out that tired horse, the national defence interest—to finish it as soon as possible. This would, of course, bring profits to Alyeska sooner, which fact is not incidental. But the men and women designated to catch Alyeska at it have their hands tied by their own fear for their jobs. Too much compliance with these stipula-tions would delay the project. Thousands of gallons of oil have been spilt along the pipeline route. Sewage has gone untreated into the tundra. Cat drivers have dug up tundra unnecessarily. Revegetation and erosion control have not been started. Alyeska subcontractors state that 'environmental stipulations are a nuisance and of low priority in contrast to construction goals.' A representative of the Alaska Department of Environmental Conservation noted that sewage treatment at Galbraith Camp was inadequate. He was fired.

189

A helicopter under charter to Alyeska heads across the Chugach Mountains near Valdez, toward Sheep Creek Camp at mile 776 on the pipeline route. Valdez is ringed with mountains such as these—they are not high, only about 8000 feet, but because of high snowfall they retain snowfields and spawn glaciers. Most of this Japanese pipe is gone now, buried beneath the tundra of the first section of the pipeline, between Valdez and Gulkana in the Copper River Basin. This 48-inch pipe, stacked in these piles since 1969, was cleaned of rust, welded into 80-foot sections and trundled on the backs of huge trucks to the pipeline sites. Alyeska had two other stockpiles, one at Fairbanks, which received its pipe via the Alaska Railroad, and one at Prudhoe Bay to which pipe was barged.

'Man always kills the thing he loves, and so we pioneers have killed the wilderness.'

Aldo Leopold

The fireweed clock stands at late August.

A land of little sun
And too much
A land of little snow
And too much
Look! A man has walked here
He left his footprints in the snow

A land of few people
And too many
For a man has come
He claims the land
See! He has cut it with roads
And houses grow in place of trees

What of this wilderness
And its moods?
This land of great warmth
And then none?
Now! We need its vast space
So our captive spirits can fly free

What of this place
With its beauty
And sense of lost time?
It existed
Once. A man has walked here
He left his footprints in the snow

GAMBELL AND ARCTIC VILLAGE

At the time of the Native Claims Settlement Act in 1971, there were nineteen Indian and Eskimo villages on reservations. These were given the option of retaining their land or taking less land and the difference in money. The Eskimos of Gambell and the Indians of Arctic Village took the land. They wanted to protect their subsistence life style as long as possible. Gambell with the neighboring village of Savoonga were given back St Lawrence Island's 1.2 million acres. Arctic Village with Venetie, farther south along the Chandalar River, were allowed to consider as theirs the 1.8 million acres of trees, lakes and rivers around the two villages. Unfortunately, it is difficult to schedule meetings between the villages, or to iron out differences on how the land should be used, because the Arctic Village corporation president is away at work on the pipeline most of the time.

Through breaks in the clouds I could just make out the shoreline of the Arctic Ocean. A gentle surf broke along the gravel beach, the gray surface of the water levelled by pancakes of ice that thickened into a solid mass to the north. Inland, openings in the stratus deck revealed a landscape of green in which were set a hundred lakes. A strong northwesterly wind drove froth from the surface of the lakes onto their eastern shores, ringing them with a necklace of foam. But this Arctic tundra east of Prudhoe was already scarred. Seismic crews had scratched its surface with a score of lines; Cat drivers connected the lines with roads that had become melted trenches in the tundra. The lower Sagavanirktok River had been turned into a giant gravel pit that had supplied Prudhoe with tons of gravel for its roads and drilling pads. Thousands of rusting oil barrels lined the beach and the lower deltas of the rivers that emptied into the Arctic Ocean. To the west of us now, welders' electric blue arcs connected the first sections of the pipeline that began south from Pump Station 1 at Prudhoe, and would follow the new gravel pad to Valdez. ARCO and BP were drilling more and more development wells into the Prudhoe basin. Offshore, a new well rose on its island out of the ice floes. Ahead of us, on Flaxman Island, Exxon was drilling a well into a new basin, the northern flank of a string of wells that overlooked the Arctic National Wildlife Range from the west bank of the Canning River. West of Prudhoe lay Naval Petroleum Reserve Number 4, ranging 275 miles from the Colville River to Point Lay. This 22 million acre area of potential oil bearing land was set aside in the '20s by President Harding, as a reserve for national defence. It was soon to be transferred to the Department of the Interior for increased exploration and development. For five hundred miles, from the Canning River to the Chukchi Sea, Alaska's Arctic was under attack.

August 1975, and again I was squeezed into the comfortably confined cabin of Lee's Super Cub, headed east from Deadhorse Airport. Deadhorse, the only airport in the world where the only service provided is not a coffee shop, or a gift shop, but a bank. We crossed the delta of the Kavik River; the clear water pushed deeply into a tundra bank and, released, spread itself over a bed of gravel. It was too early for char to be seen in the pools, and they were empty of fish. The lower Sagavanirktok had been cleared of fish the previous winter when the men at Prudhoe, using the delta for their water supply, emptied the pools of water that remained under the winter ice, killing the fish that were in them.

Lee climbed to 4000 feet to top higher swirls of the stratus. To the right the summer dark ridges of the Brooks Range rose out of the sea of clouds. We were to fly into the eastern corner of the range, into the remote valley of the Coleen River and there I hoped to find caribou. The life cycle of the Porcupine herd, the fourth largest in the world with 140,000 animals, revolves around this area of northeastern Alaska east of the pipeline corridor. The caribou had calved in early July this year along the coast that now appeared less frequently through the thickening cloud deck. With their new calves, the animals had migrated eastward into the Yukon where they crossed the British Mountains south to the Old Crow Flats. Now they should be coming back, to winter among the trees of the Porcupine flats.

I was to photograph them as part of a research project. But I was under no illusions as to the purpose of the project. The herd was being studied by consultants for Arctic Gas Pipeline Company, as part of the environmental research for their proposed pipeline across the northern part of the Wildlife Range. My pictures would hopefully be used to gain more information about the herd, which information in turn would be used to plan a pipeline that might affect them less. The decision to undertake this work was an extremely difficult one for me to make.

I have always felt that people with a love of the wilderness should be part of these projects, otherwise the work will be left to those who don't care or don't know. If I can see no way to keep the pipeliners out, and with market pressures pushing up demand for their products daily, I see no way at the moment, I want to be there when they come. I at least want to watch over the wilderness as closely as I can, and if possible contribute to the preservation of as much of it as possible. I wanted no new pipelines in the Arctic, but I knew they would be built. By providing pictures for the Arctic Gas project, I would be supporting a reality I resented. I searched the pipeline alternatives.

El Paso Company would like to run a pipeline south along the Alyeska corridor to a gas liquification plant near Valdez. This route would infest Alaska with another three-year construction project, would further destroy the lifestyle of the main population of the state, would burden the seas with a new fleet of liquified gas tankers, would waste gas in the liquification process, and would desecrate another beautiful wilderness of forest and fjord between Valdez and Gravina Point where the liquification plant would be located. A variation of this route would take the line to Fairbanks and then down the Alaska Highway to the Canadian pipeline network in Alberta. This line would not cross the Arctic Wildlife Range, and is the route most favoured by conservation groups. In May 1976 the Northwest Energy Company submitted a proposal for the Alaska Highway route to the Federal Power Commission, the agency responsible for assigning the permit to build the pipeline, thus making that route a third alternative. Either route would entail two major disadvantages. It would inflict a great social burden of workers and their families on the resources of Interior Alaska, and the presence of natural gas in the Interior would encourage industrial complexes to be developed to use that gas, thus making the impact of the pipeline

195

construction permanent.

The Alyeska project has shown the human devastation that a construction effort of this scale can bring to a small community such as Fairbanks. Today the campers with South 48 licence plates overflow campgrounds, as the Hopers and Boomers, who have fled the recession in the south, flood in for jobs on the pipeline. The pipeline corridor howls through the white nights of summer as men and women work hard for their thousand a week. This new money, three million dollars a week, is pouring into Alaska, turning her into an inflationary cauldron. After the money have come the con men, the hookers and the greedy, eager for fall out. Doors are locked where they weren't before; people are thrown out of homes they can no longer afford to rent; stores run out of items bought out by Alyeska, or shipped to the more profitable pipeline contractors; crowds jam food stores to buy inflated necessities. The golden benefits to the state of a pipeline through its middle are difficult to find, for Alaska, at the height of the construction effort, has the highest rate of increase in crime, unemployment and inflation anywhere in America.

Like most conservationists, my reasons for preserving the wilderness are not totally altruistic. It is not so much for future generations that I am concerned, but my own. I have always used the wilderness for my own ends, be they spirit or sport, and therefore resent any intrusion into 'my' domain. It is fortunate that conservationist use of the wilderness leaves it virtually intact. When industry comes the areas are changed forever. Most conservationists would not even use the land if they thought their use would cause it irreparable harm.

The amorphous masses in the south, through their high consumption of fuel, and the market pressure they have put on profit-making oil companies, are encouraging them to bring this gas out of the Arctic. The gas company is thus threatening the territory of the conservationists, the Arctic Wildlife Range. But the pipeline will go somewhere, and in 1975, there were only two real possibilities: the Arctic Gas route, or the El Paso route. Of the two, I felt at the time that the Arctic Gas line would have the least impact on Alaska *as a whole*, especially if it was located within a few miles of the Arctic coast. Now, with the Alaska Highway route a sponsored alternative, the situation is more complex. It is true that this line avoids the Wildlife Range, but it could be more expensive to build, it would affect the country along the Alaska Highway, country seen by thousands of tourists, and it would have the social disadvantages of the El Paso route that I have already mentioned. The decision for conservationists is between saving the northern strip of the Wildlife Range and the adjacent Canadian coast for the few and the future, or to try to keep industry and its associated multitudes of people away from Interior Alaska as long as possible. It is a decision that the Federal Power Commission has spent over a year of hearings and many-volumned reports trying to make, and with the introduction of the Alaska Highway proposal it will probably take another year to reach its final conclusions, that is if Congress doesn't intervene. My emotional gut feeling in the matter is simple: keep the line out of the wilderness, keep what space we have left. I realize that this opinion is selfish, narrow-minded and preservationist. As I said, it is a gut feeling. But if we conservationists want to keep pipeliners out of our territories completely, we

At any time only two or three of these rigs cut the Prudhoe Bay horizon. This one, belonging to Atlantic Richfield, is on the shore of the Arctic Ocean, drilling direction-ally under the sea. When the well has been drilled it is capped off with a 'christmas tree', a system of valves, and the rig is dismantled and moved to a new location. The month is September and the geese are beginning their migration to the south. Within the month this lake will be frozen, and a thin layer of snow will lie over the tundra. The lake will not thaw until June.

will have to convince the people of America to consume less fuel. There is no other way to keep our land intact, either for ourselves, or for future generations.

With extensive exploratory drilling taking place all along the Arctic coast, there will be pressure for more oil pipelines to bring the oil out of the area. Already there are resolutions in Congress to build an oil pipeline parallel to the Arctic Gas route. This would have a serious detrimental effect on the Arctic coast of the Wildlife Range. But the possibility of this line is another question, and one that has other answers. One solution would be to bring the oil down an increased capacity Alyeska route, using the existing oil delivery system.

So I was reluctantly working on a project that could take away more of my beloved wilderness. To stay away would mean a lack of involvement in the future of Alaska, a place that had been an important part of my life. That I couldn't do. The battle was joined; I wanted to be in the front lines.

Lee throttled back and we began our descent to Kaktovik, the Eskimo village on Barter Island about 125 miles east of Prudhoe Bay. There we would refuel and spend the night. The stratus below gradually thinned and more of the flat tundra was revealed. The rivers that drain the north slopes of the Brooks Range fan out into channeled deltas that are frequently separated from the Arctic Ocean by gravel spits. The Canning delta, almost 20 miles wide, marked the beginning of the Arctic Wildlife Range, and beyond that the ice-filled arc of Camden Bay led to Barter Island. Already the hundred-foot-high dish antennae of the DEW-line station were visible, their black shapes dominating the landscape as they stared south toward the Brooks Range. This station, one of a string across Alaska, Canada and Greenland, was built during the '50s as part of a defence network against Russian attack over the pole. The two hundred Eskimos at Kaktovik shared the island with about eighty RCA technicians who now manned the gray complex of dreary buildings capped by white golf balls of radomes. We flew over the town. It had the appearance of a place levelled by a typhoon, and from the air seemed to consist of all the old packing crates from the DEW-line site arranged into a village. This observation turned out to be nearly correct.

The Super Cub's fat rough-country wheels bit into the gravel of the airstrip which occupied most of a spit that jutted out from the village site. In fact, the airstrip *had* been the village site until the U.S. Navy, during the construction of the DEW-line station, had told the Eskimos to move. Surprisingly, they had done so without protest. Nowadays Alaskan natives don't allow themselves to be pushed around so easily. The village is now suing the U.S. Government for moving them illegally in the first place. I left Lee to check over the Cub and walked toward the village.

A sudden summer storm of rain and snow swept in on northwest winds across the green junk-splattered grass, and I bent my head against the stinging snow pellets. Between the looming warehouses of the DEW-line site and the ramshackle town was a group of graves, their crosses weathered white by a thousand Arctic gales. Around the graves were the oil barrels of the new culture, stacked to a man's height, blotting out contact with the village.

I looked up from the blurred names on the crosses but saw only gray in all directions.

198

The Tightening Sophistication

A fog bank had moved in on the strengthening gale from the Arctic Ocean. Cold, clammy and fast moving, it had come in like a creature and had taken the sky. I turned my back on the wind and walked into the village.

In spite of the weather, the street of gravel was full of people this August evening. Children in thin canvas shoes and with gloveless hands made scrap wood bridges over puddles, an old couple with oval fur ruffs outlining their weathered faces strolled along on an evening visit to friends. A three-wheeled Honda with fat balloon tires, festooned with a teenage driver and four kids, emerged from the gloom and sped along the road toward the airport. Within a few minutes they were back again and a new load was taken for a ride, this time along the road to the dump. These were two of the three available roads; the other, also about 2 miles long, led to the lake in the center of the island that was the village water supply.

Houses were made mostly from the leavings of those who built the DEW-line station. Old packing cases, flattened barrels and sheets of plastic formed buildings that fitted the tundra so closely that they seemed to grow from it. The government-supplied post office, in contrast, turned out to be a blue and white mobile structure of aluminum, complete with zip code in bold letters on its side. In a collection of out-of-place-looking ranch-style houses I found Lee, hands jammed into pockets and back to the icy wind, talking to an Eskimo. Apparently the houses were part of a long term and hesitant rehousing project for Kaktovik.

'Meet Archie, Jon. He's invited us around to his house for the night. We'll try the Coleen tomorrow, if this stuff lifts.'

Archie, who seemed to be about forty, though it was difficult to see behind the blowing ruff of his parka, led the way back through the streets lined with water and honey barrels, which illustrated both ends of a physiological process side by side. The inside of his patched-together house was warm and we were soon out of our parkas; Archie was down to a T-shirt.

On a cot by a window was a man of about twenty, fast asleep, and we were soon joined by Archie's ten-year-old daughter, just up from a nap, who tried to focus on the new arrivals with half-opened eyes. She joined her father on an overstuffed sofa and we dragged straight chairs across the checkered linoleum floor. The fellow on the cot never stirred and Archie never referred to him. A transistor radio on the kitchen table, set among a half-used loaf of white bread and a plastic cup of margarine, was tuned to a station in Inuvik, a village on the lower Mackenzie in Canada.

Archie Brower had lived in Kaktovik since 1939 and came from the extensive Brower family whose descendents populate villages all along the Arctic coast. As Land Chief for the Kaktovik area he was aware of the potential threat of a pipeline near the village. He pushed his horn-rimmed glasses up his nose with his index finger and rubbed a two-day growth of beard on his high-boned cheeks. His right hand rested on the shoulder of his daughter, and its nicotine-stained fingers supported another in the chain of cigarettes he smoked. He seemed to want to talk about pipelines.

'We need the gas in the village, but I'm worried about what the barges will do to the fishing. And the money will take all the men from the village and maybe they won't

199

come back. We have already lost a family to Alyeska.' He didn't smile. He had been through a cultural change in the '50s, when the military brought in a cash economy to replace the subsistence economy based on hunting and fishing. He could see that the pipeline might finish the process. 'And then there's the liquor. Almost none here now, but the village will have to make new laws if they bring that line through here.'

But the Eskimos of Kaktovik are now dependent on their space heaters for warmth in the long Arctic winters. Long gone are the days when seal oil warmed their sod huts. They, too, are now part of the petroleum-consuming American way of life.

'But we could sure use that gas', Archie went on, 'have to depend on the Air Force barge now, and last time all they brought us was jet fuel. That's what we're burning now. Dangerous stuff.' I moved my chair away from the space heater which had taken to making strange burping noises.

Later, braving the storm of rain and snow, we followed Archie to the village meeting place, a Quonset set up next to the post office. The building was crowded with half the village, about a hundred men, women and children. Propped on red-seated folding chairs set up in a sea of used Coke cans, the villagers were dressed for outdoors. The space heater didn't work and the place was freezing. Apparently the jet fuel had gummed up the heater works.

I sat down next to the postmaster, later to be elected mayor, Marx Sims, a white man who after working several years at the DEW-line station, married a local Eskimo girl and settled in the village. Now he is fully integrated into village life and is also the airline agent, and a school board member. He seemed happy if harried by his responsibilities, and had taken up the Eskimo habit of chain smoking.

On my right was Fenton Rexford, the Eskimo mayor of Kaktovik, who at 27 seemed young for the job. He was dressed in flare jeans and open shirt under his fur ruffed parka, and I felt he was slightly uncomfortable in his position among the elders of the village. He was the spokesman of the young in Kaktovik and tended to use words like 'fundswise'.

Fenton expressed the feeling, I gathered mainly that of the young, that industrial development would come to the Arctic and that it was in their interest to get out of it what they could. The old would rather leave things as they are, without new industry and pipelines, and leave Kaktovik alone in its isolation. But even they realize the need to support the village with cash, now that the old ways are gone.

I asked about hunting and fishing. Marx replied that snowmobile hunts in the winter brought in caribou (there was only one dog team left in the village and it was kept for sporting events) and seal hunting was good out on the ice. But his sale of frozen chickens, flown in from Fairbanks, didn't fall off when hunting time came. Eskimo tastes had changed.

Our conversation was interrupted when Fenton, after a few remarks to the group, pushed a tape cassette into the recorder and a color TV screen lit up with a film about Abraham Lincoln. This was followed by one on Arctic wildlife, of all things, showing the animals the villagers still hunt. It was supplied by the U.S. Government and I felt it was an insult to the Eskimos.

As we walked out into the seemingly endless storm, I told Fenton that I was going to try to take pictures of caribou. Fenton was indignant. 'Why do you people spend so much time on the animals? How about us? We live here too!'

It was midnight before we spread our sleeping bags out on the floor of Archie's house. Before I climbed in I took a last look out the window, but there was no change. The gray fog swirled through the village though the sky was still light. The sun stays above the horizon 24 hours a day for 72 days each summer in Kaktovik. As I lay in my sleeping bag I looked around the room. The walls were lined with dozens of photographs of Archie's relatives and friends, people scattered along hundreds of miles of windswept Arctic coastline. His orientation was to people, not things. Kaktovik to him was not the shacks or the weather, but the people that lived in it, and they made the place his home. His ancestors came from Greenland and migrated westward across the Canadian archipelago, hunting both land and sea animals, and reached Alaska centuries ago.

'Hell, let's go anyway,' said Lee peering through the fogged window next morning, 'It could be like this for days.'

In a take off roll of a hundred feet we were up, then Lee levelled out a hundred feet off the ground, just below the cloud base, and we made a sweeping turn out to sea. The snow and rain splattered against the windshield as we climbed over the ice-covered water. We rounded the edge of the low cloud that hung along the shore and turned inland again, toward the mountains. I didn't like the way this flight was beginning. The weather seemed to carry a vengeance, an Arctic whip that rocked the little Cub from cloud to cloud.

After half an hour we were between layers and our glimpses of the ground had ended. 'We'll have to go back and try it on the deck. We could get into ice up here.' Lee looked over his shoulder, his eyes glinting under his broad-brimmed hat. In another half hour we were back over the coast, dropping through a small hole in the cloud. In a moment we were skimming the tundra at a hundred feet, airspeed 65 knots, headed for the mouth of the Aichillik, a river that drains the peaks in the eastern Brooks Range.

Neither of us said much. This was going to be a difficult flight and until it was over the concentration of flying would occupy Lee fully. I spread the map on my lap and tried to be useful. 'I think we just crossed the Jago, and if we follow the fork to the left that will be the Okerokovik.' I offered. But following anything was becoming impossible. We were down to 50 feet over the gravel bed of the river; ahead the cloud seemed to merge with the ground. Lee put down some flaps and we slowed to 38 knots.

'What's the stalling speed of this thing?' I imagined us shuddering into the rushing water of the river.

The answer was brief: '28 knots.' Lee didn't have time for explanations. Suddenly, from out of the fog, the river banks closed in from both sides and we were in a narrow canyon.

'Fuck, this ain't no good!' Lee put the Cub into a tight bank, which at that airspeed and altitude was a tricky thing to do. But he is a good pilot, and we flew back down the river.

201

Hidden in a group of willows, I watch the migration pass around me; the endless click of hoofs, the snorts, the shuffle over the stones of the tundra covered hill. In threes and twos, sometimes a single bull, the passage never stops. The caribou sense my presence, vary their path slightly, and continue. The sun settles toward the distant peaks of the Brooks Range, and its orange light outlines the velvet of the caribou antlers and the hair along their backs, and streams across the red and yellow bearberry and dwarf willow that hug the ground. Ahead, down a trail worn deep by the animals that have gone before, lies the valley of the Coleen. For these three the river itself will be crossed at night.

The situation was becoming serious. I could see no way back to Kaktovik, as the rain and snow had brought the cloud to the ground behind us. We were trapped in the river bed. Lee flew as slowly as possible while we decided what to do. 'Look, over there! Isn't that a break?' I pointed to the right toward the Aichillik. The clouds seemed thinner, but the rising ground would take us higher into them. 'We'll try it.'

We left the river bed with a foot to spare over the willows along the bank. On the river we could have had a rough landing if the clouds had closed in, but now over this tussock-covered tundra, we couldn't, not without wrecking the airplane. The wheels were hanging less than 10 feet over the grass that was bent by a strong wind carrying us higher into the clouds. Then we were in them. Nothing. Zero. Lee made a gentle bank to the left and we groped our way among the tussocks. A pair of moose loomed out of the gloom, at our height, but disappeared again without even seeing us. Gradually the clouds thinned as we crested the rise between the two rivers and descended a winding creek that led down to the Aichilik. At the river we turned right and climbed to 40 feet, which seemed a great height.

As we approached the mountains the weather began to improve. The visibility ahead became several miles. We entered the mountains but were then hit by the strongest turbulence I had ever encountered. The tiny Cub, buffeted by gusts that lashed at its wings and struts, seemed to be about to fall apart. I was thrown from one side to the other against my seat belt, shoulders bruised against the sides of the cabin. In spite of all the flying I had done I was worried. The little fabric and frame airplane could only stand so much of this brutal treatment. 'Relax, Jon, it's a good airplane. Peanuts?' Suddenly the cabin was filled with a cloud of Spanish peanuts and their shells as Lee tried to hand them to me over his shoulder. 'Christ!' I cried, coughing up peanut shells.

We climbed higher as the clouds retreated above us. Slowly the turbulence died away, and ahead, through gaps in the mountains, I could make out patches of sun on the south slopes. We left the Aichillik behind and crossed the Kongakut. On its bank were two lakes, their surfaces blurred by the gale that still tore down the river valley from the high mountains. The divide was crested at 5000 feet past slopes on which were scattered the white dots of grazing Dall sheep.

The Cub buzzed into an ever clearer world; the clouds and rain of the North Slope were left behind. This was the Arctic too, but an Arctic of greater life. Below us appeared the first trees, white spruce, only 20 feet high after a century of growth, scattered along the braided stream of the upper Coleen. The mountain slopes were greener in an afternoon sun that made the showers lingering in the hills look like streams of gold.

I looked east toward the Yukon Territory, toward the direction from which the caribou would come, but saw only vacant hills. There seemed to be no animal life at all. The valleys and hillsides reposed quietly in the patterns of cloud and sun, devoid of animal movement. Perhaps we were too early, perhaps the migration was still in Canada. Or perhaps it had already passed. We lost height over the Coleen and then, on some overflow ice, Lee saw them. 'Look, down there.'

The white ice left by the freezes of the last winter was covered with the still shapes of caribou. There were at least five hundred of them, resting on the ice to escape the flies and mosquitoes. To the east I could make out more, perhaps thousands, as they streamed in long lines across the rocky hills and grassy slopes. The lines disappeared into the distant hills toward the Yukon. The caribou seemed to be coming from a limitless source, there were so many. The migration was at its peak, the centuries' old pilgrimage of the caribou had just begun to cross the Coleen.

'I'll put you on that hill over there,' said Lee pointing to a rounded bump, east of the Coleen at about 3000 feet, 1000 feet above the river. 'Where?' I was incredulous. It looked a good place to put a helicopter, but not an airplane. 'You can't land there!' 'Tighten your belt, I'll take a look.' Lee was not deterred by my frightened remark and he throttled back. We coasted almost silently toward the hill. It was a good place from which to observe the caribou, but I couldn't see anywhere to land. The tundra-covered hill-top, although reasonably smooth, fell away in all directions. No area more than fifty feet long was flat. Lee levelled out just over the hill and we drifted across, to check the wind. It was cross; we would have to land cross wind to get any length of run at all. I tightened my belt further and tried to swallow. The Super Cub climbed slightly and we came around for the landing. I had hoped the cross wind condition would have discouraged Lee, but he was determined. 'Here we go.'

We floated. The touch down was far along the crest of the hill. The wheels bumped into a dip on the edge of the slope that led down to the Coleen. But there they stopped as Lee's judicious use of the brakes prevented them from going over the edge. He carefully turned the plane around. The left wing pointed to the sky as the Lycoming roared the wheels out of the dip. But they wouldn't come. Lee tried again. I sat stone still, afraid that any movement would send us down the slope. Maximum throttle just pulled the wheels free and we were back on top of the hill.

Lee cut the engine and climbed out. I hauled my cameras and pack out and pulled them away from the Cub. 'I'll see you tomorrow afternoon down by the river. Leave your tent up so I can find you. I'm going to Arctic Village now. So long.' He settled himself back in the seat, started the engine and taxied to the edge of the hill. Lighter, he had no trouble in getting off and in a few minutes he was a speck against the mountains to the west. Then there was silence. I was alone.

Around me the mountains of the wilderness rippled for hundreds of miles in every direction. The streams, the tundra, the rock were untrammeled and unthreatened as far as I could see. Somewhere behind me were the bursting cities of Alaska, the hustling men and women in their corridors of noise welding together the steel snake. I had at last returned to the wilderness itself, that place of renewing life force that I needed. The silence and the space returned to pervade my mind and give it peace. I settled down on the lichen-covered tundra, soft and dry in the sun, and drank in the space around me. From below in a saddle came the sound of 'click, click, click'. A muted shuffling drifted up from the invisible gap in the hill. I crept to the edge. Moving through the gap were the caribou, hundreds of them. The clicking sound was made as their ankle bones hit each other. They crossed the pass and descended the slope towards the river, like pilgrims headed for a Mecca. Their heads always turned to the west, they never looked around or stopped to graze. The caribou ahead of them

205

had worn a new path over the mountain and they followed this. After a group passed, I picked up my camera and crawled down the slope toward some bushes on the edge of the gap.

I lay huddled in the willows and waited. Soon, over the skyline appeared two enormous antlers followed by a head. The eyes hesitated, looked, and then the giant bull edged around me. He was followed by another and another. And the migration was on again. One after another the caribou flowed around me, accompanied by the clicks and the shuffling of hoofs against tundra. The flow hardly stopped. I was part of a timeless stream of life that had passed over this hill for centuries, and the mere presence of a human wasn't going to alter the thrust of over a hundred thousand animals. I felt closer to the earth than I ever had been before. I was not only in the presence of the space and silence of the wilderness, but of its life as well. The picture was complete at last. The whole meaning of the Alaska wilderness was around me at that moment, and I could hardly bring my camera to my eye. My eyes wanted to absorb the experience at first hand, they wanted to drink in the primal force that manifested itself in the caribou and the space.

I lay on that hill for hours, immersed in a high of ecstasy. I hardly noticed the dip of the sun toward the black peaks of the Brooks Range to the northwest, but finally a cold wind from the high reaches of the Coleen forced me off the hill and down toward the valley. I followed the path dug in the tundra by the caribou that had passed only minutes before; their hoofs had worn a groove a foot deep. For a few minutes I became part of the pilgrimage as it rounded the hill and fed down to the flat tundra along the river. Below me caribou were scattered in their hundreds, waiting their turn to ford the rushing stream. Then, off to the right, I saw him, his tan coat glistening in the late sun.

The grizzly caught my scent and I froze. If he decided to come after me I couldn't possibly outrun him and there were no trees to climb. I hoped the scent of man would be unfamiliar to him and he would turn. Suddenly he rose on his hind legs and looked threatening, his nose wrinkled as he tried to assess the scent. Then he did, fell to all fours, and bounded away. I resumed my descent to the river, relieved.

I set up my tent in a flat area that I hoped would be suitable as a runway for Lee the next day. It was between the several channels of the Coleen and at the edge of the overflow ice. The migration continued across the ice. Animals coming down from the hill would ford the stream, accompanied by the hollow rolling of stones on the bottom, and then crunch over the melting ice. Late in the evening, with the sky a pale blue of twilight, and the deepening shadows of the valley heralding the first darkness of winter, I wandered out to a rock projecting from the center of the ice and sat there long past midnight. The caribou shuffled around the rock, unheeding of the additional figure on its top. The sky was beginning to lighten with a new day when I was finally chased back to the tent by cold and nervous exhaustion.

When I woke the caribou were gone. There were none to be seen in any direction. The ice was bare of the animals, only their tracks remained. I looked toward the hill, but the skyline was clean, no antlers cut its smooth shape. The migration had passed and it would be another year before this valley saw caribou again.

The Tightening Sophistication

The empty landscape around me glistened in the bright morning sun, silent except for the muffled flow of the river. Can we afford the luxury of a wilderness like this? I looked around, wondering.

We have built our society on a technological, material base. The aggressive frontier mentality that built the country from scratch never did give much truck to such unproductive pastimes as, for example, art. Art was a luxury for the rich or for Europeans. Americans were doers, they took the seemingly endless land and built things with it. Someday when the country was finished and running smoothly they could worry about its art. But today Americans find they have built themselves an energy consuming monster, and are trapped into providing for its fuel. The art will have to wait a little longer.

I think of the wilderness as a form of art. The canvas of mountains and valleys appeals to our sense of the aesthetic, the emotional, the organic. As a space, it is unnecessary in the technological functioning of American society. It is an art, like any, that appeals to a minority in society, an art that can be pushed aside when society needs its resources. It is an art form that a poor, unindustrialized society can easily afford.

I began to wonder if I really had a right to claim this vast empty canvas of the Arctic for my own esoteric purposes. Was I being greedy myself, an art freak, wanting the whole museum, when millions were pounding at the door, demanding fuel.

Lee was returning. The hum of the Cub reverberated from the hills, the valley was filled again with technological noise. Soon I would be back among the Boomers.

A row of 'christmas trees' grows atop three of the six wells drilled below Drill Site 2, belonging to Atlantic Richfield at Prudhoe Bay. An average of six production wells are drilled directionally from each of the eleven sites serving ARCO's eastern portion of the Prudhoe field. Each drill site occupies 7.2 acres and requires 70,000 cubic yards of gravel. The wells are drilled to an average depth of two miles below the tundra at which depth they occupy an area 2 miles by 3 miles. Gas pressure on the oil pool below the surface will force the oil, water and gas mixture through flow lines to three flow stations. Initially, each flow station will serve three or four drill sites, and will process the liquid produced by the well into its separate oil, gas and water components. The oil will flow through a gathering system of 30 or 34 inch pipe, which for the eastern portion of the field will be seven miles in length, to Pump Station 1 on the Alyeska Pipeline, located on the border between the two halves of the field (the other half is operated by British Petroleum). From here the oil will be sent through the trans Alaska pipeline to Valdez. Gas from the flow stations will be sent through the gas-gathering system to the central gas-compressor. Until a gas pipeline is built, this gas will be reinjected into the field. The water will also be reinjected into the ground through deep wells. Also at Prudhoe will be a field fuel-gas unit that will provide natural gas for fuel for the power plant, and for Alyeska's Pump Stations 1, 2, 3 and 4. The Prudhoe Bay field stretches about 45 miles east-west and 20 miles north-south. The field consists of three different oil reservoirs at depths between 5,500 and 10,500 feet, called: Kuparuk, Prudhoe and Lisburne. The Prudhoe oil pool, the largest, is located near the center of the field and is the only one being developed at present. Recoverable reserves from this pool alone are 9.6 million barrels of oil and 26 trillion cubic feet of gas.

Chapter 19

Halibut Cove

We have found the enemy—and he is us!
POGO

The 30-year-old boat chugged across Kachemak Bay toward a purple mountain of hemlock and spruce that was being swallowed by a gray, glassy sea. Between the boat and the mountain the black back of a whale briefly and silently broke the smooth surface of the water and disappeared. Beyond the churning wake of the boat a light at the tip of Homer Spit pierced the early autumn twilight.

As the boat approached the purple mountain it entered a cathedral of forest and cliff, with a floor of sea and a roof of cloud. The boat's engine was reduced to a throb and it settled against a floating dock. I jumped down.

'Thanks, see you in a week.'

The boat turned, the beat of its engine echoed briefly against the walls of the entrance channel, and it was gone. There was silence.

I picked up my pack and walked along the sloping beach toward a light glowing through the thick woods. My boots crunched on the rounded stones but there was no other sound. I was beside the sheltered lagoon of Halibut Cove, with its empty, stilted houses looking strange above a low tide. It was Wednesday. The Anchorage invasion wouldn't occur until Friday night when these shuttered houses would fill with escapees.

Alex Combs had built his studio here. It was his light that threaded its way through the branches toward me. A steep path into the dark forest ended at the log steps of the wooden studio. My footsteps thudded hollowly across the porch. I knocked. 'Alex?' There was no answer. I tried the door. It opened. Inside was a table laden with paints and brushes; four or five paintings leaned against a wall. I felt the Franklin stove. Cold. The light came from a single electric bulb over the kitchen part of the single downstairs room. A wooden stair led to bedrooms above. 'Alex?' My voice echoed around the empty house. I leaned my pack against a chair and walked back out on the porch to wait. He must be out fishing.

Below the porch the mossy ground dropped away to the edge of a cliff that plunged into a sea felt but not seen in the deepening twilight. I sat in a corner of the porch and looked up at the spruce pointing to the cloudy sky. I was at peace.

Alaska was not at peace. I had seen her reeling under the impact of new people and new money. Alaska had made a quantum jump forward into industrial development. It would take years before the full effects of the changes already set in motion by the new oil were assimilated into the lives of Alaskans, before the new scars on the land were familiar enough to be forgotten—as the Alaska Highway is now forgotten. And what of her wilderness?

Wilderness is a creation of modern sophisticated man. He invented it and can just as easily destroy it when it gets in the way of a greater need. The early Eskimos didn't think of themselves as inhabiting a wilderness. They merely lived on a land and fished in a sea. The Saharan Tuareg think they live only in a vast sea of sand and rock, but European man has defined their land as a wilderness and uses it as an antedote for the pain of his technological life at home.

Alaska is the recipient of a radical change in the trade patterns of North America, from the east-west pattern of the past 200 years to a south-north one. The new energy sources of Canada's Arctic and Alaska are replacing those of the West and Southwest, and have drawn the trade to the north. This change is the real cause of Alaska's current invasion.

Two of Alaska's non-renewable resources are energy to keep man warm and to fuel his technological life style, and a wilderness to salve his spirit tortured by that life style. To use all the energy would destroy both of these treasures, but the 200 million people in the south are insatiable.

The oil and gas already tapped in Arctic Alaska can provide enough money to run the state at least until the end of the century, and no further development of this resource is needed as far as Alaska is concerned. Oil is a capital intensive industry requiring few people to run it. When the current pipeline builders go home, admittedly leaving their finger-mark down the center of Alaska, and probably across the Arctic Slope as well, the place could be left alone. That oil and gas could buy the remaining wilderness for future generations. Alaska is in the enviable position of the farmer who has inherited a fortune and no longer needs to clear more trees to plant more crops.

Alaskans recently elected a new state administration that has brought a new approach to this dilemma. Gone, I hope, are the old ideas of resource development, based on a desire for a greater population and more money. Alaska now has more than enough of both. The mad scramble can end.

The problem is that the energy-hungry 200 million won't be put off so easily. Alaska isn't a sovereign state and her resources can be tapped by the federal government for the 'national interest'. On 21 August 1975 Governor Hammond expressed his frustration with the federal government: 'I think it is important to recognize first that serious adverse impacts will occur in all aspects of the natural and human environments of Alaska. It must be the national policy not to sacrifice Alaska and her people for oil. It is an understatement to say that the state has been virtually left out of every significant decision regarding this federal program, in violation of the intent of Congress . . . Our major frustration to date has been the manner in which we have been ignored . . .' Alaska doesn't have the power to prevent her own rape.

The drillers are already at work in the oil basins of northwest Alaska, along the Alaska Peninsula and soon they will be at the outer continental shelf. The latter, of which 66 per cent of the U.S. total is held by Alaska is currently the scene of a delaying action, in which the state is trying to keep the drillers out, at least until their impact on the fisheries and the villages along the coast can be assessed. But this action, like any in the future, or indeed like the trans-Alaska pipeline controversy in the past, can mean only a temporary respite in the struggle. The drillers will be back, and when the oil is discovered the pressure will be on for more pipelines. Alaska can only hope to delay the invasion and channel the invaders when they come, to direct the drillers to areas already drilled, and to resist as long as possible the opening of new ones.

The multitude in the south want the oil in Alaska and it is rightfully theirs. But so is Alaska's wilderness and Americans need both. Therein lies the dilemma: to take one destroys the other. There is only one solution and even it will not preserve the land. Americans must reduce their consumption of oil as much as possible, and Alaskans, as custodians of this part of the American wilderness as well as of her oil, must try to delay resource development as long as possible. Only in this way can any of the wilderness be kept, for us and for the future.

Heavy footsteps thudded on the wooden steps of the porch. Alex's white beard glowed in the gloom as he rounded the corner of the house. From his right hand hung two large salmon.

'Hello, Jon. I thought you were coming tomorrow.'

'Came down from Fairbanks a day early and I got a flight to Homer this morning. How are you?'

'Oh, tired. I must be getting old. That walk up from the beach didn't used to wear me out, the way it does now. Come on in, it's starting to rain.'

Alex put the fish on the kitchen counter. 'Why don't you make a fire. I'll cut these into steaks.'

The bottle of California claret was nearly empty, the salmon had been reduced to bones. Outside the rain increased to a persistent drumming on the shake roof, but inside the crackling fire in the Franklin stove filled the room with a suffusing warmth, combining with the wine to produce a glow of well being and delicious contentment.

Halibut Cove

'I like your new work,' I said, pointing a wine glass toward a painting leaning against the wall.

'Yeah. Did them down here this summer. Not too happy with that one over there yet. It'll come though. Well, I think I'll go to bed. You be okay down here?'

'Yes, I've got an air mattress and my bag. I'll be fine, thanks.'

'See you in the morning. Good night.'

Alex climbed up the stairs to his room. His voice came down from above. 'Say, Jon, whatever happened to that book you were writing?'

'It's finished.'

Glossary and Notes

ARCTIC: The Arctic is technically a desert, receiving only four to five inches of precipitation a year. Permafrost prevents this water from soaking into the ground during the summer thaw, and the area has a waterlogged appearance with numerous lakes. The Alaskan Arctic comprises essentially the North Slope, that flat plain, once under the sea, that stretches from the Brooks Range to the Arctic Ocean, and from the Canadian Border to Point Hope on the Chukchi Sea. The severe climate inhibits the growth of trees except for a few poplar stands in sheltered valleys, and the tundra lies exposed to fierce winter gales. A few days see temperatures in the 60's F, but the coastal strip during the summer is frequently beset by strong winds, cloudiness and rain. The average winter temperatures are higher than those in interior Alaska due to the modifying effect of the Arctic Ocean, with the coldest month, February, averaging –24°F. Frequent high winds take the 'chill factor', the cooling effect of winds on human skin, to lower effective temperatures. Sunset over much of this area occurs toward the end of November, sunrise about the last week in January. But even on the shortest day, December 21, the clear sky is not completely dark all day. Dim twilight usually lasts from about 11 a.m. to 2.30 p.m. even though the sun doesn't rise above the southern horizon. Winter darkness is considerably mitigated by the presence of the moon. During the winter months, when the moon is full, it circles the sky above the horizon for 24 hours a day, bringing an end to the darkness for almost two weeks a month, its white light reflecting brilliantly from the snow covered landscape. During these times travel over the tundra is possible, and hunting for seal can be undertaken. Bright aurora can cast a remarkable amount of light on the land when no moon is present. Twenty four hour a day sunlight begins about mid May and lasts until early August.

ARCO: Atlantic Richfield Company.

BOOMER: One who is participating in the Alaska oil boom, that is, one who *has* a pipeline related job.

Glossary and Notes

BP: British Petroleum Company.

CACHE: A small log building, frequently a miniature of the log cabin near to which it is built, about eight feet square and set on poles about ten feet off the ground. Used for storing food and equipment away from squirrels, mice and other hungry creatures, including bears.

CAT, CAT SKINNER: A bulldozer. An instance when a brand name (in this case the name of the Caterpillar Company) has moved into the language. It can now refer to any company's bulldozer. The Cat skinner is the bulldozer driver.

CHEECHAKO: A word popular in the early part of the century to describe a new comer to the North. The word is little used in general conversation today.

CRAMPONS: A framework of steel with about eight to ten spikes about two inches long that project downward and forward. A crampon is strapped to each climbing boot to prevent slipping on hard snow or ice.

EARTHQUAKE: The Alaska Good Friday, March 27, 1964 earthquake occurred at 5:36 p.m. with a Richter magnitude of 8.4 to 8.6, lasted about four minutes and released twice the energy of the earthquake that wracked San Francisco in 1906. Its epicenter was in Unakwik Inlet in northwestern Prince William Sound, 80 miles east of Anchorage, and its focus was $12\frac{1}{2}$ miles below the surface, shallow for an earthquake. This fact greatly increased the damage it caused. It produced significant property damage over 50,000 square miles, buckled ice on lakes over 100,000 square miles and was felt over an area exceeding a million square miles. Between March 27 and 30, 52 aftershocks, the largest of 6.7 magnitude, occurred between the Trinity Islands southwest of Kodiak, and a point 15 miles north of Valdez. It was these, almost more than the main earthquake, that frightened people in this area. One Anchorage woman was so terrified that she got into her car and drove to Texas. I don't know if she ever returned. Over 34,000 square miles of south central Alaska rose and fell east and west of a hinge line that ran from eastern Kodiak Island to northwestern Prince William Sound. East of this line land rose up to 7.5 feet, west of it land fell up to 5.4 feet. Anchorage itself dropped 2.6 feet. The first reported tidal wave, more accurately called a seismic sea wave or tsunami, was reported at Kodiak harbor 22 feet above mean lower low water. Two more waves followed the first at intervals of 55 minutes. The fourth and highest crested at 30 feet, $1\frac{1}{2}$ hours after the third. At Chenega, in Prince William Sound, apparent focusing of the wave around a small group of islands caused it to reach the village school house that stood on a knoll 90 feet above the sea. The water swept away all the village buildings except the school and one house, and 25 of the 76 people who lived there. Another surge of water shot into Port Valdez, struck the north shore and destroyed mine buildings 170 feet above the sea. It was then deflected back to wash 32 feet inland at Jackson Point, the site of Alyeska's pipeline tanker loading terminal.

215

HOMESTEAD: In order to open up the West to settlement, the U.S. Government gave interested citizens 160 acres of land each with the understanding that they would farm and live on it. After five years the settler would be given title to his land. This law was extended to Alaska where conditions of a short growing season, forests and poor soils made the original premises of the law virtually unworkable. Large areas of Alaskan valleys were cleared unnecessarily as the homsesteader tried to 'prove up' or fulfil the conditions of the law. Trees were cleared by bulldozers and token grains were planted. Many Alaskan homesteaders gave up after a year of so and returned south, leaving behind windrows of trees, empty land and cabins, having overlooked the fact that although the land was free, homesteading took a lot of capital. The lucky ones, those early ones who took the homesteading land around Alaska's cities, found their land valuable, but not for farming. Homesteading ended in 1974.

HOPER: Someone who has come to Alaska looking for pipeline related work.

ICE AXE: A spike about 8 inches long and a small chopper about 4 inches long comprising one unit of steel are attached to one end of a usually wooden handle, at the other end of which is a projecting point, also of steel. The chopper is used for cutting steps on hard snow or ice, the spike for the same purpose or for stopping sliding falls down snow or ice slopes. The point at the other end is used for picking up litter left by previous climbing parties.

NATIVES: The aboriginal inhabitants of Alaska, whose nomadic ancestors probably came across a Bering Straits land bridge at least 11,000 years ago. These people eventually split into four groups and today speak five distinct languages. Eskimos live along the southwest, west and Arctic coasts, Aleuts, also Eskimos, on the 1500 miles of islands that stretch across the Pacific toward Asia. In the interior and along Cook Inlet are the Athabascan Indians, with the Haidas and the Tlingits in Southeast Alaska. Today, Alaskan natives number about 60,000.

OVERFLOW ICE: Sometimes called off ice from the German *aufeis*. Formed on Arctic rivers when the river water flowing under layers of ice already frozen is forced up through cracks to spread over the ice and freeze. Layers can build to thicknesses of five feet and sometimes don't melt before new ice forms in the autumn. Frequently used as a refuge from insects by caribou.

PERMAFROST: Permanently frozen ground. The frozen mixture of ice and earth or gravel can be a few feet deep and intermittently distributed horizontally, as in south central Alaska, or hundreds of feet deep and continuous as over the North Slope. Permafrost is prevented from thawing below the top foot or two in the warm summer sun by layers of insulating tundra. When this layer is removed the permafrost melts, turning the area into a pool of mud, or, eventually a lake. Roads built on permafrost must be insulated from the ice by layers of gravel.

Glossary and Notes

PIPE, PIPELINE: Alyeska's steel pipe, manufactured in Japan, is 40 feet long, 48 inches in diameter and .462 or .562 inches in thickness depending on location of use. About 409 miles of the pipeline will be buried 'convential' between 3 and 12 feet below the surface. About 382 miles will be elevated on steel supports to prevent thawing of the permafrost. In these sections the pipe will be covered with 4 inches of resin-impregnated fibrous glass insulation jacketed with galvanized steel, and I hope painted green. Its supports will be 50 to 70 feet apart and the pipe itself will be mounted on a saddle placed on a crossbeam installed between two vertical support members placed in the ground. To prevent thawing around the supports, they will contain a refrigerant that evaporates and condenses, chilling the ground whenever the ground temperature exceeds that of the air. To take care of expansion, the pipe will be built in a zigzag pattern to convert the expansion into sideways movement. About every 1000 feet the pipe will be anchored, but will be permitted to slide back and forth across the intermediate supports. Alyeska claims that the insulation will keep the oil in a pumpable state for 21 days if the line should be shut down for any reason. The reasons could be several: a leak, an earthquake, a malfunction in the system, a threat of sabotage (the line is virtually indefensible against terrorist attack; such attack would probably come in mid-winter when repairs would be difficult, if not impossible). If the line should be inoperative for a period longer than 21 days, or the weather be unusually cold, the oil in the line would have to wait until spring before resuming its voyage to Valdez. There are 142 valves, and the entire system, with the help of satellite communication, will be monitored from a control center in Valdez, where there will also be a pair of computers. Alyeska claims that the whole thing can be shut down in 10 minutes, using remotely controlled valves. Even so, they say, oil spills could average 13,000 barrels, and as much as 50,000 barrels before the leak could be stopped.

SNOWMOBILE: A single tracked vehicle that is straddled much like a motor scooter. A broad belt with transverse cleats drives a pair of steering skis at the front. It can usually take one or two passengers, is powered by a small gasoline engine, and is capable of towing a sled. Snowmobiles, sometimes called snow machines, come in a variety of models made by many manufacturers, and have replaced dog teams in the Arctic. Their use as sport machines has rendered them unpopular with skiers whose trails they tear up, and they have been banned from various skiing and snowshoeing areas. They are the delight of teenagers, and winter nights in suburban Alaska are rent by their noise.

SNOWSHOES: Consist of a framework about 10 inches wide and 4 to 5 feet long. They are pointed at the rear, rounded and tilted up like a ski at the front, and held together by webbing, usually of hide, strapped to the feet to prevent them sinking into soft snow.

SOHIO: Standard Oil (Ohio).

217

TUNDRA: A word of Finnish origin meaning land without trees. The word is used commonly by Alaskans to refer to the mat of lichens, moss, small flowering plants and shrubs such as willow and dwarf birch, that covers much of Arctic and sub-Arctic Alaska. The tundra usually overlies and insulates the impervious permafrost and during the summer is generally wet and swampy.

TUSSOCK: Almost solid clumps of grass about 1 to 2 feet high that grow about a foot apart and can cover acres of tundra at a time. The low spaces between the tussocks are frequently wet or muddy, making walking difficult and frustrating.

Bibliography

And the Land Provides, Lael Morgan, Doubleday & Co., New York, 1974

Animals of the North, William O. Pruitt, Jr., Harper & Row, New York, 1966

Alaska and its Wildlife, Bryan Sage, Hamlyn, London, 1973

Alaska The Last Frontier, Bryan Cooper, William Morrow & Co., New York, 1973

The Alaska Pipeline, The Politics of Oil and Native Land Claims, Mary Clay Berry, Indiana University Press, Bloomington, 1975

Cry Crisis! Rehearsal in Alaska, Harvey Manning, Friends of the Earth, San Francisco, 1974

The Comedy of Survival, Studies in Literary Ecology, Joseph W. Meeker, Charles Scribner's Sons, New York, 1974

Deneki, an Alaskan Moose, William D. Berry, The Macmillan Co., New York, 1965

Earthquake! Eloise Engle, The John Day Co., New York, 1966

Hunters of the Northern Ice, Richard K. Nelson, University of Chicago Press, Chicago, 1969

Klondike '70, Daniel Jack Chasan, Prager Publishers, New York, 1971

The Klondike Fever, Pierre Berton, Alfred A. Knopf, New York, 1958

The Milepost, Alaska Northwest Publishing Co., Anchorage, 1954, 1974

My Life of High Adventure, Grant H. Pearson with Philip Newill, Prentice-Hall, New York, 1962

Oil on Ice, Tom Brown, The Sierra Club, San Franciso, 1971

Oilspill, Wesley Marx, The Sierra Club, San Francisco, 1971

Only in Alaska, Tay Thomas, Doubleday & Co., New York, 1969

Ploughman of the Moon, Robert Service, Dodd, Mead & Co., New York, 1945

Russian America, Hector Chevigny, Viking Press, New York, 1965

Wager with the Wind, James Greiner, Rand McNally & Co., Chicago, 1974

Wild Alaska, Dale Brown, Time-Life Books, New York, 1972

Wilderness and Plenty, Frank Fraser Darling, British Broadcasting Corporation, London, 1970

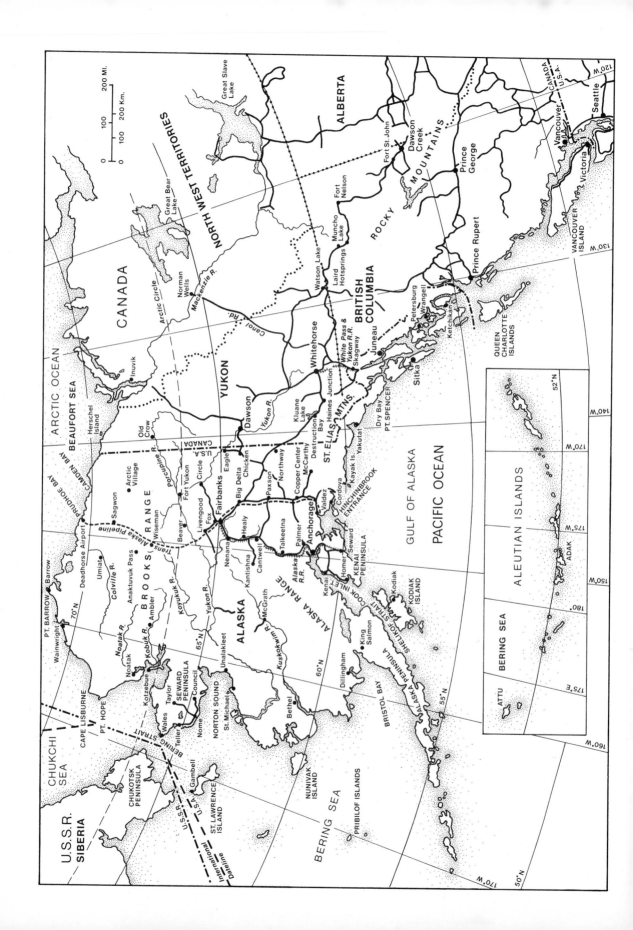